D1600799

The American
Discovery
of Tradition,
1865–1942

The American Discovery of Tradition, 1865–1942

MICHAEL D. CLARK

Louisiana State University Press

Baton Rouge

Designer: Andrew Shurtz
Typeface: Quadraat
Printer and binder: Thomson-Shore, Inc.

Library of Congress Cataloging-in-Publication Data

Clark, Michael D. (Michael Dorsey), 1937–
    The American discovery of tradition, 1865–1942 / Michael D. Clark.
        p. cm.
    Includes bibliographical references and index.
    ISBN 0-8071-3041-9 (hardcover : alk. paper)
    1. United States—Intellectual life—1865–1918. 2. United States—Intellectual life—20th century. 3. Tradition (Philosophy) 4. United States—History—Philosophy. 5. United States—Historiography. 6. Historians—United States—Biography. 7. Architects—United States—Biography. 8. Sociologists—United States—Biography. I. Title.
    E169.1.C544 2005
    973.8—dc22

                                                          2004017537

For Mary—
and for Ella,
the newest partner in the partnership
of generations

Contents

Acknowledgments ix

Introduction:
Bridging the Lethean Stream
I

CHAPTER I
Carrying the Home Outward:
John Fiske and Anglo-American Tradition
26

CHAPTER 2
Defense of the Inner Circle:
Philip A. Bruce, Lyon G. Tyler, and Virginia Tradition
66

CHAPTER 3
Tradition and Transcendence:
Ralph Adams Cram and the Tradition of the Gothic
116

CHAPTER 4
The I and the We:
Charles H. Cooley and the Tradition of the Sociologists
162

Conclusion:
Sub Specie Aeternitatis
216

Notes 227

Index 263

Acknowledgments

I would like at the outset to thank my friends and colleagues at the University of New Orleans for their support and encouragement. Gerry Bodet, Jack O'Connor, Connie Atkinson, and many others have given the History Department its own benign tradition of friendship and mutual support. Richard Collin's ironic take on all things academic failed to discourage me while keeping things in perspective; he has been a sterling friend throughout. As department chairmen during the final stages of the project, Joe L. Caldwell and Warren M. Billings are due particular thanks for helping to make available the necessary time and resources to bring it to completion. Professor Billings also gave useful advice on an earlier version of the section on Virginia; any errors I made in writing about his native state are those of a mere Marylander.

Members of the department staff deserve prominent recognition— above all Sherrie Sanders, a constant and cheerful source of assistance in all sorts of ways. Michael Baltazar has been a willing and efficient problem-solver. Members of the UNO library staff, especially Connie Phelps, Marie Windell, and Robert Heriard, helped me to obtain the sources I needed.

I am deeply indebted to Paul K. Conkin for his generous-spirited and helpful reading of my manuscript. My thanks also to the editors at LSU Press for their confidence in my project and willingness to see it through. I wish to express my gratitude especially to my excellent copy-editor, Marie Blanchard.

My son, Thomas D. Clark, possessed of computer know-how more natural to his generation than to mine, provided important tech support. My daughter, Laura Clark Brown, was indispensable in working long and hard to reformat the text in preparation for publication. My wife, Mary Dugan Clark, has as always been generous with both companionship and practical assistance—not, of course, really separable. Finally, I thank the many students who have made a career in teaching interesting and instructive.

The American
Discovery
of Tradition,
1865–1942

Introduction:
Bridging the Lethean Stream

Any study of the idea of tradition in American thought must begin with an acknowledgment of how obnoxious that idea has been to fundamental American precepts—of how strong, to invoke the obvious paradox, the American anti-traditional tradition has been. Between the American Revolution and the Civil War many Americans professed to reject tradition altogether. Europe, evidently the chief exporter of the past, was felt as a malign influence or source of moral contagion, and the Atlantic offered itself, in the words of Henry David Thoreau, as a blessed "Lethean stream." The immense space of a "new" continent seemed to cancel any remaining debt to time. To transcend—to go beyond—traditional limits has always seemed the American project: to expand frontiers, to build taller buildings, to surmount even the particulars of individual existence as the Concord Transcendentalists advised.[1]

The most prominent "traditions" of American culture authorized the rejection of tradition. It counted for nothing in effecting the salvation of the Puritan Elect, and the Puritans were bent on discarding the centuries of church tradition which had corrupted the pristine message of Christ. If faith obviated the need of tradition among Protestants, reason performed the same office among men and women of the Enlightenment. Tradition seemed only a hindrance to Benjamin Franklin's middle-class utilitarianism, and the Jeffersonian principle of the sovereignty of the present generation offered a stark contrast to the Old World traditionalism represented by Edmund Burke's idea of society as a partnership of generations. Thomas Jefferson's "strong sense of separation from the past," Daniel Boorstin points out, "made it hard for him to grasp firmly the concept of a tradition or an institution, both of which seemed illusory and transitory."[2]

I

The Romantic movement in one of its facets drew inspiration from the past, but American Romantics were more likely to look to nature than to tradition. The Transcendentalists, who in one direction epitomized American Romanticism, sought a direct access to the Over-Soul which tradition could only obscure. "Why should we import rags and relics into the new hour?" Emerson asked. "Nature abhors the old." Nature had no custom, and God delighted "to isolate us every day, and hide from us the past and the future." Whether or not this presentism was God's pleasure, it seemed sufficiently that of most Americans. R. W. B. Lewis and other critics have readily discerned in Adam, newly created in Eden, the characteristic myth of American literature—the only fitting archetype, perhaps, for a country which, as a Henry James character remarked, "denies the old at every turn."[3]

In truth, of course, American society like all others perpetuated traditions and customs of many kinds, but actual connectedness with prior generations was not entirely the point, as James Russell Lowell astutely pointed out. Lowell recognized that it was the psychology of tradition which was of first importance. "The past has not laid its venerable hands upon us in consecration," it seemed to him, "conveying to us that mysterious influence whose force is in its continuity." Americans might claim England's history as their own, but on a new continent, somehow, this did not "savor of the reality."[4]

For nineteenth-century Americans, tradition was triply dubious. It seemed, most obviously, to bind the individual in ways incompatible with the emerging ethos of personal freedom and with the possibilities of social and economic mobility which were expected to follow from it. Secondly, according to those religious and secular tenets most widely persuasive in America, tradition could only obscure the transcendent or universal truths to which the individual had unmediated access. Finally, in a way less dependent on logic than on psychology, tradition appeared to lose itself in space. Tied in Europe to associations of place and locality, it did not, as an idea or standard, travel well, and vast reaches of the new continent appeared silently to repel its jurisdiction.

During the late nineteenth century tradition gained a more sympathetic hearing among Americans, both in recognition of its ineluctable role even in a "new society," and in approval of values with which it was associated. This was not entirely the reactionary response to social dislocations which it is often made out to be; it could also authorize change, and seemed further to its proponents to widen and deepen the possibilities of human existence. Although Americans retained their reputation as a people oblivious to the past, a sense of tradition had gained enough of a foothold by the beginning of the twentieth century to play a significant part in shaping the modern American self.

What is tradition? For representative definitions one might cite David Gross, who describes it as "a set of practices, a constellation of beliefs, or a mode of thinking that exists in the present, but was inherited from the past"; H. B. Acton, who views a tradition as "a belief or practice transmitted from one generation to another and accepted as authoritative, or deferred to without argument"; or Edward Shils, for whom traditions are "beliefs, standards, and rules, of varying but never exhaustive explicitness, which have been received from the preceding generation, through a process of continuous transmission from generation to generation." Tradition has also been perceived as a reservoir of experiences, a consensus through time, or simply as the living past interpreted through experience.[5]

Such various definitions yield some common themes. Tradition, as its defenders usually emphasize, provides continuity, although this need not be absolute and may be interrupted by periods of dormancy. It is broadly agreed that tradition can, and normally does, develop and evolve. The object of tradition may be, as Eric Hobsbawm says, "invariance," but if so the vagaries of history render that intention impossible of fulfillment—or, for that matter, the vagaries of prehistory, since the assumption that "traditional" societies are static is now generally rejected. But beyond a certain degree or rate of change, it seems, tradition ceases to be psychologically or socially effective.[6]

It has been widely agreed also that tradition must contain an element of the authoritative or prescriptive. A tradition is truly a tradition, Acton argues, only when it is handed on unquestioned. This does not entail any necessary external compulsion; rather tradition elicits "a not unwilling conformity. . . . Thus, the follower of a tradition does not regard himself as being coerced. It is as though the tradition has become a part of his conscience, so that in conforming to it he is acting in accordance

with his own nature." Although they may originally have been freely chosen, traditional practices by their accumulation and perpetuation become
authoritative. The conditions of modern life have tended to reverse the
process, however, and to reduce traditions to "electives" available to enrich the individual's interests or support his ideology.[7]

Tradition is to be distinguished from other closely related terms.
"Custom" and "tradition" are similar enough sometimes to be used in-
terchangeably. Yet the distinction drawn by the American sociologist
Edward A. Ross early in the century is still useful: "By custom is meant
the transmission of a way of *doing;* by tradition is meant the transmission of a way of *thinking* or *believing.*" Other authorities have stressed distinctions inhering in temporal extension or in moral or spiritual
significance. All communities, it is acknowledged, have customs and
conventions, "but if these are not felt as possessed of considerable antiquity a community is said to have few if any traditions." Tradition implies
judgment; custom is "passively received." In a Catholic view customs can
be only "historical husks which have formed round the kernel of tradition" containing the real nourishment of revelation.[8]

Tradition is also distinguished from traditionalism, in ways almost
invariably invidious to the latter. Tradition can be followed with little or
no reflection; traditionalism is self-conscious. Further, traditionalism
connotes a reactionary activism. It is "an ideology which seeks to halt
social change and to cling tenaciously to every traditional belief and practice." Traditionalism exalts "tradition for the sake of tradition"; it is, as
Jaroslav Pelikan sums up, the "dead faith of the living" rather than tradition's "living faith of the dead." Indeed, Edward Shils suggests, in its
characteristic extremism and inflexibility traditionalism is radically hostile to authentic tradition. Defenders of tradition have been, understandably, anxious to draw the distinction. (As "traditionalism" seems too
compromised by negative connotations satisfactorily to denote mere support for tradition, I shall occasionally employ a variant form, "traditionism," to signal a more neutral meaning.)[9]

Its elements of continuity and prescription help to distinguish tradition from the closely related idea of "heritage," now an important part
of popular culture and the object of considerable scholarly attention.
Those who seek and celebrate heritage, as David Lowenthal points out,

do so unencumbered by the historian's putative goal (never attained) of objectivity; the role of the past for the purposes of heritage is unabashedly to fit the biases and serve the needs of the present. Tradition no more than heritage elicits a scholarly objectivity. But its object is not merely a self-image projected on a previous generation to create, for example, a Pilgrim or Founding Father or an Aztec tailored to early-twenty-first-century taste. While more or less distorting the past in their own way, upholders of tradition rest their case on a connection between past and present assumed to be unbroken, or at least reparable. Where heritage is characteristically "discovered," tradition is properly simply observed or maintained. And the heritage-seeker is not really looking for authority or prescription but for confirmation of his sense of himself, or of her sense of her group.[10]

Heritage was far from unknown in the last century and before—the "invention of tradition" was often really the invention of heritage, if that phrase is not redundant. But "heritage" has come into its own as a part of popular culture in the age of self-fulfillment and the identity politics that is its collective corollary. In the late nineteenth and early twentieth centuries the principle of authority loomed larger and was in better odor. The figures treated in this study certainly drew on tradition to bolster their sense of self and their pride in the collectivities with which they identified, but they looked to it also for prescriptive moral, social, and political principles on a level, I take it, above the mere celebration of heritage.

The same criteria of continuity and prescriptiveness help to distinguish tradition from the more specialized term "antimodernism." As explicated by T. J. Jackson Lears, antimodernism in the decades around the turn of the twentieth century was part of a broad "quest for intense experience," mounted in rebellion against the seeming flatness of an over-refined bourgeois world in which the process of rationalization had been extended even from "the outer to the inner life." No mere escapists, antimodernists drew on premodern symbols in an effort to recapture an emotional authenticity, but their quest ended largely, as Lears argues, in accommodation to the twentieth-century "culture of consumption."[11]

The conception of antimodernism does much to explain the appeal of tradition, but tradition belongs to a more limited category, and one which does not fall entirely under an antimodernist heading. Henry Adams's secular veneration of the Virgin Mary, although surely a classic example of the antimodernist spirit, does not appear a traditionist gesture, for instance. Adams posited a sharp discontinuity between the thirteenth-century unity which the Virgin embodied and the twentieth-century multiplicity represented by the Dynamo, with only the abstraction of force to bridge the gulf between them. Tradition furnishes not only symbols but representations of more than symbolic weight with which to confront the present, and it requires also a substantial connectedness. Those who look to it for intensified experience—emotionally heightened, more authentic, or simply "enriching"—must find it at least partly in the value of its being transmitted from generation to generation. On the other hand, social scientists who came to a sympathetic appreciation of the social role of tradition, or progressives who sought to subsume it as part of a single developmental process, do not fit comfortably under an antimodernist umbrella. Nor would the prescriptive aspect of tradition necessarily loom large in the antimodernist's backward-looking quest for emotional or aesthetic qualities missing in modern life.

Tradition is linked inextricably to other modes of temporal continuity. Even progress, often taken as the opposite of tradition, can be almost indistinguishable from it when tradition is understood as an unfolding and elaboration of venerable principles, as it was with nineteenth-century British "Whig" historians and such American counterparts as John Fiske. In the same way tradition can be perceived as a body of precepts slowly evolving, and therefore in accord with the Darwinian scheme. Values attached to both progress and evolution may assume a prescriptiveness which blurs the boundaries further; practically, however, the progressive orientation to the future and the moral neutrality claimed by science reinforce common-sense distinctions.

History plays its own role, serving sometimes as a surrogate for tradition—but studied rather than lived. An "essentially . . . cognitive reappropriation of the past," as Gross says, history turns traditional experience into information and in so doing robs it of its mystique. Indeed, according to J. H. Plumb, the rise of critical history has helped to bring about "the death of the past" by undermining the traditions by which people interpreted the meaning and purpose of their lives. Among Americans of a century ago, less steeped in undisturbed and unselfconscious traditions than were their Old World counterparts, an opposite effect can be observed, however: the growth of historical consciousness, by sharpening awareness of tradition, could stimulate a desire to preserve or restore it.[12]

More than that of progress, evolution, or history, the place of tradition in the modern scheme of things has been problematical. Enlightenment thinkers, finding it antithetical to reason, were apt to consign it to the realm of the premodern and antimodern. It retained this stigma among many later intellectuals, although some have found its nonrational qualities negotiable or even reason for support. Max Weber sharply distinguished tradition from reason (as well as from charisma) as a basis for legitimate authority; conservative thinkers have recognized the same opposition from a different point of view. Michael Oakeshott characterized the rationalist as profoundly hostile to tradition. The rationalist mind, Oakeshott observed, "has no atmosphere, no changes of season and temperature"; consequently, it entertains "a deep distrust of time" and "falls easily into the error of identifying the customary and the traditional with the changeless." Even the moderate proposition that tradition and reason are complementary ways of coping with human problems has needed to be actively defended, as it has been by Edward Shils.[13]

Yet efforts to banish tradition from modernity have failed. While it has lost much of its authoritative character, in keeping with the temper of the times, it has been appropriated on many levels as a resource for the enrichment of life. "Tradition is the well-spring of human fulfillment and not its enemy," according to George Allan, "for under the tutelage of the past values are created that are richer, deeper, more intense than could ever be otherwise attained." Philosophers as different as Alasdair MacIntyre and Richard Rorty treat traditions as necessary contexts for the pursuit of truth. Making perhaps a virtue of a necessity, Gross offers the pregnant suggestion that in the modern world tradition is valuable for its very aspect of otherness; it offers a stance from which to criticize modernity.[14]

There are different ways of living in tradition. It should be clear that I am not concerned here with "traditional society" as described for instance by Daniel Lerner—illiterate, rural and isolated, resigned and incurious, regarding change as shameful—except as knowledge of this kind of society impinged on the modern consciousness. In "traditional society," tradition was an all-pervasive atmosphere, and observance of it, if not entirely unselfconscious, required little contemplation. For educated Americans of the late nineteenth or twentieth century, of course, the situation was far different. Living sufficiently outside of tradition to be conscious of it as a discrete phenomenon, and one of evidently declining importance, thoughtful moderns were driven to consider its role in their lives.[15]

Even within the modern context, the failure to make some rather elementary distinctions has resulted in endless confusion and in much indiscriminate use of "tradition" as a positive or negative token. Tradition, for example, is not identical with its physical traces. Nathaniel Hawthorne and Henry James famously lamented the lack of ancient monuments in America, and foreigners were understandably led by the raw newness of the "American scene" to suppose Americans traditionless. It is true enough that medieval cathedrals and ruined abbeys can powerfully convey a sense of tradition, and that human beings live largely by tangible signs and symbols. But the message does not depend entirely on the age of the messenger. American society like all societies has always been governed very largely by the traditions which inhere in the law, in political institutions, in religion, in folklore, in the myriad ways in which people conduct their lives—most of them of Old World provenance. When tradition became fashionable, it did not have entirely to be invented.

Tradition, moreover, endures or expires on many different levels. A people may swiftly abandon the "traditional" horse and buggy for the automobile but cling tenaciously—perhaps all the more tenaciously—to Lockean traditions of political philosophy or to Christian or Judaic traditions in religion. As a number of recent writers have pointed out, tradition and innovation are not opposites, and certainly not mutually exclusive; to conceive of them in such a way is a fallacy of a "unilinear conception of progress." In developing countries, tradition and modernization can be mutually reinforcing; traditional family units can support industrialization, for instance, and technically advanced forms of communication can disseminate traditional ideas.[16]

The apparent shallowness of American commitment to tradition provides reason to doubt that such patterns would persist as strongly in the United States. But conscious attitudes toward tradition are not the same as actual social behavior. It is as possible to disdain "tradition" while following in traditional paths as it is to evoke it in defense of the radically new. The ascendancy of the "Party of Memory" in American culture after the Civil War was marked less by increased observances of fundamental social and cultural traditions—which in some respects at least declined—than by increased conscious respect and nostalgia for traditional values and standards. In large degree, it seems, the late-nineteenth-century discovery of tradition was symptomatic of its loss.

Looked at in another way, however, what may have been at work was simply a modernizing of tradition, through which its observance became more eclectic and more often elective, more self-conscious, detached to a degree from the physical contexts of custom, association, and labor which gave premodern traditions their presumptive inevitability. Inundated by modernity, perhaps, a traditional way of life had finally to yield to a traditional way of mind—possibly to endure on "higher" ground, certainly somewhat disembodied.

Some students of the subject have insisted that authentic tradition must be followed unreflectively; thus awareness of living in tradition, like the awareness of Adam and Eve of their nakedness, spoils it. This seems too purist a view, and certainly one that would too severely circumscribe the role of tradition in the modern world. Even the best educated of modern people spend much of their lives in unreflecting obedience to custom and tradition, certainly, but in some more detached moments they are aware of this as a general necessity or convenience of life. If any historical or even prehistoric people has ever lived in tradition with entire lack of self-consciousness, this surely was becoming difficult or impossible by the late nineteenth century, a time when traditions were being actively revived or invented.

Although the "invention of tradition" summons to mind the concoction of folk dances and patriotic rituals, the term could apply as well to the more active intellectual participation of the modern person in responding to the offerings of tradition. "If earlier ages still have a hold on us," Brian Stock points out, "it is through our thoughts about them."

These thoughts can be marvelously potent, enough so perhaps to justify the definition of tradition as a mental construct available to the individual regardless of the continuities and values cherished by society. "'Belonging to a tradition,'" Stephen Spender suggested in 1963, "means simply living spiritually on a chart where you are aware that your physical existence is but a small point in the whole of the life that has reached us from the past, and being able to have a realization of the equal intensity of past living with present existence, so that you can measure present life against the lives of the dead."[17]

Although this seems at first glance a radical attenuation, a thin intellectual broth drained off from the thick stew of traditional life, it can also be seen as a distillation rendering tradition more potent. Aware that traditional influences shape his life, the individual finds it natural to search for congenial traditions. If modernity promised to liberate the individual from tradition, modern self-awareness offered to liberate tradition, extracting it from the tedium of blindly repeated actions. It became accessible as an actively chosen agent in personal or collective endeavors, in quests such as those engaged in by the subjects of this study for aggrandizement, vindication, transcendence, and enrichment of life.

In a country like the United States, where the physical traces of tradition were sparse and its social threads less knotted in the ties of generations than in older nations, the idea that tradition could be actively chosen or engaged was of considerable importance. It was possible by the 1890s to suggest that Americans had become more tradition-minded than their European contemporaries. In his presidential address to the American Historical Association in 1895, William M. Sloane delivered a sweeping and optimistic exposition of the prospects of history in the United States, characteristic of its time in associating progress, evolution, and "race life" as totems of historical continuity. "No university class-rooms are more thronged than those where instruction in history is given," he observed. The popularity of his discipline served to refute the notion of Americans as a people with neither history nor historical consciousness, Sloan thought—a view encountered, he noted, among both Europeans and those narrow domestic patriots who discounted the relevance to their country of other places and times. "We are Europeans of ancient stock, and a change of skies did not involve a new physical birth for our society," he pointed out. Americans had built upon the past, and were continuing to do so at a time when many Europeans seemed intent on breaking away from it. Continental democracy was "young, radical, and fierce," lacking the tempering experience of the Anglo-American tradition. In art as in politics, the Old World seemed weary of the past, and drawn to experimentation "on untried paths." This was not yet the case in America, he was pleased to conclude.[18]

If Sloane's Americans were truly people of tradition, those described later by Van Wyck Brooks were only traditionist "wannabes." In The Wine of the Puritans (1908), Brooks admitted that Americans were starved for tradition; in pursuit of it they had "almost invented that insatiable and infinitely pathetic habit of mind called 'sight-seeing,'" he observed. Indeed, he doubted if anyone understood "the sentiment that lives in crumbled castles . . . [or] the very quality of the picturesque as we Americans understand it." But all this was to be on the outside looking in. Completely discounting the cultural continuity of America with Europe to which Sloane had called attention, Brooks felt it to be only a "pleasant delusion that we can graft ourselves upon ancient, finished, mellow, decaying civilizations. . . . No amount of taking thought can make us anything but the products of a rude, vigorous race, which has not yet finished laying its material foundations, imperfectly civilized. We have nothing to do with tradition." The best that Americans could do was simply to "be American," responding originally to the real conditions of American life and thus, perhaps, to "make Broadway a tradition to our descendants."[19]

These assessments were separated by half a generation, and whatever their other differences, Brooks reflected post-Victorian currents of cultural nationalism and rebellion against tradition which would have been foreign to Sloane. But the two seemed to share an assumption that tradition was less a matter of actual continuity with the past than of a certain disposition of the mind. Sloane perceived this as largely a conscious disposition. Although more conservative and content than the restless Europeans, the Americans whom he described embraced the Anglo-American traditions into which they were born with active eagerness, as indicated by the enthusiasm for the tradition-minded history of his day. For Brooks, on the other hand, authentic tradition was unreflective. He would presumably not have denied the actual cultural links between America and Europe, but he discounted these by the simple expedient of making American civilization a separate entity, one in which tradition had no metaphysical weight. It became in the New World the kind of false consciousness that caused Americans to go to Europe to press their noses forlornly up to medieval stained-glass windows to seek a genius not their own. Real tradition, he suggested, must be inhabited, or at least engendered, unawares, and he advised his countrymen to forget about it so that it might, in time, come of itself.

Although William Sloane's promotion of a seamless and paramount Anglo-American tradition seems now very dated—to say nothing of his talk of "race life"—Van Wyck Brooks's confidence in American traditionlessness seems scarcely less so. As the antebellum myth of Americans as a people without a past was demolished by historians like Sloane, so more recently has been the subtler myth of Americans as a people in any simple way indifferent or hostile to the past and its traditions—as Brooks suggested when in their right minds they were. From nineteenth-century antiquarians and antimodernists to the post–World War II pursuit of heritage, the search for meaningful connection with prior generations has been a major theme of American culture. Indeed it can be concluded, as a recent reviewer put it, that "in the business of memory, heritage, roots, and tradition, as in industrial production itself, America leads the world." If much of this carries the odor of commercialization, perhaps this merely validates its appeal in true American coin—it pays. Yet the breadth and persistence of the appeal, its attraction to scholars as well as tourists, suggests that the interest in tradition and its cognate ways of relating to the past rises above its often superficial and evanescent manifestations.[20]

Even during the early national history, when the Adamic myth was at its most potent and the impossible American ideal of self-genesis and autonomy seemed most within reach, rejection of the past was seldom seriously entertained without qualification or ambivalence. Efforts to deny actual continuities with the Old World could only be rhetorical or radical beyond the bounds of reality. In one way or another, the past had to be given a hearing. Jefferson sought to eliminate primogeniture, entail, and other vestiges of the feudal tradition, but invoked earlier precedents romantically derived from the liberties and allodial land tenures of the Anglo-Saxons. Emerson did not after all hold the past irrelevant, but urged its student to "transfer the point of view from which history is commonly read, from Rome and Athens and London, to himself." He would have made the study of the past subjective, but believed man to be "explicable by nothing less than all his history."[21]

Most tellingly, perhaps, Americans' sense of the significance and importance of their national mission did not allow them truly to reject the past. Even while proclaiming their liberation from it, they readily imagined themselves, in a phrase from Alfred Tennyson's "Locksley Hall" that became something of a cliché, as the "heir of all the ages." If the line struck a chord on this side of the Atlantic, it was not surprising. Americans were quicker to accept Tennyson than the poet's own countrymen, and responded to him with remarkable independence from British criticism. They discovered in his poetry American themes of democracy and optimism, and even—in the vision in "Locksley Hall" of a "Federation of the world"—the foreshadowing of an American empire. In a frontier society, where several races clashed and mingled, the narrator's contemplation of a new life far from English shores must have had special resonance: "Mated with a squalid savage—what to me were sun or clime? / I the heir of all the ages, in the foremost files of time."[22] In "Locksley Hall," Henry Kozicki explains, there is a larger dialectic of "convulsive cyclicity" and "linear progressivism"—the hero is "never sure whether he wants to be part of a wondrously evolving 'Mother-Age' or to blow it up in revolution." America, committed to "linear progressivism" but interpreting revolution as independence, posed a less apocalyptic dialectic: that of novelty and continuity. For Americans, Tennyson's line was supremely equivocal: were past ages dead, that they should require an heir, or did they live on to consummation in the inheritance? To those who paused to consider the problem, it seemed resolvable, with little of the "strangely modern angst" that Kozicki finds in Tennyson's poem.[23]

For such a historian as George Bancroft, whose professional career spanned the decades between the age of Jackson and that of Benjamin

Harrison, continuity and innovation were readily subsumed in a German idealist framework. In Bancroft's lifework, *The History of the United States from the Discovery of the Continent*, the nation represented the culmination of history, the capstone of the progressive design of Providence, even something new under the sun—but not a break with the past. Democracy, come to fruition in the United States, "makes no war on the past," Bancroft wrote. Willing to discard the erroneous and the outworn, she nevertheless "garners up and bears along with her all the truths that past generations have discovered; she will not let go one single idea, not one principle, not one truth."[24]

Bancroft's acknowledgment that earlier generations could instruct the present took too purely instrumental a view of the past to make him in any sense a traditionalist. But the work of the historian was part of the nineteenth-century "discovery of time," from which issued, in the postbellum United States, a more particular discovery of tradition. This meant a new scholarly interest in its role in human affairs as well as a broader sympathy with its positive functions. The fascination of the age with temporal continuity and development, apparent in its enshrinement of history and progress and culminating in the master-idea of evolution, could only suggest as well the importance of the traditionary (often perceived as the social counterpart to heredity).

This new time-consciousness looked both ways: by heightening the sense of difference with the past it magnified progress in confident Western eyes, but it also fostered a "culture of retrospection," which seemed at times to eclipse the forward-looking impulses of Western society. By the 1920s it seemed to the idiosyncratic but perceptive Wyndham Lewis that a mainly backward-looking "cult of Time" had come to dominate the West, on popular as well as sophisticated levels. "All the most influential revolutions of sentiment or of ideologic formula to-day, in the world of science, sociology, psychology," Lewis maintained, "are directed to some sort of return to the Past." Americans had followed well behind Europeans in adopting the retrospective gaze, and the United States did not cease to be a progressive-minded, forward-looking country, but it became also, as Michael Kammen puts it, "a land of the past, a culture with a discernible memory."[25]

A natural consequence of the retrospective mood, the interest in tradition gained force through the very consciousness of its opposition to modernity. Perception of tradition was framed by an odd paradox. Anglo-American "Whig" historians as well as evolutionists understood change as gradual and continuous—a conception readily applicable to the persistence and slow modification of traditions. Actual personal and social experience in the late nineteenth and early twentieth centuries, on the other hand, produced a sense of radical discontinuity. This was sometimes not so much the exhilarating liberation represented by the New World Adam as a jarring and disorienting consciousness of disconnection. Startling juxtapositions of old and new, of the traditional and the unheard-of, appeared on all sides. In Europe the changes wrought by industry crowded upon traditional village societies; in Asia, Africa, and the Americas seemingly changeless cultures retreated before the abrupt advance of the railroad, the telegraph, and the Gatling gun. Promises of liberation from environing circumstance and the "trammels" of the past coexisted with the assurances of physical and social scientists that all was determined—radically continuous.

But confusion did not prevent a new and fruitful investigation of traditionary phenomena, especially in the social sciences. While such scholars as Herbert Spencer, John Fiske, and William Graham Sumner emphasized the continuity of traditions and customs, or folkways and mores, the shock of discontinuity was of greater immediate impact. The breakup of the old order of things, Robert Nisbet has pointed out, made thoughtful people acutely aware of the significance of the loss of traditional communities and sources of authority. Nineteenth-century thinkers like Auguste Comte and Robert de Lamennais feared that the loss of tradition led to a social emptiness. Later sociologists invented such dichotomies as status-contract (Sir Henry Maine) and gemeinschaft-gesellschaft (Ferdinand Tönnies) to differentiate between ways of life characterized, in part, by continuity with the past, and those which disavowed an obligation to it.[26]

An interest in the traditionary was not limited to social scientists; historians have treated a wide range of retrospective movements and interests in the United States between the Civil War and World War I.

Despite their diversity, these quests for the past shared a sense of the significance of tradition, and in most cases a sympathy with it. An upsurge of interest in genealogy was accompanied by a proliferation of patriotic societies, and these activities combined in organizations like the Daughters of the American Revolution and its cognate societies for "Sons" and "Children." New historical and antiquarian societies were founded in states and localities, capped on the national level by the American Historical Association. Historical novels enjoyed increased popularity in the 1890s, and the arts and crafts movement, imported from Britain, sought to recapture a traditional craftsmanship endangered by machine technology. Historical pageants became remarkably popular during the first quarter of the new century, although those who planned them were notably uncertain whether to portray a continuous progression from past to present or to accentuate the gap between the two. The preservation movement, with a root in the antebellum Mount Vernon Ladies' Association, gained strength after the Civil War with a new determination to save old houses and historical sites and to promote traditional values.[27]

In such ways did Americans "discover" tradition in the decades after the Civil War. Tradition of course was not previously unknown. But it does appear that significant numbers of people became more conscious of themselves and their society as the products of tradition, and more likely to look to tradition for emblems of their hopes and ideals and for affirmation of values which earlier Americans had sought precisely in liberation from tradition.

Historians with good reason have emphasized the reactionary elements in late-Victorian and Edwardian appeals to tradition, which often issued from those whose power and status were most threatened by change. Traditionalist movements shored up the self-esteem of those who felt besieged by unWASPish immigrants and upstart millionaires, or, in the South, by blacks and poor whites. Not necessarily the last refuge of a "dispossessed elite," tradition was as readily the weapon of well-entrenched social groups in struggles over values and power. It could be a psychological anodyne offering a sense of stability in the midst of unsettling change and the feeling of time-hallowed certainty in the face of religious or metaphysical doubt.[28]

The strength of motivations rooted in disappointment and frustration should not be minimized. The painful sense of life gone awry could lead into odd culs-de-sac—to Jacobite enthusiasm or the demonization of Abraham Lincoln, as well as to more serious idolatries of genealogy, race, and regional or national aggrandizement. Yet the meanings of American traditionism are not exhausted by the label of reaction. Tradition could be used to validate as well as to oppose change. Accepting a degree of continuity with the lives of their forebears, Americans who were so disposed found it easy to discover authorization for innovation in past experience. Some Americans came to view tradition as extending rather than merely limiting the possibilities of individual and collective life. They defended it variously as instrumental, relational, and iconic. Thus traditions provided practical social resources; they alleviated the isolation of time and place by bringing one into communion with other generations; and they served as the vehicles of transcendent qualities of being.

Whatever the uses they found for it, expositors of tradition to a remarkable extent adhered to core American values. They offered not alternatives to those values so much as alternative routes to them. This was logical enough; the keepers of tradition could hardly turn their backs on the very principles from which American tradition derived. But it attested also to the oft-noted American ability to tame and absorb contrary views, to make even the most disaffected bend the knee with the claim of defending, after all, only the "true Americanism." This malleability in turn gave the somewhat suspect notion of tradition an entrée to the sensibilities of the country which it might not otherwise have possessed.

American values began with the American home, and hometown. Neither of course lived up to its often sentimentalized ideal, and rebellion against both was a familiar theme of American literature, but domesticity and locality were touchstones for artists, social scientists, politicians, and many others. Middle-class Victorians, protective of the family and nostalgic for the small town, were especially inclined to locate the sources of individual and civic virtue in these limited venues. Inevitably traditions were associated with these old-fashioned aspects of the nineteenth-century world, as opposed to the big city, the business corporation, and the nation-state. But serious defenders of tradition were not content to consign it to sentiment or nostalgia; they wished to show its continuing potency in shaping society, or at least its superiority as a source of value. This meant bringing tradition into play in the expansion—territorial, economic, demographic—which so largely defined America. It meant also joining it to general principles which would often lift it above the level of local or archaic custom. Differing in many respects, traditionists were similar in the direction of their thought: finding the source of tradition in the close and intimate, they traced its significance through broadening circles, into larger polities and toward transcending goods. They wanted to carry the home outward, as was said to be the special talent of New Englanders—or upward.

Tradition presents a varied mental landscape, into which the home seems comfortably to fit. Tradition is never pure stasis, or a simple linear continuity or evolution; it should never be regarded as finished or complete, Stephen H. Watson observes. Arising from particularities rather than from abstractions, it properly inheres in the roughness and contingency of experience rather than in the artificial smoothness or unity proffered by deterministic envisionings of progress or invocation of the "laws of history." The very derivation of the word—from *tradere*, to hand down—suggests the physical proximity of familial or other close relationships, as Theodor Adorno pointed out. The metaphors used to describe tradition, in negative as well as in positive terms, express this defining immediacy. Those hostile to it have called it a "burden"; those who live by it have been advised to throw off its "shackles"; it has even been described as a state of paralysis or catalepsy. On the other side, the great defender of tradition called direct attention to its source: "we begin our public affections in our families," said Edmund Burke. More recently tradition has been characterized as a dialogue or "conversation" with the past. Its domesticity persists even to the grave; as Spender put it, members of a living generation are "tenants" in "the houses of the dead."[29]

Less straightforwardly apprehended, at the opposite pole, is the tendency of tradition to seek the transcendent. Superficially the two are antithetical: one plods in tradition's narrow ruts or one soars above them. Yet many commentators have seen in the one a way to the other. "My freedom must mime the choices of my ancestors so that I can participate fully in the enduring values which they have fashioned and which have made me who I am," George Allan explains. "The purpose of my culture's myths is to give vibrant immediacy to my link with transcending importances." Often such transcendence is perceived in the form of the sacred. Tradition "establishes contact between the recipient and the sacred values of his life in society," Edward Shils remarks. It makes possible a "communion with past powers" comparable to any act of communion with a "timelessly transcendent symbol such as divinity or truth or goodness."[30] "Tradition is not only remembrance of ancestors, but also openness to God," or even "the extension of revelation through time," according to other formulations. Jaroslav Pelikan puts it most trenchantly when he characterizes an authentic and living tradition as an icon which "points us beyond itself" and thus indicates "the way that we who are its heirs must follow if we are to go beyond it—through it, but beyond it— to a universal truth that is available only in a particular embodiment, as life itself is available to each of us only in a particular set of parents."[31]

There is inevitably a tension between the immediacy of tradition and the timelessness or sacredness to which Pelikan's icon points. "The more precisely we imagine society as a series of concrete human actions in time, and time in terms of the sequence of such actions, the more we seem to move away from imagining society in terms of the sacred," J. G. A. Pocock observes. At extremes, in Pocock's view, tradition may be perceived either as immemorial or as an expression of the sacred, the latter deriving from one's conception of its creative or charismatic origin. S. N. Eisenstadt similarly notes a partial antithesis between the continuity of tradition and the "charismatic qualities and activities" it entails.[32]

The conception of tradition as immemorial came naturally enough in a country like England, where the origins of tradition and custom seemed often to be lost in the dim recesses of time, and it was effectively used by Edmund Burke to describe "the constant and continuous transformation of past into present." In America, where origins seemed not obscure at all, and could plausibly be attached to Pilgrims, Cavalier immigrants, or Founding Fathers of definite historical status, the charismatic emphasis was the more natural. Yet to those who chose to extend their frame of reference to Anglo-American experience entire, the Burkean option was always available. Americans of the period under consideration embraced tradition in both aspects, some appealing to national institutions inspired by timeless truths and truthbearers beholden only to the eternal, others to immemorial Germanic social and political genius, many to both with no apparent sense of contradiction.[33]

This polarity framed others of more limited definition. Home and locality were readily associated with the immemorial, with shiremotes and village communities held to be the forerunners of modern political entities. Larger polities and institutions, in the United States, were more plausibly identified with the transcendent or "charismatic." The home, however, was the starting point.

The idea that tradition arose in the domestic sphere and spread to wider circles of life was far from new. Johann Herder was among those who gave expression to it in the eighteenth century: "Nations may be traced up to families; families to their founders: the stream of history contracts itself as we approach its source, and all our habitable Earth is ultimately converted into the school of our family, containing indeed many divisions, classes, and chambers, but still with one plan of instruction, which has been transmitted from our ancestors, with various alterations and additions, to all their race." But Herder's riparian figure of gradually broadening tradition hardly applied to the United States. American tradition had to persist across several centuries of radical change in the conditions of life and the great divides of emigration and revolution. Within the same span, in a boisterously expansive country, it had to stretch between small-scale political and social organization, such as that of the town, and the large-scale organization of the nation or empire.[34]

It was therefore the problem of tradition to find the middle ground, or the linkages, which would plausibly bind immediate to transcendent, past to present, local to imperial. Traditionists were at their most creative in inventing or adopting these linkages. Sacramentalism offered a venerable way to transcendence, but even evolution, infused with religious teleology, could supply tradition with a transcendent destination. In a quite different way a cyclical theory of history could bring past and present seemingly closer. Most common was an unacknowledged but marked typological pattern of thought, adapting to modern and mundane history the method long employed to identify Old Testament prefigurations of the New. Also serviceable (and usually more explicit) were the federal principle, used to connect local tradition to its continental embodiments, and the sociological conception of the "primary group" as a school to prepare the individual for larger venues.

To illustrate such strategies I shall cite many different figures, but I intend to devote my primary attention to a few who exemplify the modes and uses of tradition with particular clarity. These few were born between the 1840s and 1860s, and were contemporaries at least to the extent that all were active in their careers during the 1890s. They show, however, a rough progression of thought.

The oldest of them, John Fiske, championed an Anglo-American tradition fixed on New England as the port of entry for "Teutonic" institutions and established liberties. Fiske was in the last decade of his life during the nineties. The most completely Victorian of the group, he readily conflated tradition with progress within an evolutionary process which took the place of the Calvinist eschatology of his upbringing. He found a more worldly mission for tradition in territorial expansion. Taking its departure from the ordinary association of tradition with place and rationalized as the realization of an adventurous and freedom-loving English genius, expansion seemed a natural way to keep faith with preceding generations. If Americans remained wary of the hold of the past—the "empire of the dead," as Comte called it—they hardly hesitated to locate tradition in an empire of the living. Within this spatialized tradition domestic and local institutions, epitomized in the New England town, provided the models for their national and imperial counterparts. And if the distance from the traditional New England town to the frontiers of modern empire seemed too great to bridge, Fiske offered the mediating principle of federalism as the ultimate flower of Teutonic genius.

Philip Alexander Bruce and Lyon Gardiner Tyler were among the most determined defenders of Virginia tradition—part of a southern "exceptionalism" indispensable for any study of the idea of tradition in American history. Like Fiske, Bruce and Tyler recognized the spatial context of tradition, but they unsurprisingly disagreed with him on the nature of that context, on the meaning of federalism, and on the strategy required of traditionists. Where New Englanders might still look for the traces of tradition in the project of "carrying the home outward," the Virginians located it in the "defense of the inner circle." This defensive stance was not entirely a negative one, although it was steeled with bitterness. Speaking self-consciously for the Old Dominion, reputedly the most tradition-minded of the states, they sought vindication for her role in the sectional struggle. But Virginia tradition, they found, was properly American tradition, the Virginia cavalier the type of George Washington as well as of Robert E. Lee. In different ways—Bruce emphasizing that Virginians were more English than the English, and Tyler that they were more American than the Americans—these two historians ended by endorsing, in the main, the same enduring Anglo-American precepts as their New England colleague John Fiske. These were precepts, indeed, that Virginia claimed first to have established on this continent. Although burdened with troubled memories of slavery and defeat, tradition seemed to offer a vindication which was at the same time a means of reconciliation with the state's Civil War adversaries.

Ralph Adams Cram discovered the authentic American tradition in the Middle Ages, centered on the glory of Gothic architecture and a society which was a paradigm of true democracy. As the country's leading neo-Gothic architect, Cram worked professionally in a tradition which in its ineffable medieval triumph had transcended, he believed, all tradition. As an Anglo-Catholic he perceived a sacramental relationship between the mundane particularities of stone and mortar and the eternal spiritual and aesthetic verities to which they pointed—somewhat in the way that for Fiske the federalist principle mediated between the town community and the universalizing thrust of nation-building and Anglo-American world leadership. But Cram rejected altogether the progressive evolution in which Fiske placed his faith, along with its ugly harvest of "imperial modernism." In place of linear schemes of change and development which rendered the recovery of the Gothic an absurdity, Cram proposed a cyclical theory of history which made tradition renewable. The quasi-typology with which he fleshed out this hope found in medieval institutions models and foreshadowings not so much of their decadent modern counterparts as of the communal institutions "on a human scale" which he believed once again possible with the latest turn of the cycle. Rescued in this way from the past, tradition could become the wave of the future.

The nineteenth and twentieth centuries most jarringly collided in Charles Horton Cooley. Cooley brought a soaring Victorian idealism and a painfully Victorian sense of duty to an American sociology of which he was one of the professional pioneers. He shared a Progressive agenda with such colleagues as Lester Frank Ward and Edward A. Ross, but far more than they he valued traditions as bonds of the social order and as necessary contexts of innovation. Cooley was a man of the twentieth century in viewing tradition less as prescriptive and constraining than as providing elective means to the enrichment of life. But with Cooley tradition was in danger of becoming disembodied. He rooted it less in any particular place than Fiske rooted it in New England, the Virginians in their state, or Cram, in a different way, in the sacred space of church or monastery. He relied on the "primary group"—family, neighborhood, and other such counterparts of Burke's "little platoons"—to provide the nurturing soil of national and human virtues. The problem of sociology for Cooley was the problem of the Christianity of which he had abandoned only the theology: the problem, as he put it, of the "I" and the "We." But this was not a problem reducible, he realized, to that which was amenable to the expertise of social scientists operating in the isolated present. On the contrary, he found inspiration in those, like the Old Testament prophets and the Christian mystic Thomas à Kempis, who seemed able to combine membership in the "common life" with an intensely personal yet transcending vision.

Victorians by birth, these figures all retained in varying degree a Victorian mind-set. Yet they all participated in the shaping of the modern self with its distinctive attitude—both positive and negative—toward tradition. Fiske did so only within Victorian confines, the Virginians in spite of themselves and minimally, Cram and Cooley most substantially. On one level they anticipated twentieth-century concerns for heritage and preservation; related sentiments promoted the enshrinement in public esteem of the New England town, the revival of the Gothic, and the restoration of colonial Williamsburg. On another level they shared ground with the Modernist movement in art and thought. (Although Modernism is often sweepingly characterized as anti-traditional, some leading Modernists did not so much reject tradition as render it ahistorical; thus T. S. Eliot and Ezra Pound sought to collapse chronology to make all traditions immediately accessible to the trained intelligence. Traditional recourse to such devices as typology and historical cycles represented a not entirely dissimilar rebellion against the tyranny of linear time.)

The subjects of this study were of course farther removed, and not only in time, from Postmodernists and their "arbitrary appropriation and imitation of the past." Fiske, the Virginians, Cram, Cooley, and others differed on what parts of the past should be "imitated," but there was little that was arbitrary in their use of tradition. Tradition a century ago still was rooted in "home" experience and still pointed as well to fixed goods. But its appeal to the generations between the Civil War and World War II owed much, I think, to a conjunction of these older with newer connotations: not only with Modernist foreshadowings but with an expansive, quasi-consumerist promise of a richer, more "fulfilling" life for the individual.[35]

This study seeks to analyze rather than to advocate. It does no doubt reflect my general bias in favor of the kind of tradition that arises from a generosity of spirit—which is based, that is to say, not on a narrowness of sympathy or fear of novelty but on a sense of the accumulating plenitude of human experience and of the connectedness of the peoples and generations from whose lives that experience arises. I am aware of the obvious: that particular traditions can be judged good or bad, and that the traditionary often serves selfish or otherwise pernicious interests and may impede necessary or desirable change. Yet I believe that a society lacking in a sense of tradition is a society impoverished, truncated most sadly in its recognition of community with other human beings. Intelligently embraced, I would suggest, tradition both binds and liberates. Resisting the modern tendency to sort people out as interchangeable parts, it can also help to free the individual from an unreflective thralldom to the things of the present. If history extends the life of the mind, participation in tradition extends the field of one's shared experience, intimating that in however dim and limited a way one's life touches the lives of the townspeople and planters, serfs and slaves, cathedral builders and prophets, of other generations.

In America, however, not even such a simple connection could be taken for granted, and the discovery of tradition was in the first instance the discovery that the voyage across the Atlantic did not sever all ties to ages past, that Thoreau's Lethean stream could be bridged.

CHAPTER I

Carrying the Home Outward:
John Fiske and Anglo-American Tradition

Perhaps few nineteenth-century biographies are now more obscure than Augustine Jones's *Life and Work of Thomas Dudley, the Second Governor of Massachusetts* (1899), yet few can display more starkly the extraordinary ambivalence of Americans of that time toward their past, and particularly toward the notion of tradition. The biography fairly represents much nonacademic historical work at the turn of the century. It was a frank defense of Dudley from latter-day calumniators of the Puritans, from partisans of John Winthrop and Roger Williams in their differences with the second governor, and against the general imputation to Dudley of the more narrow-minded and bigoted aspects of Puritanism. The book was a filiopietistic effort by an author who had been assisted in the attainment of his education by the governor's descendant, David Dudley. Despite the limitations of the work, Jones's determination to exalt the Puritan forefathers as, simultaneously, men who broke fearlessly with the past and men who were the bearers of proud and ancient tradition, reflected a division in historical consciousness which ran deeper than boundaries of professionalism or section.[1]

Jones was clearly oblivious to the contradiction, as he was to the genealogical piety in which it was rooted. He assured his readers of the need to study the heroes of the past without imbuing them with superhuman qualities. Yet he glorified them in spite of himself, and partly by trying to have it both ways on the matter of genealogy. Jones pointedly noted the contempt of the Puritans themselves for lineage, and concluded that as one of them Dudley "regarded all human distinctions founded on family and blood as worthless." At the same time the biographer was at pains to point out that Dudley was of "gentle blood," as evidenced by his youthful service as a page. Pagedom, Jones noted, had had its origins in knighthood and chivalry. Although there was no logical contradiction in this, the discordancy conveniently allowed Jones to present Dudley as a sturdy forerunner of American faith in the unbeholden individual, and at the same time as a man ennobled even against his will by his ancestry.[2]

This personal perplexity reflected in small Jones's double view of American Puritanism as representing at once a completely new start in the world and as the fruition of a long tradition. So sharp was this ambivalence that it could be encompassed within a single sentence. The Massachusetts Bay immigrants "were reasonably convinced that the only true and safe course was to break at once totally with the past," Jones wrote, "taking the best of everything that it had produced, and to transplant it on virgin soil beyond the sea, a glorious heritage for succeeding generations."[3]

The idea of breaking completely with the past while taking the best of it with you might be dismissed as a manner of speaking were not the theme so often repeated, and were it not so intrinsic to Jones's conception of the Puritan mission. He spoke in glowing terms of the Puritan achievement in transplanting English civilization to America, and noted that Old and New England had much in common. Yet he judged the transit of the Massachusetts charter to have been "really the first declaration of independence from British supremacy." Thomas Hooker and his associates in Connecticut had "proceeded to construct in America the ideal state, freed largely from the useless trumpery which has adhered to and incumbered old and worn-out systems of church and state." Nevertheless Americans were "'the heir of all the ages. . . .' Our fathers had the wisdom and discretion to take, as bees select their honeyed sweets, from sources many, strange, and curious, but they always secured the useful, life-saving, life-sustaining thing for their hives."[4]

These were, indeed, different facets of the American experience: political independence and cultural continuity, altogether a selective transplanting of European civilization. But Jones seemed to feel the force of each side of the proposition too strongly to be content with a moderate formulation: his America had to be both an immaculate new beginning and the culmination of all tradition. And despite his suggestion of a colonial eclecticism not hesitant to derive cultural enrichment from the most exotic sources, Jones himself was content to fall back on the Anglo-Saxons, those paragons for all seasons who furnished a ready-made tradition for immigrants and revolutionaries. Jones, however, placed his emphasis not on the original Anglo-Saxon emigration to Britain as a forerunner of the English migration to America, as Thomas Jefferson had, but on the mission of Augustine of Canterbury to heathen England in the early seventh century. He even speculated that the Puritans might have recalled Augustine's evangelism in their own mission among the Indians. (It was notable, Jones thought, that "in both England and America, Christianity had been planted before the arrival of the masterful spirits who were destined to achieve its first real conquests"—so much for Celts and Virginians.)[5]

The parallel was important because the Puritans, Jones made clear, were appointed to carry on the Anglo-Saxon tradition. It struck him as fitting that departing immigrants had often passed the ancient Anglo-Saxon capital of Winchester, for the Puritans could be regarded as "the rising and triumphant remnant of that Saxon race which, vanquished at the battle of Hastings under Harold, and in the fens of Lincolnshire, had returned to grind to powder in succeeding years the residue of the feudal system, with its oppressive tenures, and to preserve this continent from its baneful tyranny." It would have been especially appropriate, Jones added, if the emigrants had paid homage at the grave of Alfred the Great before departing "to plant on another continent that liberty denied to them at home, which their ancestors had struggled and died for" under the Saxon kings.[6]

In the end history came full circle, as "the battle won at Hastings was lost at Marston Moor. The victorious Saxon was uppermost alike in the commonwealth of England and in the other one of Massachusetts," Jones exulted. But ancient tradition issued finally in the revolutionary sundering of a people. Jones noted that Dudley's old mansion had been razed and used to make Patriot fortifications a few days after the battle of Bunker Hill. "If the glorious old Saxon was permitted to witness that desolation of his home and hearth," the biographer speculated, "that invincible spirit which inspired his life work responded, Grind it as fine as dust to construct bulwarks to resist the tyranny of the British throne and defend American liberty!" The American preference for the break with the past firmly consecrated by tradition—and during this period at least by the ties of "race"—could not have been more clearly evidenced.[7]

If there was anything in Jones's account which in any measure resolved its ambivalence toward historical continuity, it lay in the typological pattern the historian introduced. The employment here of a method so important in Christian thought is hardly surprising. By the nineteenth century typology had outgrown its original meaning of an Old Testament prefiguration (the type) of a New Testament person, event, or institution (the antitype). Applied to history, literature, and the natural world, it had shaded into allegory, symbolism, and mere parallel without quite relinquishing the assumption of a transcendent purpose or design against which type and antitype made sense. It became pervasive enough and diffuse enough, certainly, to be used without conscious reference to its intellectual provenance. Apparently unaware of using typology as such, the figures under study here nevertheless found it natural to comb history, not merely for evidence of development but for prefiguring models—leaders and prophets, migrations and revolutions, organs of local government—of more modern characters, events, and institutions.[8]

Thus in Jones's history Augustine's mission to pagan England served as the type of the Puritan mission to the Indians, and Dudley was at once the antitype of the defenders of Saxon liberties against Norman feudalism and the type of the American Patriot of 1776. Seemingly without placing its American subjects in bondage to the past, this device dignified their mission with the solemn bond of the typological foreshadowing. That Jones had substituted Saxons for Israelites as favored type would have surprised the Puritans themselves, but their modern champion retained a sense of providential purpose at work in history.

This resolution was perhaps inadvertent, but weightier thinkers struggled with the same dialectic of continuity and discontinuity, and not always with even Jones's degree of success. Nowhere other than in New England did thesis and antithesis stand in such sharp contrast. Perhaps the root was theological. The transcendent Puritan God and His human creature confronted each other directly and without strict need of the mediation of society or tradition; thus any liberation from the mundane authority of past or present became possible. Yet there could be no breach of continuity with the will of a predestining God. It was perfectly in keeping with the Calvinism of his ancestors for George Bancroft to restate the puzzle in the terms of German idealism and Jacksonian Democracy, the unbreakable plan of Providence working through history to free humanity from all which constrained the equal freedom of individuals.

The Adams brothers gave more modern articulation to the problem. Charles Francis Adams, Jr., tracing the history of Massachusetts, applied a characteristically Adamsian image to the theological rupture represented by Unitarianism: "The continuity in the process of human development was distinct and clearly to be traced,—no less than the break in it, corresponding to what in geology is known as a 'fault.'" Charles Francis scorned the "filio-pietistic" proclivities of Massachusetts historians like Augustine Jones, but fell into the same kind of doublethink in describing the emergence of the idea of legal equality in the Bay Colony. Acknowledging that this liberating concept had sources in the English Commonwealth, he evidently saw no difficulty in proclaiming also that it went against all law, usage, and tradition. Searching nature and history for an intelligible "sequence of force," Charles's younger brother Henry found images of continuity in the stubbornly unevolving pteraspis and the glacial inertia of Russia, yet at the Paris exposition of 1900 famously discovered his "historical neck broken by the sudden irruption of forces totally new."[9]

Composing not merely a New England conundrum, the claims of continuity and discontinuity became the bases of opposed myths of American history, classically supported in the late nineteenth century by the historical scholarship of Herbert Baxter Adams and Frederick Jackson Turner. There was for Adams no question of an American break with the past. Writing to Johns Hopkins President Daniel Coit Gilman in 1882 in support of an Anglo-American historical magazine, he insisted that "the history of the two countries is one. The whole tenor of our researches at the J.H.U. is to show the continuity of English institutions in American." In his study of New England towns, Adams described this continuity with a luxuriant organic imagery replete not only with his notorious germs but with seeds, roots, branches, and even protoplasm. It was, indeed, more than imagery; to Adams it was "just as improbable that free local institutions should spring up without a germ along American shores as that English wheat should have grown here without planting."[10]

The celebrated riposte to the "germ theory" was Frederick Jackson Turner's essay "The Significance of the Frontier in American History" (1893). Turner captured the American historical imagination with his suggestion that civilization had had to be born anew on the frontier. He did not argue a complete break with the past; he balanced and qualified carefully. "For a moment, at the frontier, the bonds of custom are broken and unrestraint is triumphant," he asserted. "There is not *tabula rasa*. The stubborn American environment is there . . . ; the inherited ways of doing things are also there; and yet, in spite of environment, and in spite of custom, each frontier did indeed furnish a new field of opportunity, a gate of escape from the bondage of the past."[11]

It is indicative of the convolutions of this American puzzle that it has been possible to regard Turner, quite contrary to his general reputation, as a preeminent defender of tradition. Writing in 1938 the erstwhile Southern Agrarian Donald Davidson argued that the frontier thesis was properly subsumed in Turner's interest in sectionalism. From this perspective it seemed clear that Turner had assumed "the continuity of multiple traditions within one general tradition." Davidson compared Turner not with Herbert Baxter Adams but with Charles A. Beard—a fellow progressive but, unlike Turner, an advocate of "extreme centralization." In Davidson's view Beard's interpretation of American history assumed discontinuity, as it entailed "the impermanence of all factors except the economic."[12]

The problem actually admitted of no easy solution. In the judgment of later historians neither Adams's germs nor Turner's frontier provided an adequate explanation of the national history. Adams seemed to his successors to exemplify the unfortunate consequences of historical scholarship pursued with too dogmatic a devotion to Darwinian conceptions and to Anglo-American and "Teutonic" precepts of government read backwards into the remote past. The notion of Anglo-American cultural and institutional continuity had much to support it, and has been revived and restated by recent historians, but Adams seemed oblivious to genuine historicism in slighting the equally real claims of change.

Turner has retained far more professional respect, but later historians perhaps regretfully concluded that his portrayal of the almost mystically liberating and democratizing effects of the frontier is not sustained by the evidence. But Turner won the battle of the myths. Whether or not the Turner thesis was closer to the institutional facts, it was closer to experiential realities; America seemed to Americans to constitute a far sharper disjunction from Europe than Adams would allow. Turner's conscientious qualifications did not obscure the appealing vision of the frontier as "a gate of escape from the bondage of the past" and into the fresh and happy fields of democracy. It was this historical epiphany which captured the public imagination—not the traditionalism nurtured by sectional diversity and not the grim anomic social discontinuity that Davidson seemed to impute to Beard's urban, industrial America.[13]

As the question of the frontier demonstrated, the problem of continuity and discontinuity in time was also a problem of continuity and discontinuity in space. As fields of passage for westering emigrants, in particular, were the Atlantic and the Alleghenies to be seen simply as parts of homogeneous space, or did they have the special property of effecting disjunction, of causing a "fault" in time or of breaking the American's historical neck? That Americans were pleased to possess "the best of time and space," as Bronson Alcott had put it in 1834, perhaps obviated the need for more than rhetorical answers to such questions. But by the 1890s, when time had been thickened by evolutionary ideology and the official closing of the frontier had diverted spatial expansion into retrospective or overseas venues, they had a different resonance, one which could lend a glamour of jingoistic ebullience even to the profession of which Herbert Baxter Adams and Frederick Jackson Turner were members.[14]

Emerging in the late nineteenth century as a full-fledged professional discipline in America, history itself was partly the product of a national search for continuity amidst the disruptions of social and technological change. Seemingly validated by evolutionary ideas, American historical consciousness underwent a remarkable awakening in the decades following the Civil War. "Works on American history are descending upon the country in a flood," an *Atlantic Monthly* reviewer exclaimed in 1890. Once "eschewed by common consent as the dullest of topics," the national history was now being pursued by Americans "with the same wholesale ardor with which they have extirpated Indians, felled forests, built railroads, crushed rebellion, and populated a continent."[15]

This conflation of the energy of the historian with that of the frontiersman nicely represents a confusion of time and space noted over a century ago as a natural issue of nineteenth-century patterns of thought. "In place of a heterogeneous duration whose moments permeate one another," Henri Bergson argued in 1889, the determination to objectify and measure had elicited "a homogeneous time whose moments are strung on a spatial line." Ricardo J. Quinones has drawn on Bergson to explain the character of numbing uniformity which historical schemes of progress and evolution assumed for twentieth-century Modernists: "When the predictive, controlling aspect of time triumphed in the late nineteenth century, and triumphed so thoroughly and one-sidedly, it paradoxically produced its opposite effect, the triumph of space. Predictive time, without innovation or simple freshness of human appeal, leads to a kind of repetitive sameness."[16]

Bergson's distinction between "heterogeneous duration" and "homogeneous time" helps to define tradition as a particular kind of temporal phenomenon, one which did not fit so comfortably with spatial expansion. "The thinking American," Stephen Spender observed, "was divided between history—his roots within the English and European tradition—and geography—the immensity of America and the sense of his own being expanding to embrace that immensity." Space to expand could compensate for a paucity of tradition. The "homogeneous," measured time of which Bergson wrote meant above all to Americans the more or less smooth course of progress which was an article of the national faith. This kind of time positively summoned Americans to expansion. And insofar as Americans perceived their continent as "empty"—leaving its aboriginal inhabitants out of account— the space to be traversed and consumed was from a human standpoint equally homogeneous. The frontier line could advance with as much temporal and spatial evenness as inevitable natural and historical contingencies would permit.[17]

Efforts to spatialize tradition by identifying it with expansion, however, were bound to miscarry. The affinities of tradition have long been recognized as being with place rather than space—with the definite rather than the abstract. As Sir Walter Scott put it, "tradition depends upon locality." This was a problem for American traditionists. George Perkins Marsh early encapsulated the withering effect upon tradition of the mobility so central to the national experience: "antiquity, and the reverence with which it is regarded, necessarily partake of a local character, and an emigrating people leaves behind it, with the localities, the associations and the traditions upon which that reverence is founded," he observed in 1843. And when locality yielded to a space which is everywhere and nowhere, it would not be surprising if the lumpy specificity of tradition resolved itself accordingly into a smooth and abstract time. In such a time the future was readily identified with progress, but the past ran the risk either of becoming alien—a "foreign country"—or of being absorbed by founding national ideals perceived as timeless and universal—consequences familiar enough among ahistorical Americans.[18]

American historians provided little serious analysis of tradition before the twentieth century. For both Herbert Baxter Adams and Frederick Jackson Turner, tradition was an epiphenomenon of history, to be embraced in the celebration of Anglo-American heritage or rejected for the sake of liberation from the past. For neither did tradition carry any genuine authority. For Turner it was to be escaped, at least provisionally, but even Adams offered only a quasi-tradition, narrowly conceived and based on Anglo-American identity and biological analogy. The organic mode of germs and seeds was after all better suited to the transplanting of wheat than to the vicissitudes of human institutions. It was particularly inappropriate for a phenomenon so subject to human acceptance or rejection as tradition. Burke's metaphor of society as a partnership of generations better captured the spirit of tradition; partners may converse, agree, disagree, negotiate, cooperate—even in extremities dissolve their partnership. For Adams tradition, manifested in the spreading over the sea of cereal grains and townships, was as unnegotiated and inexorable as the evolution of a species of conifer.

Other historians sought to escape the stark polarities represented by Adams and Turner and to define in better tempered terms the role of tradition in an expansive American society. Edward Eggleston traced the evolution of this society in *The Beginners of a Nation* (1896) and *The Transit of Civilization from England to America in the Seventeenth Century* (1901). Eggleston had proclaimed at an 1890 meeting of the American Historical Association that "American institutions were all historical developments from colonial germs." This seemed patented H. B. Adams language, but Eggleston made more generous provision both for the American mutation of these germs and for tradition as a distinct social phenomenon. At a time when race, culture, and tradition were commonly scrambled together (and served with a sauce of progress), Eggleston's relative clarity and specificity in dealing with tradition was significant. "What are loosely spoken of as national characteristics are probably a result not so much of heredity as of controlling traditions," he surmised. "Seminal ideas received in childhood, standards of feeling and thinking and living handed down from one overlapping generation to another," shaped the individual to a particular nationality.[19]

Americans were no less subject to these shaping customs and traditions—in their case predominantly English—than any other people. But Eggleston did not portray his early American as tradition-bound; on the contrary, he was "more open-minded than his ancestors," and more prepared to break "the conservative crust of centuries of English life." The historian noted "the thralldom of the age to tradition" in such areas as medicine, but took a balanced view of continuity and change. Two principles worked through human life, he perceived. "Athwart the warp of traditional continuity there is woven the woof of variation; the pattern changes by degrees, but the web is without break or seam."[20]

The New England town was a case in point. Eggleston pointed out that the "town commune" could be traced in England as far back as the fifth century, with presumably even earlier origins lost to historical view. The town seemed a prime example of social continuity: "it shows how far human development can be carried without breaking an ancient shell of society." With some modification New England had followed "the immemorial usage of the English township." Society was a delicate transplant on American shores, Eggleston observed, and "the town community held it together in common helpfulness."[21]

The town community was central to the American discovery of tradition—and probably the preeminent American institutional "type." Custom and tradition exercised their sway in communities, and the effort to recover or preserve community was a hallmark of the late-nineteenth- and early-twentieth-century period, as it is of our own age. Among intellectuals the ideal of the transcendent individual, and the sense of society as an aggregate of individuals, gave way after the Civil War to the "concept of community," R. Jackson Wilson points out. Appreciation of community in the abstract was reflected in an increased interest in actual local communities. During the course of the nineteenth century, almost every New England town became the subject of a local history. Such endeavors were accompanied by the publication of records, the organization of state and local historical societies, a vogue for genealogy, and "a new appreciation of 'customs.'" Mid-century Whigs, especially, had sought to recover ties of memory to bind a society threatened with the incoherence of unrestrained freedom and materialism. The impulse proved an enduring one. Even acknowledged superstitions became "legends" or "traditions" of value. Much of this was of a merely antiquarian or filiopietistic interest, a limitation which caused local history to fall into disfavor among the newly professionalized historians of the turn-of-the-century period. (It enjoyed a resurgence in the community-oriented 1960s.) During its Victorian efflorescence, however, the study of local history was well in keeping with the main concerns of Anglo-American historical writing.[22]

Although the town community theme had a strong attraction for New England historians, they perceived the need to adapt its traditionalist cast to the frontier conditions and individualistic spirit which seemed to distinguish America from the Old World. William B. Weeden's *Economic and Social History of New England, 1620–1789* (1890) developed a panoramic yet particularized picture of English institutions transplanted and adapted. It depicted a traditional community which both nurtured American individualism and generated American expansion. New Englanders, in Weeden's account, had possessed the "power of carrying the home outward," and thereby of establishing the bases for new communities. Employing the inevitable biological imagery, Weeden suggested that "there was in every body of emigrants from the old world a communal germ, a society in the bud: if it matured well, the colony succeeded; if it grew awry, the colony failed. This communal life developed according to its hereditary tendencies, and even more according to the local conditions of its new home."[23]

The town then was fundamental, and the town was steeped in antiquity. It was founded on three institutions, Weeden explained: (1) freehold land "regulated by the best usage of many centuries"; (2) a town meeting expressive of "religious life and family culture"; and (3) "a representative, democratic gathering, corresponding to the old folk-mote of the Germanic races." Economic life showed perhaps the least breach of continuity. In particular, "the old Aryan custom of [common] herding, handed down through many countries and long periods of time, brought to the new continent the social order and fellowship of the Teutonic races."[24]

Weeden's New England was a fine balance of inheritance and adaptation to environment. The colonists "swept away feudalism, but kept the best features of the old land tenure." They democratically enlarged the folk-mote. They modified "English traditions of rank and prestige" and developed "new codes of manners." Even biblical prescriptions based on Jewish history and precedent evolved into distinctively Yankee courses of law and custom.[25]

Most fundamental of all was the balancing of community and individual. "The communal principle—deep-grained in the English and Teutonic races—planted the first towns," Weeden explained. "Individual freedom was never absent, but it was directed by a strong compelling force proceeding from the body politic, which tended to fuse individuals into a common union." Custom fostered a spirit of order and common purpose, which became preeminently New England's contribution to the national genius. By the time of the American Revolution, the historian thought, the "social impulse underlying the New England town as a political entity, forming the community, . . . was putting forth a larger organism,—a union of the colonies, which ultimately worked out the imperial unity of the United States of America."[26]

Weeden failed to define the functions of tradition so clearly as Eggleston, and was more typical of the period in his confusion of culture with race. It seemed to him that a "fusion of race characteristics and previous experiences has been going forward and working itself out" in America. "Combining blood, hereditary experience and national tendency, it has formed the solid amalgam of the American people." Central to this development in its racial aspect, he thought, was "the Anglo-German tendency to self-government." Yet Weeden did not insist on racial hierarchy; he perceived a benign combination of peoples, races, and nationalities. His final vision was that of individuals graduating into larger communities, achieving in the process broader opportunities and more complete freedom. Nurtured in the local community, the American was prepared for wider circles of action after the Civil War: "the national or imperial impulse carried the citizen higher and widened him out." And the American people, "having burst the swaddling clothes of local government, . . . grew into imperial government."[27]

Weeden touched on concerns of cardinal importance for his time: the reconciliation of individualism with community, the balancing of tradition with adaptation and innovation, the linkage of the local unit of society with the cosmopolitan scale of new economic and technological realities. Above all he treated with the "organic" expansion of the community from town to empire—"carrying the home outward." Other historians elaborated upon these themes. Lois Kimball Mathews, in *The Expansion of New England* (1909), viewed American society as the product of interaction between "the conservatism of the established community and the radicalism of the frontier." Citing Turner's frontier thesis in support of pioneer willingness to change, she sought to give equal weight to the continuity of the Puritan tradition, identified closely with New England. Characteristically for this school, the tradition had deep and quasi-racial roots: "the *Wanderlust* in the Anglo-Saxon blood had been potent in urging Englishmen to a part in the Crusades and later to voyages of exploration and discovery," she observed. The pattern was repeated by emigration overseas and once again on the frontier. Migrants often sought, indeed, to escape "tradition or habit," but necessarily brought much of it with them. The results were "institutions transplanted and transformed," and the spreading of New England civilization—church, school, and town meeting—from the Atlantic to the Pacific. "Wherever Puritan blood has gone, Puritan traditions have been carried"; that seemed to Mathews "the essential thing to note."[28]

In important respects historians like Eggleston, Weeden, and Mathews refined Augustine Jones's naive juxtaposition of social continuity and discontinuity. They reconciled the two in delineating patterns, suggested or validated by evolution, which combined tradition with variation, and the transplanting of ways and values with their adaptation to new environments. The result was to associate tradition, not with a static society, but with progress through time and expansion through space—a conception well fitted to American circumstances and values. These refinements hardly concealed an impulse to typology similar to that of Dudley's biographer. Long-ago Anglo-Saxon migrations foreshadowed the settlement of New England and the advance westward of its civilization; the town served also as the type of larger and more complex communities.

Although the resulting scheme of history was well adapted to growth and change, it assumed behind all flux universal standards of social well-being. New England church, school, and government, although they might differ in Massachusetts and California, stood for constant qualities of spirituality, learning, and self-rule. Tradition, in America, was yoked to transcendent values as well as to progress and physical expansion. In no prominent figure do these linkages appear more clearly, perhaps, than in the popular philosopher and historian John Fiske (1842–1901).

Fiske served up a mixture of scientifically-gilded idealism, high-minded expansionism, and infectious curiosity about the past which struck a responsive chord with the late-nineteenth-century American public. The British historian William Stubbs might have been thinking of Fiske and his followers when he suggested that a codification of manorial customs might serve to demonstrate "the continuity of English local institutions from the earliest times, to last until our American cousins have annexed us; and possibly longer still, for those cousins, even more than most of our own countrymen, show a very lively interest in everything, legal, customary, or historical, that illustrates the cradle of the race, out of which evolution is going to produce the ideal man."[29]

Fiske was a "popularizer," as his leading biographer describes him, who drew on more original thinkers to fashion an account of history as evolutionary progress. Standard treatments have emphasized the conservative outcome of this project: beginning as a rebel against religious orthodoxy, Fiske ended by constructing a defense of orthodox values based on Spencerian and Darwinian precepts. But Fiske can also be considered the other way around, as a traditionalist who vitiated tradition. Identifying an anciently rooted "Teutonic Idea" of political development with unlimited Anglo-American expansion, he universalized that which took its life from particularities of place and time, and discounted those other traditions for which this expansion left no room. Fiske shows the traditionist impulse in late-nineteenth-century America to have been in no simple way reactionary, but as capable rather of an aggressive, characteristically modern, and ultimately self-defeating rendering of time as space.[30]

A native of Connecticut, Fiske graduated from Harvard in 1863. He lectured briefly at his alma mater and served as assistant librarian at the Harvard College Library for seven years, but was disappointed in his ardent hopes of winning a permanent faculty position. Religious heterodoxy initially damaged his prospects. While an undergraduate he had abandoned the Calvinistic religious faith he had accepted in adolescence—denouncing the Geneva Reformer himself as "a sort of incarnation of the Devil he talks about"—and in consequence had drawn unfavorable notice as a rebel. Without the scholarly discipline that academic affiliation could have provided, his thought developed little beyond his youth. Proclaiming himself a positivist during his college years, he later tried with limited success to "shake off the label." (He insisted, "I have always been a positivist in just the same sense that Wendell Phillips has been a celebrated pro-slavery orator.") Although nettled by the persistent misunderstanding, he settled comfortably into Herbert Spencer's "synthetic," evolutionary philosophy.[31]

Fiske was a stout, hearty Gilded Age American, uxorious and companionable, full of hope and cheer. "His personality had a sort of manifold simplicity, or was built in laminae of unconsciousness, which you could penetrate to the last without finding any taint of distrust or suspicion," William Dean Howells recalled in a eulogy for Harper's Weekly. Long and wearying lecture tours yielded wordy letters to his wife Abby, sentimental in the Victorian mode, yearning for domestic comforts, and often signed with the pet name Hezekiah, or "Hezzie." His personal habits ran to excess, whether of work, play, smoking, or eating; on forays abroad he laid waste to English beef and ale with the same gusto with which he inspected Gothic cathedrals and schmoozed with Charles Darwin and Herbert Spencer. Fiske's enthusiasm seemed to flag only on an occasion when friends held him by the ankles so that he could kiss the Blarney Stone; he drew back in fright at the airy depths below. The indefatigable lecturer and conversationalist needed no help with the gift of gab, and posterity could hardly fault his trivial failure of nerve; more serious, from a later perspective, was the Victorian optimist's reluctance to stare into the darker abysses of the human condition.[32]

Fiske's personal expansiveness was emblematic of much that was both most and least attractive in his work and in his society. His interests ranged over the whole of time and space, and were capable of narrow focus as well as wide. His faith in progress combined with what has been characterized as "an extreme reverence for the past"—not a reactionary stance but a sympathetic fascination with tradition, customs, and folklore quite different from the dismissive attitude toward such phenomena of some more confirmed positivists. An early work, *Myths and Myth-Makers* (1872), described folk stories—"some of them familiar to us in infancy, others the delight of our maturer years"—as "the débris, or alluvium, brought down by the stream of tradition from the distant highlands of ancient mythology." This was not a merely antiquarian interest, for Fiske sought to draw broad conclusions from his data, and especially to account for myths as pre-scientific ways to explain natural phenomena. But the same confident spirit could lead him to exalt the "Aryans" over less progressively inclined "races," and to become a spokesman for political as well as cultural imperialism.[33]

Fiske's expansiveness fitted well with the appetite of the age for grand systematizing, which he most ambitiously indulged in his *Outlines of Cosmic Philosophy* (1874). Impelled by financial need into his career as a public lecturer, he eventually rendered many of his largely historical topics in book form. Works like *The Discovery of America*, *The Beginnings of New England*, and *The Critical Period of American History* effectively combined vivid narrative with a clear and edifying interpretive scheme, and made Fiske "the best-selling historian of his generation."[34]

Fiske's reputation among his countrymen—he placed impressively in contemporary lists of "immortals"—made it seem fitting that his death, in 1901, should come on the Fourth of July. To this solemnity was added a note of pathos deriving from his long fascination with the evolution of Anglo-American institutions, for his demise cost him a chance to speak at the millennial celebration of Alfred the Great in Winchester, England. But contemporaries like Howells recognized his limitations as a thinker, and after his death his reputation began quickly to erode. The shrinking of Herbert Spencer's stature from its Victorian dimensions inevitably contributed to the diminution of that of his disciple. Academic historians, more laudatory of Fiske's style than of his substance during his lifetime, faulted him with less restraint afterwards for lack of originality and research methods insufficiently grounded in primary sources. His philosophy, despite its "cosmic" reach, seemed increasingly provincial—that of an "ethnic historian" who celebrated the English heritage in New England and its achievements in the building of the nation, as Milton Berman put it in 1961. Most fundamentally, perhaps, his vision of progressive social evolution became a casualty of Modernist sensibility and twentieth-century disillusionment. Yet in his articulation of the themes to which Bishop Stubbs called sardonic attention, and particularly in his dexterity in rendering the traditional virtues of home and community as a summons to national expansion, Fiske illuminates a phase of American thought in which a retrospective mood ran in tandem with imperial aspirations.[35]

For a well-educated American coming of age in the 1860s, and possessed of the normal desire to make sense of the course of human development, Herbert Spencer was an inescapable presence. Evolution, which could be made plausibly not only to explain the past but to guarantee the future, offered the most comprehensive way of tying up natural and social phenomena with human hope and faith, and those who explained and guaranteed most comprehensively, like Spencer, could have overwhelming impact. Fiske, encountering the philosopher as a Harvard undergraduate, was permanently captivated.

The captivation was not complete. Hewing closely to Spencer's synthetic philosophy in most respects, Fiske departed from it most significantly in adapting it to theological precepts. In contrast to Spencer's bleak allowance for the "Unknowable," the quondam American rebel came to espouse a much more positively religious "Cosmic Theism." This lofty faith purged Christian doctrines of gross anthropomorphism but recognized their essence in the keeping of a deity immanent in nature and human consciousness, who worked through evolution to elevate the human race from brutality to an eventual reign of peace and altruism. It was a theism which did not reject the Protestant conception of the access of the individual to the universal, but which allowed for the discovery of transcendent truths through the properly understood continuities of social development.[36]

This religious infusion certainly served to make evolutionary doctrines more palatable to the American public, as has often been pointed out; it was what Vernon Louis Parrington meant in his unkind description of Fiske as "a philosophic hippopotamus, warming the chill waters of Spencerian science with his enormous bulk." But the thermal effects of this theism were more complex. Not merely easing the accommodation of evolution to American religiosity, they included also the legitimizing of tradition as a mediator between the individual and the transcendent.[37]

For Fiske personally, cosmic theism clearly filled a need. Following his youthful religious apostasy, he had seized upon positivism in part, apparently, because it offered a quick replacement for Protestant orthodoxy. In the first flush of enthusiasm he described it as "both a philosophy & a religion which met all my wants, & filled me with such joy as I had never known before." Yet positivism, although it provided a system of thought comparable to a theology in its claim to comprehensive validity, had the disadvantage of lacking religious substance, of any opening to the transcendent.[38]

A return to an orthodoxy which Fiske no longer found credible, on the other hand, was hardly possible. This had a bearing on his attitude toward tradition. As he was aware, his original faith was in itself profoundly hostile to the very idea of tradition. Rejecting Catholic sacramentalism, and making salvation a transaction directly between God and the individual, it had rendered all mundane relationships ultimately insignificant. Immediate obedience to divine will obviated the importance of the partnership of generations which for Edmund Burke defined society. Tradition represented, further, the long-accreted errors of

Catholicism from which Protestants had struggled to break free. However tight community and generational bonds actually were in Puritan New England, the theological premises it bequeathed were more favorable to the expansion of society—if not in the service of God at least in the service of individual gain or "Manifest Destiny"—than to the maintenance of its traditions.

Fiske retained much of this Protestant animus against tradition. Christianity itself had begun, he remarked sympathetically, "as a kind of Protestantism, in which old heathen ideas of conformity to tribal requirements as to doctrine and ritual were utterly discarded, and in which religion was presented as something which concerns the individual alone in the presence of the infinite God." But the rejection of tradition on an ultimate level of saving knowledge and grace could without contradiction become itself a tradition on a human and worldly level. As a historian, Fiske came to value Calvinism not as a theology but as a tradition which, liberalized and secularized, had culminated in American democracy. Like George Bancroft and others, Fiske reconciled the country's Puritan heritage with its libertarian ideals through a kind of paradox. Despite its absolute demands, "Calvinism left the individual man alone in the presence of his God." Fortified in this awesome company, he was prepared to defy kings and bishops in the service not only of God but of human progress.[39]

Fiske acknowledged in this tradition a "vein of mysticism," which he traced through Jonathan Edwards to the Concord Transcendentalists. Yet this was not a cloistered spirituality, he emphasized, but a devotion which was fruitful of good works in the world. Edwards, in emphasizing the distinction between the converted and the unconverted rather than that between the elect and the non-elect, had provided a warrant for human effort. Retaining an ultimate allegiance to truth despite its sometimes bigoted narrowness, this modernized Calvinism could develop "towards light and stimulus and exaltation of life as typified in an Emerson," Fiske concluded.[40]

In this way Fiske the historian placed tradition at the service of Protestantism and liberty. For Fiske the "Cosmic Theist," on the other hand, tradition was a problem resolvable only in terms of a doubleness in tradition itself: its nature both as a set of ideas and usages developed and maintained in practical response to social needs and interests, and as a signpost for what were held to be ultimate or absolute truths. This doubleness was reflected in Fiske's religious sensibility, an uneasy mixture of idealism and empiricism, as H. Burnell Pannill described it, which compounded the transcendent purpose of the "Absolute" with its radical immanence in the world.[41]

Even in his early "positivist" phase, Fiske displayed this ambivalence. Having abandoned an orthodox reliance on the Bible, he looked to the universe itself as his "Revelation"—an "'open secret,' written in *hieroglyphs*, in a *sacred* language, which science is daily translating into the dialect of mankind." The media of this revelation included mathematics, physical nature, and "the great social Organism." Yet if science provided evidence of a purposive intelligence immanent in the world, as this formulation suggested, Fiske was led necessarily back to the conception of a transcendent deity. Physics showed nature "quivering with energy," indicating, as he later concluded, "that all the myriad phenomena of the universe . . . are the manifestations of a single animating principle that is both infinite and eternal." As that eternal force could not itself be material, the only consistent conclusion seemed to be that it was the same power which appeared in human consciousness.[42]

Immanence and transcendence had been at two poles of Christian theology throughout the history of the church—never of course mutually exclusive, but representing different notions of God's relationship to His creation. Among Protestants, as Jon H. Roberts points out, the immanentists gained strength during the last quarter of the nineteenth century, encouraged by the idea that science might be understood as revealing divine activity in the universe. Fiske found particular support in Alexander V. G. Allen's *The Continuity of Christian Thought: A Study of Modern Theology in the Light of Its History* (1884). An Episcopal priest, Allen traced the history of two opposed Christian traditions, one based on a "Latin theology" emphasizing divine transcendence, the other a "Greek" school of thought which envisioned God as immanent in His creation. After a long Latin predominance, the nineteenth century was witnessing a profound shift to the Greek conception of God, he contended. Manifested in the evangelical belief that God was immanent in the conversion experience, this theology also invited demonstration of His presence in the laws of nature. It might be possible, Allen suggested, to construct "a science which shall embrace all knowledge, because it sees all things in God."[43]

Fiske was impressed by the congruence of Allen's "Greek" theology with modern science, which fitted well with the evolution of his own thought. Certainly it provided reassurance that Christianity might after all have a message for the modern world. And despite Fiske's determination to eschew anthropomorphism, his scientifically validated deity grew increasingly to resemble His original of Christian tradition. Christian doctrines reappeared in scientific garb. Overcoming original sin became a matter of "throwing off the brute-inheritance," and "true salvation" the evolutionary perfecting of human nature. Even personal immortality seemed implied by a soul-generating evolutionary process. Evolution, it transpired, had worked no alteration in the essential Christian message. It had simply provided a new revelation of the scope and complexity of divine immanence, replacing, as Fiske emphasized, "as much teleology as it destroys."[44]

Most crucial was the proposition that God was immanent in human consciousness as well as in nature itself. Joining the inwardness of Protestant spirituality to the laws governing outward processes, this permitted Fiske to assume an "essential kinship between the human soul, as it was evolving, and ultimate reality," as Pannill points out. It was the "evolving," absent in the original Protestant nexus of God and individual, which made room for tradition. An ineluctable means of social evolution, tradition provided a linkage between the particulars in which Allen's "Greek" deity was immanent and the transcendence which Fiske's idealism never permitted him to abjure. Tradition was fitted to serve, indeed, as the bearer of this increasingly apprehended transcendence. If Fiske did not entirely jettison a Protestant-progressive sense of tradition as a drag upon human betterment, his theism also afforded a framework within which tradition could function both as a practical accretion of beliefs and usages and as a harbinger of the "Absolute."[45]

Fiske's religious impulse prompted him to a notably more positive assessment of the function of tradition than that of his mentor Herbert Spencer. In the Spencerian view customs and traditions played necessarily an ambivalent role. Requisite to social development, they were apt also to be frustrating and intractable. They accumulated in society in accord with Spencer's celebrated law of evolution "from an indefinite incoherent homogeneity to a definite coherent heterogeneity." In the early stages of society, Spencer observed, the "coercive influence of . . . traditional beliefs must be strong"; there was little way other than through tradition and custom to organize human beings effectively to cope with the conditions of their lives. Even in more progressive stages of development tradition could act as a necessary brake on too-rapid change.[46]

Yet what was necessary was also a tyranny. For primitive man there was no escape from the imperative of custom. "In all cases habits of life, when continued for many generations, mould the nature," Spencer pointed out, "and the resulting traditional beliefs and usages with the accompanying sentiments, become difficult to change." The rule of custom and tradition became nothing less than "the rule of the dead over the living," which it was the task of social evolution to overthrow.[47]

Following Spencer's lead, Fiske acknowledged primitive men to have been broken to the "yoke of tyrannical custom"—a bondage entirely necessary, and yet contrary to the destined ascendancy of the individual. But as oppressive as the intense social conservatism of early societies had been, custom and tradition had made possible a truly human life, Fiske emphasized, one distinguished by enduring social relationships which nurtured the growth of moral sentiments from generation to generation. In keeping with the Spencerian law of evolution, moreover, accumulating customs and traditions made the social environment increasingly heterogeneous, and this heterogeneity was "the chief proximate determining cause of social progress." Human society came to be distinguished by "the permanent character of the relationships between its constituent members," Fiske believed. "Enduring from birth until death, these relationships acquire a traditionary value which passes on from generation to generation," nurturing in the process fundamental moral sentiments.[48]

For these reasons Fiske recognized the prehistoric invention of tradition as a decisive event in human development. Citing the French philosopher Émile Littré, he concluded that the study of humanity revealed "a new phenomenon unknown in biology or in psychology pure and simple. That new phenomenon is Tradition, or the bequeathing of all its organized intellectual and moral experience by each generation to its successor. Here for the first time we have an environment which is rapidly changing in a definite order of sequence, and changing by the very activity of the community itself." Fiske's ready association of tradition with change—rapid and evidently progressive change—is especially revealing.[49]

It is no less noteworthy that the one insight Fiske claimed as his own contribution to the theory of evolution imputed to tradition both a biological and a domestic basis. He proposed a theory emphasizing the importance of the prolongation of infancy in human beings—a contribution not accorded much importance by later investigators, but one which Fiske (on Spencer's assurance) regarded as his guarantee of immortality. A long childhood, combined with the development of language, increasingly permitted education to supersede mere heredity as the means of passing on ancestral experience, Fiske argued. Humanity was thus enabled "to accumulate a fund of tradition, which in the fulness of time was to bloom forth in history and poetry, in science and theology."[50]

Made possible by slow evolutionary processes and the placid nurturing of the family circle, tradition became a dynamic force in human development. Fiske so closely identified tradition with progress as seemingly to reduce them to facets of the same grand process of social evolution. He could praise Francis Parkman for his unequalled skill in depicting American Indian society in the "ancient stages of its progress," and as readily note that when barbarism was overwhelmed by civilization "its vanishing is final; the thread of tradition is cut off forever with the shears of Fate."[51]

Fiske perceived some of the difficulties of fitting human social development to a scheme of general evolution. He disclaimed any "crude" identification of biological evolution with progress, noting that organic development tended to subordinate individual members to the whole, while in social development the reverse obtained. He understood that evolution in the natural world did not necessarily converge with human goals, that evolution could give way to dissolution and that even progress was "contingent and partial" rather than "necessary and universal." It was obvious, further, that tradition and custom could become static. The restraints of custom, while necessary to concert human efforts at an early stage of social development, had to be relaxed if the race were to advance, he pointed out; the problem was to relax them "without entailing a retrogression toward primeval lawlessness."[52]

None of these caveats seriously vitiated Fiske's faith that "the law of progress, when discovered, will be found to be the law of history," as he stated it early in his career. And if inexorably progressive in its ultimate direction, the social process was dependent on the accumulation of tradition in its provenance. Sheer continuity seemed able to resolve any difficulties. Although he could contemplate the severing of barbarian tradition with fair equanimity, Fiske was a gradualist when it came to changes in civilized society. He accordingly adapted Walter Bagehot's famous metaphor to bind tradition and progress in a different way: "in a progressive society the cementing and breaking of the 'cake of custom' must go on simultaneously," he suggested.[53]

Yet the breaking, it appeared, never quite kept pace with the cementing. The effects of the traditionary were cumulative, and to make the point Fiske availed himself of another image from the stock ideas of the century, at once more imperial and more somber, and as darkly ironic in its implications for expansion as in those for progress. "As Comte expresses it, in one of his profoundest aphorisms, the empire of the dead over the living increases from age to age," Fiske noted in his Cosmic Philosophy. In the earliest phases of human experience, as he explicated Comte, conditions of physical environment were largely determining; with the advance of civilization "the organized experience of past generations" was of ever-increasing importance. Consequently, Fiske concluded, "the environment of each generation consists to a greater and greater extent of the sum total of traditions bequeathed by all past generations."[54]

Americans, Fiske included, were in actuality more interested in creating an empire of the living than in living in an empire of the dead. Yet the one could authorize the other. Whether conceived as Pelikan's "icon," pointing beyond itself to the universal benefits to be conferred by American expansion, or as part of Bergson's "heterogeneous duration" transformed into "a homogeneous time" lending itself to spatialization, tradition could readily serve the needs of empire-building. Although to many of Fiske's countrymen it implied constraints uncongenial to a frontier society, it could also suggest the continuity of venture and endeavor represented by expansion—the seeds of community life giving forth at length into the federal republic and eventually into imperial and perhaps even global embodiments. And at the end of the process of social evolution Fiske envisioned a society based on peace, altruism, and voluntary cooperation. Tradition for John Fiske was not only a "communion with past powers," as Edward Shils put it, but a promise of things to come, and the final antitype of the town community, it appeared, was to be a quasi-City of God.[55]

However stated, this was for Fiske a natural sequence. Unwilling to jettison the traditions of place and home to which he was wholeheartedly devoted, he made it his mission to find a way in which they might be generalized. With him as with many Victorians domesticity comported easily with empire—and even with cosmos. Having become full humanity only with the emergence of the family, the species in Fiske's view had a social destiny tied to the extension of the "sympathetic" feelings—those the family had fostered—to broader and broader areas of life. Fiske's increasing recourse, if not to an anthropomorphic God at least to one recognizable in terms of human values and purposes, partook also of this familial sense. "The human soul shrinks from the thought that it is without kith or kin in all this wide universe," he observed. Even an acceptable afterlife was unimaginable "without the continuance of the tender household affections which alone make the present life worth living."[56]

In *The Idea of God as Affected by Modern Knowledge* (1885) Fiske more graphically linked home with eternity: "As in the roaring loom of Time the endless web of events is woven, each strand shall make more and more clearly visible the living garment of God." Associated traditionally with women's hearthside labor and cottage industry, the loom became the emblem here of a universal design. Processing yarn or thread into an expanse of cloth with the forward motion imparted by the machine, it suggested as components of that design both linear progress and the translation of time into space as proposed by Bergson.[57]

Striking as was the figure of the loom—as majestically inexorable in its workings as Henry Adams's dynamo—expansion could be more precisely represented in ways which drew on a contemporary Anglo-American absorption with the processes of constructing large units out of small. Referring primarily to England, J. W. Burrow alludes to "a sensibility . . . characteristically mid-Victorian, in its feeling for the obscure and provincial, and its fascination with the structures fabricated, coral-like, by countless almost imperceptible creatures." There was something of this fascination in Fiske and other American scholars, appearing in myriad narrowly focused ventures in local history and antiquarianism. Joined to equally Victorian expansionist impulses, the comfortable assurance of tradition slowly accreting in domestic and local venues could foster a version of history which, as Bishop Stubbs had suggested, regarded this locally rooted tradition as the bearer of transcendent purpose, progressively realized in time and space. Yet despite Stubbs's amusement at American ebullience, it was largely Stubbs himself and other of the later British "Whig" historians who supplied the rationale for Fiske and other transatlantic expositors. "Ideas of progress and the Burkean conception of tradition" were the "warp and woof" of Whig history, in Burrow's words. The Whigs emphasized the continuity of English legal and political institutions, their roots in the local community, and their long progression from Anglo-Saxon and even earlier times.[58]

Of the Whigs, Fiske found Edward A. Freeman—both as a "very lovable" friend and as a historian—particularly congenial. Freeman's belief in the Teutonic origins of Anglo-American democracy and his view of the United States as a third England—after the original Anglo-Saxon home on the European mainland and "Middle England" in Britain—could have been especially calculated to win the American's approval. Like Fiske, Freeman believed firmly in the congruence of progress with custom and tradition. "Let ancient customs prevail; let us ever stand fast in the old paths," he urged. "But the old paths have in England ever been the paths of progress."[59]

These customary paths, according to a widespread view, began at the "mark community." In his influential *Village-Communities in the East and West* (1889), Sir Henry Maine characterized this kind of habitation by "the arable mark, divided into separate lots but cultivated according to minute customary rules binding on all." If these primitive communities were customary and traditional to an oppressive degree, they also harbored a democratic impulse, Maine thought. In the village council in particular, as he elsewhere explained, lay the "embryo" of Parliament and other Anglo-American legislative bodies.[60]

As remote as the mark community might have seemed to American society, British scholars were quick to acknowledge its transatlantic relevance. Maine himself noted as a "remarkable fact" that early English colonists had grouped themselves in traditional communities. Contemporary British interest in corporate pluralism and federalism provided a larger historical context for such communities, further, which was of direct interest to Americans. Freeman, entranced by the persistence of ancient local liberties in Switzerland, was especially insistent upon the advantages of federalism. In America, he believed, the federal model had been most fully realized in New England, where local self-government had flourished most vigorously.[61]

Such themes, emphasizing the continuity of democratic institutions from traditional local communities to modern continental or imperial embodiments, were pervasive in the writing of American history during the last third of the nineteenth century. Fiske himself depicted America as a modified but greater England, the product of an unfolding, progressive transatlantic tradition. He traced the Virginia colonial assembly to the old English county court, and the New England town meeting to ancient Germanic institutions. Notions of the country as a new beginning were wholly set aside; those traditions most deeply rooted in English history usually turned out to be the ones that had best served the cause of liberty, and that had therefore flourished most freely in America.[62]

Fiske predictably agreed with Freeman that such usages were preeminently those of his native New England, the section of the country he deemed at once the "most completely English in blood and traditions" and the "most completely American" in its political principles. One reason for this, he believed, was the settlement of much of New England by the migration of communities rather than by mere individuals or even families. Through generations the civil procedures of town life had accustomed New Englanders to democratic modes of debate and self-government. Fiske took rare exception to Freeman in insisting that the Swiss cantonal assemblies, which had impressed the English historian as pure survivals of Germanic democracy, were no more venerable or egalitarian than their New England counterparts—even if they were held in the open air and attended by a pageantry eschewed by austere Yankees.[63]

Fiske admitted that New England town governments might have been established without "conscious reference to precedent," but it seemed clear that they embodied usages extending far back in time. The most primitive self-governing body known, he contended, was the "village-community of the ancient Teutons, of which such strict counterparts are found in other parts of the Aryan world as to make it apparent that in its essential features it must be an inheritance from prehistoric Aryan antiquity." Americans had simply brought to fruition a tradition they had transplanted from England.[64]

Fiske's idealized representation of the town was colored by his personal ties to particular New England communities. In his place of residence, Cambridge, Massachusetts, he perceived the traces of "the ancient threefold partition into town mark, arable mark, and common." But the founders of Cambridge, he emphasized, were not the same as "the rough followers of Alaric or Hengist"; they were the heirs too of classical civilization, of English law, and the learning of the Middle Ages and Renaissance. Fiske pointed especially to a bond with the town's English namesake, "the beautiful city on the Cam," forged not only of the personal ties of those graduates of Cambridge University who had emigrated to Massachusetts, but also of a mutual commitment to scholarship, godliness, and freedom. The founding of Cambridge, then, had not been merely the establishment of a new town in a new world; it had been the realization of "a rich inheritance."[65]

Fiske saved his most affectionate encomium, however, for his boyhood home of Middletown, Connecticut (which as a young man he had sought to escape as an unenlightened backwater). In an address in 1900 commemorating the two hundred and fiftieth anniversary of the founding of the town, Fiske observed that its history, extending back "over one fourth of the interval that has elapsed since the death of Alfred the Great," refuted the notion that America had no history. Middletown was clearly for Fiske the very model of the New England community, the heir of the past and yet representative of social life at its most felicitously developed. That some of the town's "old-time charm" remained, he thought, was due "to the preservation of old traditions and mental habits," shining through strong individual personalities. Fiske's sentimental vision of "the sweet domesticity of the old New England" was coupled with a reminder of the seminal role of the town meeting in generating American democracy.[66]

Village domesticity was not the ultimate end; the great project, as William Weeden had suggested, was to "carry the home outward." Not condemned to be cramped within the town, tradition entered naturally into the vast spatial dimensions which seemed more and more to define the United States. Although Fiske manifested the Yankee tendency to see America as New England writ large, he sought to give the section's institutions a broader American base. "Something very like the 'town-meeting principle' lies at the bottom of all the political life of the United States," he wanted to show. The "admirable" manorial institutions of early Maryland had established a sort of rural counterpart to the New England town before being eclipsed by the growth of slavery, he suggested: "These manors were little self-governing communities. The court leet was like a town meeting. All freemen could take part in it." Transplanted without alteration from England, these institutions were well adapted to preserve a measure of liberty on manors which were otherwise, he acknowledged, little "patriarchal" worlds in themselves. Indeed, he thought, they provided the "democratic" element in the Maryland constitution. In South Carolina, Fiske noted, elected vestries "discharged many of the functions which in New England were performed by the town meeting." Virginia institutions (which included vestries which were self-perpetuating rather than freely elected) were more difficult to assimilate to the town principle, but Fiske could at least enlist Thomas Jefferson in testimony that "the town meeting is the best form of government ever devised by man."[67]

No matter how impressive the institutions of local self government, however, Fiske believed that the ultimate problem of political history had been to find a way of combining them with the greater security and concert of efforts made possible by large-scale organization. The solution, upon which he elaborated in *The Beginnings of New England* (1889), had been found in the "Teutonic Idea of political life," which it had been preeminently the work of New Englanders to bear to America and nurture on the new continent. Despite its racial nomenclature, Fiske described the Teutonic Idea as essentially a political and social tradition, inhering not only in ideas but in beliefs, values, laws, customs, and institutions which the historian ascribed to the Germanic and especially the English people. It was for Fiske the paramount tradition of Western political development because it provided the nexus between tradition and expansion, community and empire.[68]

The Teutonic Idea represented the highest phase of statecraft. In Fiske's analysis, the "Oriental" method of nation building had been one of "conquest without incorporation." The Roman method had provided for incorporation, but not for representation. It had been the Teutonic genius to follow expansion with both incorporation and representation, making it possible to achieve national unity without sacrificing local self-government. Although the struggle between centralizing and localizing forces had been a general one in Europe, it was only in England, Fiske thought, that the representative principle had been fully established, and it was there that local independence had been most effectively preserved. But the problem was a continuing one. "From the days of Arminius and Civilis in the wilds of lower Germany to the days of Franklin and Jefferson in Independence Hall, we have been engaged in this struggle," he observed.[69]

The continuity of the struggle was unbroken. Fiske explained the apparent American discontinuities of emigration and revolution by making such breaks with the past themselves traditional—the habitual recourse of a wandering and freedom-loving race—and further through his perception that the circumstances of emigration had resulted in a distillation and strengthening of salient national traits. The ancient "Aryan" invaders of Europe had been "the pioneers or Yankees of prehistoric antiquity," in whom changing circumstances had fostered resourcefulness and flexibility. The fifth-century Anglo-Saxon migrations to Britain had accentuated these qualities. Physical isolation had allowed the later English to remain more independent of Roman law and ecclesiastical authority than their German cousins and had enabled them more effectively to exercise their Teutonic aptitude for local and representative government.[70]

English emigrants to America had worked out the Teutonic Idea even more fully. The Atlantic Ocean served as a wider English Channel, a shield against foreign despotism which obviated the need for a domestic one. Powerfully strengthened by the Puritan disposition to personal liberty and self-government—despite Calvinist theological absolutism—English traditions of liberty had taken ready root, and were given new scope by the vast reaches of the continent. Not even the War for Independence could break the transatlantic cords of continuity. Regarding that conflict as a conservative revolution in defense of English liberties, Fiske agreed with Freeman that the result had been simply the creation of another England, prepared to work alongside its parent "with might and main toward the political regeneration of mankind."[71]

A favorable environment had enabled Americans to perfect a principle which was embryonic in English and Germanic modes of political organization, and thereby to supply the capstone of the "Teutonic Idea." This capstone was the federal principle of government. Federalism was for Fiske no mere expedient, and its significance transcended that of formal constitutional arrangements. It rendered time as space; it linked type and antitype. Fiske's enthusiasm for the principle distinguished him from Herbert Spencer, whose evolutionary philosophy offered a model of seamless development requiring no such mediating terms. His views were re-enforced, however, by the Whiggish British scholars who viewed federalism as a way of preserving the political participation of the citizen in an age of massive and leveling social institutions. As a protagonist of the New England town, Fiske no less than Freeman was disposed to look to federalism for "a chance of perpetuating at least some shadow of the virtues of the polis in an age of large states," as Burrow puts it.[72]

Federalism, in Fiske's view, was a natural product of social evolution, of the progressive "integration of communities, originally mere tribes or clans, into social aggregates of higher and higher orders of complexity." The historian applied the term not merely to the division of powers between states and nation, but more broadly to polities which in any way combined local self-government with more general authority. He acknowledged foreshadowings of modern federal forms in the ancient Greek leagues, the Swiss cantonal system, and the Dutch Republic. But it was the English branch of the Teutonic race which had realized the principle most fully. Fiske described the historical evolution of the English state as a sort of cellular construction of small units into large. Thus village-communities made up the shire, and the kingdom was composed of a union of shires. Conflating federalism with representation, Fiske cited the practice, as far back as the time of Alfred the Great, of sending men from each township to participate in the proceedings of the county court—"the parent," he thought, "of all popular legislatures." Parliament later recapitulated the process on a larger scale.[73]

Full germination of the federal principle required, however, abundance of space as well as of time: "*first*, a vast extent of unoccupied country which could be settled without much warfare by men of the same race and speech, and *secondly*, on the part of the settlers, a rich inheritance of political training such as is afforded by long ages of self-government." These, of course, were precisely the advantages Americans enjoyed. Transplanted to the New World, federalism showed its vitality in the seventeenth-century Confederation of New England, and more fundamentally in that region's early-developed practice of representing towns in a general court or assembly. Fiske was especially proud that his native state of Connecticut had played a key role in elevating the principle to a continental plane. Connecticut's colonial system of electing its governor and council by a majority of the voters, while towns were represented equally in one house of the legislature, had created a kind of "tiny federal republic," he argued. It had also provided a broad precedent for the "Connecticut Compromise" on congressional representation at the Constitutional Convention of 1787—an accommodation enabling the United States to combine "imperial vastness with unhampered local self-government."[74]

This was the solution to what was politically the "chief problem of civilization," as Fiske reiterated it: "how to secure concerted action among men on a grand scale without sacrificing local independence." The local was as important as the grand. Although Fiske's best-known historical volume, *The Critical Period of American History, 1783–1789* (1888), portrayed the government established by the Articles of Confederation as unacceptably weak, and he regarded the Civil War as a crucial vindication of federalism, he cautioned against too much consolidation. A purely national government, after all, would destroy the local roots from which Anglo-American government was fed.[75]

Federalism thus fitted the continuities of Anglo-American political life to the specific American realities of immense space and rapid expansion. It generalized the principles of liberty and democracy which arose from the closest traditions of the people. It joined the increasing empire of the dead to the also increasing empire of the living, and in so doing enabled modern man to become—Fiske echoed Tennyson's catchphrase—the "heir of all the ages, in whose making and perfecting is to be found the consummation of God's creative work."[76]

The note of universalism in this was not an aberration; Fiske was confident that the political genius which had inspired the Connecticut Compromise was not yet exhausted. Vindicated and strengthened by the Union triumph in the Civil War, the federal principle seemed poised to give the Teutonic Idea "a hundred-fold power and seminal influence in the future work of the world." A federated Europe, and even an eventual world federal union, appeared as reasonable prospects in this great unfolding. Globalized, the traditions of the English village and the New England town would construct a peaceful, "truly Christian," world.[77]

So defined, of course, this vision was only provincialism universalized. Fiske had noted the advantages of flexibility which an American federal union offered in bringing into comity states so diverse as Maine, Louisiana, and California. Yet the accent was on commonality—of race and of political tradition. That accent became even more pronounced when Fiske sought to project the federal principle beyond national bounds. He proposed his world federation in a lecture appropriately entitled "Manifest Destiny," delivered at Boston in 1879 and published unchanged six years later. He left no doubt as to the inspiration and provenance of such a federation. The contemporary vigor of the English-speaking peoples seemed to him ample indication that "the work which the English race began when it colonized North America is destined to go on until every land on the earth's surface that is not already the seat of an old civilization shall become English in its language, in its political habits and traditions, and to a predominant extent in the blood of its people. The day is at hand when four-fifths of the human race will trace its pedigree to English forefathers, as four-fifths of the white people in the United States trace their pedigree to-day." Clearly the federation which was to preside over a future so envisioned would represent the triumph of one very particular tradition. We hear nothing here of any others, but only the implied concession that a non-English "old civilization" might be permitted its residual existence. The ideal of world union seems hardly to conceal a heady mixture of imperialism and racism.[78]

Actually these terms cannot be applied to Fiske without serious qualification. He was indeed heir to a centuries-old Anglo-American legend which exalted the Anglo-Saxons as lovers of liberty and fathers of free institutions. In the nineteenth century the legend had become strongly racialized, and in the United States had served to justify American expansion at the expense of Indians and Mexicans. "Survival of the fittest" notions, of course, had added further intoxicants to the brew.[79]

The residue of these spirits was thicker in Fiske's terminology and rhetoric than in his considered arguments. Yet there seems no escaping the fundamental confusion of the time about the term "race." With "culture" not yet fixed in its modern meaning, "race" often did double duty, hovering uncertainly between biological and cultural categories. Fiske preferred "English" to "Anglo-Saxon," but he accepted easily enough the conventions which used such terms as "Teutonic" and "Aryan" to denote "dominant races" and sort out historical developments. Thus William Pitt the Elder was not simply a British statesman but, in preparing the way for the occupation of the Mississippi Valley by English-speaking people, the peer of Charlemagne "in the annals of the Teutonic race." In his own time Fiske welcomed what seemed to him the increasing "solidarity" of that "race in its three great nationalities—America, England, and Germany."[80]

Fiske was neither a vulgar racist nor a model of racial enlightenment. He knew that there were no "pure races" on any large scale, and no necessary correlation of race with social advancement. He warned as early as 1876 of "the fallaciousness of explaining all national peculiarities by a cheap reference to 'blood.'" Deeming the "New Immigration" of the late nineteenth century insufficiently selective, he accepted the honorary presidency of the Immigration Restriction League in 1894, but contrary to hard-core nativists, he believed American society capable of absorbing any particular "race." While well aware of the role of force in the growth of the British Empire and the American republic, he attributed the success of those polities fundamentally to superior Anglo-American political traditions and organizing principles, and despite his rhetorical mating of spread-eagle with rampant-lion, he expected the future enlargement of their sway to be benevolent and pacific. He was consequently dismayed by the war with Spain in 1898, although he was persuaded to endorse the annexation of the Philippines after initial opposition.[81]

Despite relatively moderate views on such issues, Fiske illustrates a mind-set of his time in which race could act as a surrogate for tradition. In this role it was satisfying at once to modern and antimodernist sensibilities. It offered pleasing intimations of the primordial qualities ascribed to "immemorial" customs and traditions; it appealed to a romantic tribalism; but it claimed at least by implication a hardheaded and empirically supported biological underpinning. In reality such underpinning might be wholly lacking, as it was in Fiske's discussion of the "Teutonic Idea." His actual argument went no further than to claim special merit for a political and social tradition which had emerged and developed among certain Germanic peoples.

The racial terminology was not trivial, however. Aside from its association with contemporary and later enormities, it fed what in Fiske's case was a more insidious system of abstraction. Fiske falls short of later standards of tolerance and pluralism less because he was touched by racism and jingoism than because he subordinated considerations of culture, tradition, and race alike to a unitary scheme of progressive social evolution. Relying on anthropologists like Louis Henry Morgan, Fiske accepted the view that human cultures advanced toward higher levels of civilization by passing through universal stages of development. Consequently one might observe among the Iroquois customs and beliefs characteristic of the early Greeks, for example. Fiske determined without hesitation that the inhabitants of the Aegean region had reached a stage of development by ca. 6000 B.C. which it had taken the North American Indians until ca. A.D. 1700 to attain.[82]

The theory of universal stages of development was not inherently racialist, and might even imply a racial equality: a people detained in its ascension of the great developmental ladder by adventitious factors or adverse environmental circumstances could still in the normal course of social evolution expect to make its way up. Fiske gave point to his comparison of the Iroquois with prehistoric Europeans by arguing that Indians were eminently capable of "learning civilization." But the unilinear scale of development accentuated perceived inequalities of culture, and submerged the integrity of particular traditions in a preconceived plan of progress. It would be difficult to rescue Fiske from Edward Said's strictures upon the "Eurocentric culture" which "relentlessly codified and observed everything about the non-European or peripheral world," with the limits of understanding such a project entailed.[83]

On the American continents, where the Teutonic Idea had entered upon its culminating phase of development, surviving Indians might "learn civilization" and in this way accelerate their social progress, but native traditions that the prescribed course of ascent could not accommodate were readily severed by the "shears of Fate." Fiske did not contemplate this denouement with any lack of interest, or even of sympathy. In what was probably his most impressive and successful work of history, *The Discovery of America* (1892), he devoted considerable attention to the Native American cultures. His interest derived in the first instance from the assumption that these societies could throw light on those of Europe at an equivalent stage of development, but he was clearly impressed by the brilliant arts and urban amenities of the Aztecs and the attainments in social and political organization of the Incas. He acknowledged that the Spanish conquest of Mexico and Peru had had no more of right or morality about it than the springing of the "lion . . . upon his prey," and he decried—with a certain Anglo-American self-righteousness—the heinousness of Spanish methods of empire building.[84]

Yet in their encounter with indigenous American societies the Spanish had after all represented civilization, whereas according to Morgan's classification even the Aztecs and Incas had never risen above the middle level of barbarism. When "two grades of culture so widely severed" came into contact, the destruction of the lesser was to be expected, and Fiske could not feel that this was truly to be regretted. Even the Spanish Inquisition was preferable to the human sacrifices of the Aztecs, and the Spanish use of torture more palatable than the Native American. At least the Inquisition tortured with a moral purpose in view; this seemed to Fiske—innocent of the dedicated cruelties of the twentieth century— somewhat less repugnant than "wanton" Indian atrocities.[85]

However the moral scales were to be balanced between conquerors and conquered, the extirpation of peoples and traditions Fiske described suggests to the present-day reader a different and grimmer meaning for the phrase "empire of the dead" than that which Auguste Comte intended. Within the new empires of the living—Spanish or English— there was little chance of any equitable coexistence of largely incommensurate traditions—as incommensurate, perhaps, in their cruelties as in their virtues. Not even the federal principle, efficacious among Connecticut towns or the states of the Union, could guarantee comity among such differing cultures.

Indeed a unilinear scheme of social development, especially when it issued in the spatialized form of imperial expansion, almost precluded such comity. It also distorted the nature of tradition, as it had previously been understood. For earlier defenders of tradition such as Edmund Burke, the traditional had had a particularistic and motley quality; for them, indeed, its very value to the accumulation of human experience arose from its lack of assimilability to any abstract or universalizing principle. Burke's "little platoons" could encompass the domestic and community felicities Fiske defended, but hardly such a hypertrophy of tradition as the "Teutonic Idea" with which he tried to give those felicities universal scope.

The racial terminology and rhetoric were symptomatic of this miscarriage of traditionism, even if there was little substance behind them. Racialism yielded only ersatz tradition, a cowbird's egg in the nest which customs and traditions had constructed. Seeming to provide scientific validation for social continuity, it smoothed out the uneven heterogeneity which Fiske himself had recognized as inherent in tradition, and proffered a biological solidarity in place of rough cultural adhesiveness. Beguiled by the ambiguous vocabulary of race, Fiske shows the extent to which, even in a benignly conceived scheme like the "Teutonic Idea," respect for traditions might be overwhelmed by the chauvinism of one tradition.

Even within the confines of "Teutonic" experience, as Fiske depicted it, the particular succumbed to a monistic scheme of history. From a modern and technical point of view, this was a failure of historicism. Belatedly gaining a foothold in American scholarship between the 1870s and 1890s, historicism required, as Dorothy Ross puts it, that the past "be both decisively different from and causally linked to the present"— a posture incompatible with a history in which continuity overwhelmed change. Yet judged against old-fashioned patterns of thought, Fiske does not necessarily fare any better. If he fell short of historicist standards, he equally exemplified the weakening of the typological imagination. Typology proper did not confuse type with antitype, Jonah with Christ, or even—despite some New England imitation of Old Testament ways—Israelites with English Puritans. With Fiske the comparable distinctions between Arminius and Jefferson, and between the Aryans who were the Yankees of antiquity and the Yankees who were the Aryans of modernity, were less clear. A transcendence which provided a universal frame within which the values of type and antitype were fixed yielded to an immanence which worked toward uniformity. The law of evolution, especially when articulated with the rhetoric of race, further reduced the rough edges of real history, and of real tradition.[86]

By the time of Fiske's death tradition subsumed in a scheme of progressive evolution, whether racially tinctured or not, was coming to seem as constraining in its way as tradition understood as a purely static phenomenon had seemed to the American "Party of Hope." Franz Boas and other anthropologists abandoned the theory of universal stages of development even as they affirmed the necessary functional role of tradition. Modernists like T. S. Eliot resolved to break up the sheer continuity of nineteenth-century time to permit the timeless to impinge upon everyday experience; they rejected as well the spatial expression of that continuity. "Was not Modernism . . . an attempt to put a brake on the linear movement of the will toward simple expansion?" Quinones asks.[87]

Since Fiske's time exponents of tradition have been inclined to view it as a defense precisely against the tyranny of the narrowly progressive, the universalizing, and the mindlessly expansive—against "empire" of either the living or the dead. During the first half of the twentieth century it retreated from its imperial dimensions into such spatial embodiments as Josiah Royce's "province," Ralph Adams Cram's "walled town," and the yeoman's farm of the Southern Agrarians. As removed from reality as they sometimes were, these intellectual models at least attempted to restore to tradition its proper specificity of place. (So also did such tangible reservations of memory as Colonial Williamsburg and Old Sturbridge Village.) At best perhaps they sought something akin to the old typological linkages between different times.

The ascription to tradition of an imperial destiny was simply a corollary of overreaching moral and epistemic claims. Some recent thinkers have like Burke concluded that the value of tradition is intimately connected to its limitations. Alasdair MacIntyre, for instance, commends tradition as a version of moral inquiry arising from acknowledged "membership in a particular type of moral community," in contrast to the "encyclopaedist" aspiration to provide "timeless, universal, and objective truths" (and to the "genealogical" dismissal of reason as a mask for interests in their quest for power). A tradition conceived as a necessary context for moral inquiry may grow by transcending itself and extending its reach, but has no warrant to imperialize or condescend.[88]

John Fiske was a model "encyclopaedist" both in an ordinary sense referring to the range of his interests and in keeping with the more specialized meaning employed by MacIntyre—in his confidence in the availability of universal truth. The advocate of "English" tradition, as he understood it, he failed to recognize its limits. With his vision fixed on the "ideal man" toward which this tradition guided the course of social evolution, he shared the encyclopaedist inability, as MacIntyre describes it, to "enter imaginatively into the standpoint of those allegedly primitive and savage peoples" who stood in the way of this consummation. But Fiske in truth was hardly able to enter imaginatively into the diversities even of his own civilization. To spatialize a tradition, it seemed, was not only to extend its dominion, but to flatten the variegated landscape in which traditions can endure and flourish.[89]

This of course was not Fiske's intent. While he and others used Anglo-American tradition to justify expansion, the reverse is equally true; they used expansion to justify tradition. In some ways the latter project was the more urgent, most Americans requiring less encouragement to applaud national growth than to respond enthusiastically to invocations of the past. The family hearth had no doubt a sentimental appeal, but if home were to be more than a nostalgic memory it must be validated, some of its defenders seem to have thought, by its assumption of imperial dimensions.

When growth was rendered, in effect, as part of a universal process, the mutual justification of expansion and tradition was raised to another level. As Fiske sought to salvage essential Christian truths by inflating the old-fashioned anthropomorphic God into a scientifically viable "cosmic" deity, so he invoked the evolutionary scheme to rekindle a kind of sacredness in the traditions and customs of home and town and parish and shiremote which might otherwise have seemed of no more than antiquarian interest. That it might deaden rather than vitalize tradition to lock it into a unilinear and deterministically conceived process was not a possibility he was of a generation easily to entertain.

CHAPTER 2

Defense of the Inner Circle:
Philip A. Bruce, Lyon G. Tyler,
and Virginia Tradition

Quintessential missionary of New England values though he seemed, John Fiske won a respectful readership south of the Mason-Dixon line. His *History of the United States for Schools* elicited some complaints from southerners ever sensitive to Yankee pedagogical bias, including a group of Confederate veterans meeting at Culpepper, Virginia. But historians who were habitually quick to detect sectional prejudice regarded Fiske's major works as relatively fair and attentive to southern claims. His two-volume *Old Virginia and Her Neighbours* (1897) made due acknowledgment of the traditions of the Old Dominion. He defended the credibility of Captain John Smith's account of his rescue by Pocahontas, and attributed to the "Cavaliers" (judiciously defined as a largely middle-class party) the "greatness of Virginia." Reviewing *Old Virginia* for the *American Historical Review*, the pugnaciously anti-Yankee president of the College of William and Mary, Lyon Gardiner Tyler, questioned Fiske's description of Virginia as more aristocratic and less educated than New England, but nevertheless thought the work deserving of the "highest praise" for its general fairness and "profusion of knowledge." Fiske had not long before scored what he deemed "a No. 1 Knock down success" with an address at the University of Virginia. "I am getting on beautifully with the ex-rebels," he boasted.[1]

The friendly response to Fiske in Williamsburg and Charlottesville is not really surprising. The New Englander's membership in the Association for the Preservation of Virginia Antiquities evinced a respect for tradition which transcended section, and his version of history was largely congruent with that favored by southern colleagues. The southerners endorsed wholeheartedly the notion of Anglo-American continuity, even if they traced it primarily through Jamestown rather than

Plymouth or Massachusetts Bay. There was nothing in the "Teutonic Idea" to offend southern racial views, and Fiske's scheme of political evolution culminating in American federalism was eminently acceptable despite an ultimate disagreement about the application of federal principles to state secession. Virginians who perceived in Alexander Spotswood's 1716 expedition to the Blue Ridge Mountains the harbinger of the continental triumph of American democracy had no quarrel with Fiske's vision of expansion. Virginians too celebrated the carrying of the home outward, although they might locate the home on the farm or plantation rather than in the town.[2]

Virginia writers were at least as proud of their English ancestry as New Englanders like John Fiske. In his home area of Virginia, the novelist and popular historian Thomas Nelson Page observed, English names and traditions predominated, and "old habits of thought and old customs of speech and of life survived for generations, almost without change." Even the political rupture with Great Britain had marked no real breach of continuity, for the South had emerged from the Revolution, Page assured his readers, with the "Anglo-Saxon spirit" only intensified.[3]

The suggestion that Virginia represented the best of England—so similar to Fiske's estimation of New England—needed little encouragement. In his *Local Institutions of Virginia* (1885) Edward Ingle had alluded to the axiom of the British historian Edward Freeman that "if you wish to see Old England you must go to New England." With equal justice, Ingle thought, it could be said that "if you wish to see Old England you must go to Old Virginia." It seemed to him that "the colonists were unconsciously led by their English instincts to reproduce . . . old customs, laws and institutions" such as the hundred and, with some modification, the parish. The result, he thought, was that "in social, civil, and religious relations Virginia resembled, more strikingly than any of the other American colonies, the prominent and superior side of old England."[4]

The most illustrious Virginia historian of the very early twentieth century, Philip Alexander Bruce, concurred with this assessment. Continuity of customs, laws, and institutions between the mother country and her oldest American colony was the central theme of Bruce's most important works. "The [early Virginia] community, from a social point of view, was as if some shire of England, with its whole population, had been moved bodily over sea," he thought. "There was not the smallest desire to leave the old privileges and customs behind." No other colony "so closely resembled the parent stock as Virginia did under British rule," Bruce believed. The Virginia population had been drawn not from a narrow section of English society as the New England population had been, but from all sections, he pointed out. Virginians could therefore remain "true to all the hearty and generous customs and habits of their English forefathers. The isolated situation of the colony and the secluded life of the plantations only confirmed these inherited traits."[5]

Bruce agreed with Fiske that it had been the very loyalty of Americans to English tradition which had led to their break with the erring mother country. Although he was careful to point out that Virginians had been more devoted to king and country than their New England cousins, he added that they were for this reason at least as resentful of policies which struck at English liberties. The War for Independence, consequently, had been simply a response to Britain's abandonment to her colonies of her own proper political genius, and therefore a British defeat which proved "the most glorious of all England's triumphs."[6]

These were not sentiments directed merely at a past connection; they lived on in contemporary habits of life and thought. Bruce was a practicing Anglophile, personal inclination as well as research interests drawing him to extended visits in the mother country. He delighted in bird-watching in his English "water meadow," and as naturally championed the "special relationship" between Great Britain and the United States. The First World War, an early test of that relationship, heightened consciousness of the more particular Anglo-Virginian connection. Lyon G. Tyler was quick to take sides in the war. "My sympathies have been, from the first, pro-British, and they have increased in intensity as the war has developed," he wrote to Bruce during the carnage of 1915. "I can't understand how any Virginian tracing his ancestry back to Great Britain can feel other than I do." Bruce certainly concurred. He was furious with the native Virginian and "invertebrate school ma'am" Woodrow

Wilson when the president failed to respond to the sinking of the Lusitania with the mettle of "our Confederate fathers."[7]

The enduring Anglo-Virginian tradition, especially as rendered by Whiggish historians, provided a reassuring frame for the Old Dominion's social and political development. Any signal political event, even if it seemed to mark a decisive break with the past, suggested one or more analogues with past experience—analogues formal and weighty enough at times to suggest the sequence of type and antitype. Emigration to America inevitably recalled the arrival of the Anglo-Saxons—or the Normans—in Britain. The London Company charter of 1618 served as the "Magna Charta" of the Virginia colony, although James I played an early George III as readily as he did a late King John. Historians easily located the English Civil War in the long struggle for freedom which included the American Revolution and the War for Southern Independence. No sympathy for the Cavaliers deterred Thomas Nelson Page from invoking the Parliamentary cause of 1642 in token of the "liberty of the subject" dear to the hearts of Virginians.[8]

The racial rhetoric with which John Fiske gilded his treatment of "Teutonic" and Anglo-American traditions had of course a more serious counterpart in Virginia. Bruce was proud that early immigrants to the colony had brought and maintained the English diversity of class, as well as a diversity of type and character which he believed well exemplified by Robert E. Lee and Stonewall Jackson. Yet he was also proud that the white people of the southern states, as he argued in *The Rise of the New South* (1905), "were sprung from an unmixed Anglo-Saxon stock," and saw no incongruity in attributing to this circumstance "their own complete homogeneity as a people."[9]

No more than John Fiske were the southerners able to "enter imaginatively" into traditions not recognizable as their own, however. That Virginia tradition might include, in its own integrity and dignity, an African American strand was not a possibility which even the more liberal of Virginia historians of the period were prepared to entertain. Beyond the dialect level of folklore and custom—and in fact, even there—blacks were simply annexed to white tradition, and used to explain its development and permutations. It was not that white historians were oblivious to the problems raised by race; both Bruce and Page, most notably, wrote books defending the reality and necessity of white supremacy. In *The Plantation Negro as a Freeman* (1889) Bruce portrayed the post-slavery black as reverting to a childlike African type, incapable even of maintaining the civilization with which he had been endowed by white tutelage. (Bruce's views moderated considerably in later years, when he was even able to contemplate equality and intermarriage as eventual solutions to the racial problem.) Page, in *The Negro: The Southerner's Problem* (1904), was characteristically sentimental about the "old-time Negro" and marginally more optimistic about the prospects of individual blacks than Bruce, but also skeptical of the capacity of the race for civilization. Bruce and Page in their earlier pronouncements on the subject both subscribed to the covertly hopeful view of many whites that the black race might eventually become extinct in America—Page more explicitly.[10]

But Virginia historians were unable to make blacks disappear from the future, and they were no more able to make them disappear from the past. They acknowledged slavery's obvious and increasing importance in early Virginia history but made no effort to defend it in principle; the institution, Tyler admitted, was "unjustifiable morally." Yet they mitigated such fleeting strictures with equally brief assertions that slavery as it had existed in the Old Dominion, at least, had been a civilizing blessing to the Africans themselves. Pondering its historical significance, they invoked it either as an explanation of the establishment of a planter aristocracy or as a prerequisite of white equality, depending on the needs of the case. However applied, the pragmatic argument ended by eclipsing the moral. "Our slavery business may have been all wrong, but it produced a society which we will never see again," Tyler remarked to Bruce. His sense of loss seemed here to outweigh his moral scruples.[11]

This formal ambivalence—or confusion—was reflected in an uncertainty about the place of slavery in Virginia tradition. Historians could not decide if it was intrinsic or an alien and intrusive element. Philip Bruce described it as rooted in the depths of familial and community existence. It had been in large measure the "deep seated conservatism of the people of Virginia, and their love of a country life, and devotion to their rural homes," which had perpetuated slavery, he thought. Bruce elaborated in his biography of Robert E. Lee: "The institution, having been in existence since the foundation of the country, was inextricably interwoven with the whole social life of the Southern people; to make an end to it, was to destroy a social fabric consecrated by all their historical memories, domestic traditions, and intimate personal affections. Indeed, the working of habit and custom through two centuries and a half made it hard for them to conceive of their ability to live under a different order." Yet placed in the larger context of the great Anglo-American tradition, slavery appeared as a starkly alien factor—not without serious consequences, to be sure, but essentially an aberration, "incongruous," as Bruce concluded, "with the genius of English institutions." As Virginia represented purportedly the highest development of those institutions, it would logically have followed that the incongruity was magnified there. This was not an argument which Bruce pursued, however.[12]

Although race was hardly a divisive issue between northern and southern champions of Anglo-American tradition at the turn of the century, the shadow of the sectional struggle still fell between Fiske and Virginia scholars like Tyler and Bruce; the triumphalism which came so readily to the New Englander was replaced in the Virginians by a never-satisfied quest for vindication. Tradition, when not followed blindly, always in some measure solicits vindication. It is a vindication which, strictly speaking, is tautological: the followers of tradition seek to vindicate the present through adherence to the ways of the past, and the past through the ascription to it of qualities which can be validated in the present. This double need of vindication is magnified when traditional ways are threatened or defeated, when not only the present seems in jeopardy but also the present's vision of the past.

Fiske needed little effort to vindicate what seemed to many self-evident; the New England town could still pass as a model for the world. But even in the antebellum South fear of the future and sensitivity to outside pressures had accentuated the vindicating function of tradition. Southerners sought most urgently to validate slavery by presenting it in a romanticized context of custom and tradition, as part of a time-hallowed way of life. But by the end of the nineteenth century the substantive foundations of Virginia particularism had largely been lost, their provincialism confirmed by defeat. Jefferson's self-sufficient yeoman farm had fallen prey to inhospitable economic realities; the plantation had become romance, and was no longer a home which could be carried outward. Slavery was acknowledged to be indefensible per se, however strenuous the efforts to show it to have been benevolent in practice. State sovereignty had been overruled by main force. Vindication had first to show that Virginia tradition was not revealed in error, calamity, and ruin. Beyond this work of salvage, the invocation of salient traditions provided a defense against the encroachment of Yankee values or, often, a drapery within which the presence of those values could be disguised. And it could lend the appearance of dignity and necessity to the establishment of white supremacy which was completed during the Progressive Age.

If the South provided the largest public constituency for tradition in the late-nineteenth-century United States, this was due as much to the need to make sense of military defeat and cultural siege as to the actual character of southern society. The antebellum plantation system had offered something perhaps as close to "traditional society" as had existed on a large scale in this country, aside from the Indian tribes, and had perpetuated a traditional, premodern culture of honor. Traditional elements had been combined with a progressive, capitalistic agriculture in a way which prefigured the New South alloy of tradition and economic progress. But the post-Appomattox need for vindication, bound up with the need for sectional reconciliation, evoked a traditionalism which transcended social realities.

Virginia was the chief fountainhead of this traditionalism. Identifying closely with the mother country, it was even more thoroughly identified with the beginnings of the United States. It furnished the standards for the regional customs and traditions of the South—the antebellum planter in Alabama or Mississippi aspired to the estate of the Virginia gentleman, as Wilbur J. Cash pointed out. Altogether Virginians seemed to live in the ways of tradition as most other Americans did not. Yet tradition was beleaguered even within the Old Dominion following the Civil War. Few actually opposed industrial development and urban growth, although these features of a relatively progressive economy tended naturally to undermine traditional ways. Traditionalists like Philip Bruce and Thomas Nelson Page were more alarmed by General William Mahone and his Readjuster movement of the 1870s and 1880s, which threatened to break down the more undemocratic traditions of the Commonwealth, and which conservatives perceived as being based on the support of blacks and ignorant whites. And of course the degree of political power which blacks retained from Reconstruction was to many itself an affront to Virginia tradition.[13]

Historians have found that the reform impulse which crested in the Progressive movement in the South and the rest of the nation in the early 1900s was in part an effort to salvage and preserve traditional values and a traditional order in the face of change and feared cultural and political anarchy. This was true perhaps most of all in Virginia, where, as Raymond H. Pulley contends, Progressive reform of the period strongly evoked the "Old Virginia mystique" and sought insofar as possible to reconstitute the paternalistic antebellum order—in part through the disenfranchisement of blacks and many lower-class whites. Virginians who felt themselves to be living in the shadow of a heroic age struggled to be worthy of their Confederate fathers, and to perpetuate their authority, in whatever ways were available to them.[14]

The resulting traditionalism had naturally a defensive character, a stance seen most clearly when placed in a spatial context. Southerners found it as natural to spatialize tradition as did other Americans, and antebellum Virginians played a leading role in settling the South and West. After the Civil War the expansionism which space evoked so readily for John Fiske was inverted for some tradition-minded Virginians, however. The outward-moving frontier yielded to a many layered defense of that which was nearest and dearest. This issued frequently, of course, in a mere nostalgia centered on "the old home" or other specially consecrated place. Sentiment found prolific expression in the many recollections of old times in the Old Dominion which poured from the presses in the late nineteenth and early twentieth centuries, along with the fictional renditions of Thomas Nelson Page and other storytellers. Colorful characters like the old colonel, the down-at-the-heels gentleman, the rough but honest yeoman, and the faithful slave (or ex-slave) slipped easily into the abstractions of archetype and stereotype, but they were meant to evoke familiar specificities of time and place.

The innermost of the widening circles of loyalty on which the Virginia traditionalist looked out, almost as upon the concentric spheres of the Aristotelian universe, was that of the family on its farm or plantation. This rural habitation was the sacred space of Virginia tradition as historically rendered, the counterpart of the New England town, the home to be "carried outward" before the Civil War, to be defended in remembrance thereafter. When the home rose in memory to the dignity of a "plantation" (already an old-fashioned usage as applied to contemporary Virginia, as a writer of the 1890s remarked), it stood with particular force for local independence and domestic pieties. It was common among historians of otherwise divergent views to describe the early plantation as a little principality or kingdom in itself.[15]

Yet it was not really all to itself. It became a truism that the rural home, whether plantation or farm, joined love of place with respect for social traditions, and was accordingly the root of wider loyalties. In his sentimental *Brave Deeds of Confederate Soldiers* (1916), Philip Bruce emphasized the role of old country homes, "invested with the sacred interest of ancestral traditions and personal association alike," in fostering social unity:

> It was this love of home, with its thronging recollections of the past both near and far,—this clear vision of a house surrounded by ancient trees, perhaps, and standing in the midst of a wide rural domain, or of a few acres only,—that nerved the arm of many a Southern soldier and strengthened his soul in repelling invasion. Love of the South was inextricably mixed up with this love of the family hearth, whether imposing or humble of character. Love of one particular spot, of one neighborhood, of one State, was the foundation stone of the love of the entire region.[16]

For Bruce here, wider loyalties were strictly southern, and the same writer demonstrated that familial customs and traditions could divide as well as unite. Even a common Englishness could become a bone of contention between Virginia and New England. In an early editorial for the *Richmond Times-Dispatch*, Bruce pointedly suggested that Yankees and cavaliers derived from different Englands, distinct even in their holidays.

"Thanksgiving Day is a festival transplanted from the barren hills and cold hearthstones of Puritan England," he insisted, "but Christmas comes down to us from our Virginian fathers, who received it from their remotest English ancestry," presumably less bleakly environed.[17]

For a champion of sectional reconciliation such as the *Louisville Courier-Journal*'s Virginia-born editor Henry Watterson, on the other hand, the "domestic spirit" of "provincialism" was properly "the spring not of national divisions but of national unity." And Thomas Nelson Page found Yankee hills and hearthstones decidedly more welcoming than did his brother-in-law Philip Bruce. In an address in New Hampshire Page placed the "Home-passion" in broad historical perspective as "one of the basic principles on which the life and vigor of a people is builded." Briefly invoking the *lares* and *penates* which sanctified ancient Roman hearthsides, Page hurried on to consider the love of home as a primary characteristic of the Teutonic "race," regardless of where Teutons might be situated. He agreed with Bruce that domestic felicity inspired the fighting man to strength and courage. For "our fathers," he concluded, "the home was the temple of Liberty, the fortress of Freedom. From this sprang the hundred, the hamlet, the town, the state, the union." Page paused to worry about the domestic failings of the contemporary "Smart Set"—distressingly prone to divorce and infidelity—but retained his confidence in the average American home. This home had been carried outward, he noted, by both northerners and southerners, who yet remained true to its original embodiments. He offered his New England audience the image of westward migrants as they gazed back toward the eastern seaboard: "the light which they catch," he felt sure, was no "false glitter," but issued rather "from where the rays of the sun touch the old plantation-houses of the South, or the little white homes upon the granite hills." Such a reconciling vision made Bruce's carping about Thanksgiving seem petty.[18]

Beyond the charmed domestic circle, in its centrifugal ramifications, lay local loyalties which might be directed toward even so seemingly prosaic a division as the county. This unit was important enough in early Virginia to give rise to "a sort of county sovereignty which was the forerunner of the State sovereignty of a later era," Moncure Conway noted. But the Old Dominion itself provided the real political circle of liege-loyalty. Beyond lay the Union, to which the New South pledged allegiance, and the wider circles of Anglo-American or at least Anglo-Virginian community; finally the vestiges of a Jeffersonian universalism shone with the wan light, it sometimes seemed, of distant stars.[19]

Fundamental to the entire scheme was the principle, enunciated by Philip Bruce in an editorial for the *Richmond Times-Dispatch* in 1889, that "local patriotism is the root of all political excellence." Northerners like John Fiske, taken with the radiating virtues of town and parish, might not have disagreed. But of course the Civil War had defined an important sectional difference on the practical application of this precept, one which indicated the more defensive quality of Virginia traditionalism. For Fiske the Union triumph in 1865 had been the consummate vindication of the "Teutonic Idea" which culminated in representative and federal government: "The good fight begun at Lewes and continued at Naseby and Quebec was fitly crowned at Yorktown and at Appomattox." For the Virginians the true expression of the "Teutonic" tradition resided in state sovereignty and local liberties. The Confederacy had represented, as Thomas Nelson Page put it, "the basic principle of the Anglo-Saxon civilization . . . the defence of the inner circle against whatever assailed it from the outside"—a principle "nowhere . . . more absolutely established than in Virginia."[20]

Defensiveness could issue in a traditionalism in the true pejorative sense—resentful, bitter, obstinate. These qualities appeared at times even in the otherwise illustrious figures of Lyon Gardiner Tyler and Philip Alexander Bruce, respectively long-time president of the College of William and Mary and author of impressive works on Virginia's social and economic history. Neither Tyler nor Bruce can be dismissed as a simple reactionary. Tyler was in certain respects at least a liberal reformer, most notably in his advocacy of rights and opportunities for women. He successfully fought for the admission of women to William and Mary and, as early as 1896, actively supported woman suffrage. He was a member of the Equal Suffrage League of Virginia, addressed Suffragette meetings, and wrote letters which provided ammunition for the movement from Norfolk to Baltimore. There was "no sense," Tyler thought n 1914, "in denying to any one who has the proper intelligence the right of the Suffrage. That sex has nothing to do with intelligence is admitted, I believe."[21]

Bruce, by contrast, was politically most active in supporting the constriction of the voting rolls in the state constitution of 1902, which had the avowed purpose of eliminating the least intelligent of both black and white voters. (This was viewed in the South as a progressive reform.) But in England Bruce could come across less as a southern traditionalist than as an up-to-date Yank. He criticized the British for an "unconscious hatred of change," manifest in "an almost slavish adherence to conservative methods which the spirit of American progress condemns."[22]

Such comments demonstrate both the hold of American shibboleths even upon those who seem least under their sway and the tendency of living abroad to make one conscious of one's national identity. But Bruce struck a different tone in his voluble correspondence with his friend and fellow Virginian Lyon G. Tyler. Tyler and Bruce were not entirely of one mind. They assigned different weights to the aristocratic and democratic components in Virginia tradition, differed in the degree of their attachment to England, and evinced the shades of temperamental difference one might expect between a professional academic and a gentleman scholar and farmer. Tyler's was the more polemical spirit. Bruce once addressed him as "My Dear Old Bucking Broncho," although his name suggested another quadruped and he sometimes used stationery identifying his roar as from the "Lion's Den." Yet the two were quick to agree on the fundamentals of Virginia tradition and in identifying the assaults modernity levied against it. Neither was hesitant in flaying Yankee impertinence and defending the preeminence of the Old Dominion.[23]

A sensitivity to sectional affronts was pervasive among southern intellectuals of Tyler's generation, spurred by personal and professional grievances. Even such prominent southern scholars as Archibald Henderson and John T. Latané complained that institutions like the American Historical Association and the Academy of Arts and Letters slighted or excluded them. But Tyler, with some private encouragement from Bruce, went far beyond such irritations in a sustained polemical campaign against Yankee abuse of history and misappropriation of American tradition. Northern colleagues otherwise respectful of Tyler's scholarship reacted with dismay and amusement. "I am amazed that a man who has rendered such great service to the history of his justly celebrated commonwealth should be spending his time now in trying to perpetuate old animosities and revive new ones between fellow-countrymen," Albert Bushnell Hart wrote Tyler in 1929. Worthington Chauncey Ford had earlier essayed, with no more effect than Hart's missive, a bantering tone: "You do claim the earth and all the heavens for Old Virginia. I suppose as a mere Northerner I ought to be thankful that you have left hell open to us. My impression, however, is that we will make more out of hell than you will out of the earth and heavens."[24]

A quarrel which seemed preposterous to Hart and Ford was deadly serious for Tyler, because it was a battle for the present and future as well as the past, and for the outer circle of the United States as well as for the inner one of Virginia. Heroes and other symbols were chess pieces in this fight for tradition, and no sign of change in their standing seemed too trivial to require attention. Aside from the mythic hegemony of the Pilgrim Fathers, nothing enraged Tyler and Bruce so much as the national adulation of Abraham Lincoln. Lincoln was "one of the greatest malefactors in history," Tyler was persuaded, and a man of "vulgar instincts" to boot—certainly no gentleman, as he informed William E. Dodd. What was most galling was to see the Lincoln cult make inroads even among the sons and daughters of the Old Dominion. A proposal in the Virginia legislature to observe Lincoln's birthday aroused Tyler to an ire public enough to receive attention in *Time* magazine. "I don't wish to make your flesh crawl," Bruce apologized to Tyler on another occasion, no doubt correctly anticipating his correspondent's reaction to the news that a *white* high school in the state had been named for the Great Emancipator. Tyler was appalled to hear that the native Virginian Nancy Astor had praised Lincoln in the British Parliament, and he resigned from the New York Southern Society over the appointment of a Lincoln admirer as historian. "The Yankees have the whip hand over the world," he lamented.[25]

Behind the cantankerousness which made the president of the College of William and Mary at times a caricature of the diehard

Confederate was a deep-seated anxiety, a fear shared by Bruce and perhaps most clearly articulated by him in a letter to Tyler in 1926:

> As our communities drift further away from the social traditions of
> the past,—as the public schools get in their work of Democrization
> [?] more effectively,—as people from a different social order creep in
> from the North,—the old social landmarks will grow less and less
> venerated, and in time, I am afraid, will entirely disappear—Persons
> with no ancestry behind them will look upon the old Virginia ways
> and claims as so much rubbish. . . . I am afraid that the day will come
> even in our own beloved state when Lincoln will be nearer the social
> ideal of the people at large than Robert E. Lee.[26]

The struggle for tradition was most serious when it became a struggle over education. Virginia historians had long chafed at the tutelary
legends of American schoolbooks, which they felt gave southern contributions to the building of the nation short shrift. Tyler devoted a
lengthy tract to exposing the multitudinous errors and misrepresenta-
tions he found in David S. Muzzey's *History of the American People*.
Apparently incorporating every debater's point its author could think of,
Tyler's polemic ranged from colonial New England bundling practices
and illegitimate births to Benjamin Franklin's materialism and immoral-
ity to the felicities of slavery and the iniquities of "Lincoln's War." For a
prominent academic, it was natural to suppose that the war of traditions
would be decided in the classroom. But Bruce clearly agreed, going so
far as to suggest to his friend that the schools should teach traditional
principles in the same way that the Roman Catholic Church inculcated
its doctrines.[27]

Tyler and Bruce perceived this new battle of the books as between
North and South, but more particularly as between Virginians and New
Englanders. Only those two sets of stubborn regionalists seemed to have
adequate claims to the fountainheads of American tradition; they were
therefore natural rivals. Lamenting the lack of the sense of "historical
continuity" among Americans as compared to Europeans, Bruce felt able
only to cite Virginia and Massachusetts as partial exceptions. The
Yankees, of course, had the upper hand: "I sometimes feel as if the whole
country, North and South alike, were in collusion, either actively or

passively, to exalt New England and to depress Virginia," the historian complained. As in the case of Lincoln, even minor annoyances rankled; thus a proposal to name a hotel at Virginia Beach "The Mayflower" could cause serious consternation. (Bruce breathed easier when he learned that upon reconsideration the establishment had become "The Cavalier.")[28]

As historical scholars, the Virginians kept up a steady barrage intended to force recognition of Virginia's claim to priority in the making of America. They took a special satisfaction in stealing New England's thunder by subsuming the Pilgrims of "North Virginia" in the original colonial enterprise. For Bruce the Mayflower Compact was only a "rehash" of Virginia charter provisions, and Tyler put the First Thanksgiving in perspective by noting that Plymouth might have starved in 1622 had it not received provisions from Jamestown. In fact, he surmised, the Pilgrims would have gone to Dutch Guiana in the first place, had not the southern colony been established.[29]

Although Tyler seemed to regret that the Pilgrims had missed their South American destination, the salient fact was that Virginia—or South Virginia—was first. In a letter to the *Richmond Times-Dispatch* in 1926, Bruce praised the newspaper's "constancy" in defending "Jamestown's priority over Plymouth, not simply in the date of its settlement, but in its right to be considered the political fountain-head of the American people, and the real source of their institutions on this continent." Bruce was here preaching to the choir, of course, but he had not long before had recourse to the columns of the *Springfield [Mass.] Daily Republican* to attack the "stale old statement that the Puritans of Massachusetts founded the American commonwealth." Claiming to recognize the "great qualities" of the Puritans, Bruce nevertheless asked a rhetorical question: "Has it been the spirit of the Puritans, or the spirit of Jefferson, the Virginian, as expressed in the immortal Declaration of Independence, which has been most instrumental in fostering our American democracy, which, in time, is certain to broaden out into the democracy of the whole world?"[30]

It was clearly the combination of defeat and a close and proprietary identification with American tradition as a whole which made the need for vindication so intense. It was almost as if the Virginians had been conquered by themselves. Washington the champion of federal union had bested his putative alter ego Robert E. Lee; Jefferson the apostle of liberty and equality had prevailed over Jefferson the slave owner and defender of states' rights. The ferocious resentment of Abraham Lincoln, especially marked in the son of another president, Lyon G. Tyler, was perhaps a measure of the anguish entailed in this sense of doubleness. Lincoln, elevated to the most exalted rank in the national pantheon, challenged Virginia's identification with the nation. A native of the Old Dominion's first offspring among the states, Kentucky, and the man who had sanctified the central passage of Jefferson's Declaration of Independence as the national creed, Lincoln might have qualified as a "cavalier" along with George Rogers Clark, Woodrow Wilson, and other unlikely candidates upon whom the title was bestowed. Indeed, New South publicists like Henry Grady and Henry Watterson were wont to say that Lincoln combined the virtues of Puritan and cavalier, and some prominent Virginians graciously invoked his name. But for Tyler and Bruce the arms of reconciliation would not reach so far. Lincoln was not only "no gentleman" but, least forgivably, had directed the very invasion of the Commonwealth—and so the sixteenth president could only appear as a sort of anti-Lee.[31]

Lincoln marked, finally, too sharp a break with the past for tradition to contain. Not even typological devices would have availed, at least for Tyler and Bruce, to bring him within the compass of the ancestral experience to which they appealed: who could have served as the type of Lincoln? And Lincoln fractured continuity twice, once in the 1860s, but again in the twentieth century, the two historians feared, as the younger generation threatened to slip from the old allegiances and join in the civil pieties founded on their state's defeat.

Even without the goad of vanquishment in war to prompt reaction, it was always a temptation for defenders of tradition to carry continuity to the point of changelessness; Tyler and Bruce sometimes wrote as if they were comfortable contemporaries of Thomas Jefferson or Nathaniel Bacon. At worst this propensity could lead to a form of mythmaking more insidious than that which was most notorious among Virginia traditionalists, the celebration of a cavalier aristocracy. Most competent historians saw at least partially through that conceit by the early twentieth century, as potent as the cavalier remained as type or icon. But some were strongly inclined to make exaggerated claims for the emergence of democracy in the early years of Virginia history, projecting an image of the present upon the past to bolster the Old Dominion's claim to primacy in the making of the nation. Thus for example Mary Newton Stanard's invocation of Queen Elizabeth I: "the influence of this absolute yet democratic monarch planted and nurtured the liberty loving spirit which English colonists brought to America."[32]

This tendency was illustrated most fully, perhaps, by Alexander Brown, author of *The First Republic in America* (1898) and *English Politics in Early Virginia History* (1901). Brown was an assiduous scholar but, as Philip Bruce pointed out, more an "indefatigable collector" than a historian. Bruce suggested that a true historian would combine Brown's talent for research with John Fiske's "vivid capacity for presentment," but Brown's deficiencies went deeper than weakness of narrative or bashfulness of interpretation. Rather, in his zeal to show the continuity of Virginia tradition, he assumed too readily that continuity meant constancy.[33]

Reviving and restating the thesis of the eighteenth-century historian William Stith, Brown argued that the primary purpose of the Jamestown enterprise had been to establish a refuge from Stuart tyranny. To make his case he did not hesitate to impeach the veracity of the locally lionized Captain John Smith, whose account of the early settlement and the circumstances of the dissolution of the Virginia Company of London reflected, Brown thought, an obsequious deference to King James I.[34]

In the face of royal despotism, Brown contended, the company had attempted to institute a popular government, complete with guarantees of civil and religious liberty. Making copious use of the biological figures so favored in the historiography of the period, he recalled the patriots who "first deposited in the womb of the great North American wilderness the germ of the vital principle which has sustained this nation since its birth—'Vox populi, vox Dei!'" Alternatively the seedling of republican liberty grew "into the political system of the new nation until our forefathers could rest under its shade, and under its expanding branches the sons of the cavaliers learned to defend the liberties of the subject from the encroachments of the crown." King James having failed to destroy the "tender plant" of liberty, the task of the patriots of 1776 had been simply one of protecting what had become "a great tree . . . from the axe of the royal woodmen."[35]

Arboreal imagery has appealed to defenders of tradition since at least the time of Edmund Burke, combining as it does continuity with gradual growth and development. How treacherous this metaphor is for the vagaries of actual tradition, and actual history, is apparent in Brown. His acorns grow into trees, but the organism is no less oak at its inception than at its maturity. Patrick Henry is all too readily whisked back a century and a half: "'Give me liberty or give me death!' was the inspiration of our foundation as well as the battle-cry of our Revolution." In this history, not only Patrick Henry but the barons of Runneymede and even the Lincoln of the Gettysburg Address seem to be in attendance at Jamestown. The present is linked to the past not merely in spirit, but even in detail. Brown found it curious that many of the issues which had exercised the Virginia founders still agitated the American republic—"free trade, protection, monopolies, free elections, tobacco taxes, the negro, etc." Tradition is reduced to a sort of enlarging stasis.[36]

Brown's thesis dominated the historiography of the subject for a generation or more, until called into question by Wesley Frank Craven and others. It had perhaps less influence on Virginia tradition as broadly received and celebrated, as it slighted the aristocratic elements in that tradition. But Brown still offered an image of the cavalier rocking the cradle of liberty which could gratify pride of ancestry. Far more disturbing to keepers of the tradition like Bruce and Tyler was the work of some younger historians which seemed to call into question the very substance of the ancestral types.[37]

Chief among the revisionists was the native Virginian Thomas Jefferson Wertenbaker, in whose groundbreaking *Patrician and Plebeian in Virginia* (1910) the emphasis seemed to traditionalists to fall all too heavily on the plebeian. In his preface to a new edition in 1957, Wertenbaker took satisfaction in his contribution to a new interpretation. "The old belief that the Virginia aristocracy had its origins in a migration of Cavaliers after the defeat of the royalists in the British Civil War has been relegated to the sphere of myths," he pointed out. And indeed, in 1910, Wertenbaker had argued that few real cavaliers had crossed the Atlantic to seventeenth-century Virginia. He contended that the largest part of the "Virginia aristocracy" derived from "the English merchant class," but pointed out also that many former indentured servants had risen to be elected to the House of Burgesses.[38]

Bruce himself had considerably tempered the cavalier interpretation, as had others. But Bruce, very much an insider of Virginia society, kept space for tradition within the bounds of respectable history. Wertenbaker was a much less comfortable historian for the keepers of the lares and penates of the Old Dominion. A correspondent named Tunstall Smith wrote to Bruce's wife in 1919 that Bruce's *Social Life in Virginia in the Seventeenth Century* "simply smashes flat the very ridiculous statements of one Wertenbaker (or some such Teutonic name)" suggesting that many of the Virginia aristocracy, whom Wertenbaker "would not know . . . if he saw them," derived from the servant class. Another writer, Fairfax Harrison, coupled Wertenbaker with the novelist Ellen Glasgow as traducers of the Old Dominion.[39]

Tunstall Smith remarked to Betty Bruce that he doubted that her husband had ever heard of Wertenbaker, but of course Bruce was quite familiar with the younger historian's work. Two years previously Wertenbaker had thanked Bruce for his "kind review" of *Virginia under the Stuarts*, as well as for some praise of an article. Wertenbaker had also thanked Tyler for favorable professional notice. Yet if they respected Wertenbaker as a historian, Bruce and Tyler, as they settled together into the crochets of age, were increasingly disturbed by the threat to Virginia tradition which he seemed to embody. Having heard that Wertenbaker was saying that "practically no gentle people settled in Virginia," Bruce was as quick to play the ethnic card as Tunstall Smith, a card of heightened value in the wake of the World War. "I like him personally," he remarked to Tyler, "but I am afraid that he is a descendant of the Hessian stock which was imprisoned near Charlottesville in the Time of the Revolution."[40]

With such considerations entering into historical discourse, it is not surprising that an opening for a chair of historical research at the University of Virginia in 1926 became for Tyler and Bruce more a question of tradition than of professional competence. It was essential to "avoid 'the new school,' represented by [Hamilton James] Eckenrode, [Charles Henry] Ambler, Wertenbaker and Co., who use research to write down

Virginia instead of writing it up," Tyler wrote to Bruce. The only person fit for the chair was Bruce himself, he added, because his friend had "a true Virginia heart, and can be relied on to hunt up the forgotten good things in Virginia instead of the evil things." Bruce responded two days later with bitter animadversions upon an unnamed "Virginian by birth at Princeton" who was "the most detestable representative of the new ideas," and who he feared would get the appointment in question. "No one has less sympathy than I with the old exaggerations and inflations of our Virginia history," Bruce assured his friend, but to go to the other extreme was equally wrong. Adverting in a familiar vein to "descendants of Hessians and Yankee settlers . . . who have no more inherited and intuitive insight into the social history of our state than the black crows that roost in the wood near my house," Bruce remarked that he had come "very near to blows" with the obnoxious Princeton historian the previous year while the professor was visiting Charlottesville.[41]

Even if there was an element of professional jealousy in such extreme reactions, they seem disproportionate and unprovoked. Wertenbaker could appear dangerously iconoclastic only from the standpoint of the old "exaggerations and inflations" of Virginia history which Bruce disavowed and which his own best historical writing eschewed. No doubt anticipating bruised sensibilities, the younger historian had sought to deflect criticism of *Plebeian and Patrician* in terms calculated to have maximum appeal to state pride:

> Thinking Virginians of today cannot but be gratified that the old erroneous belief concerning the origin of the aristocracy is being swept away. Why it should ever have been a matter of pride with old families to point to the English nobility of the 17th century as the class from which they sprang is not easy to understand. The lords of that day were usually corrupt, unscrupulous and quite unfit to found vigorous families in the "wilderness of America." How much better it is to know that the aristocracy of the colony was a product of Virginia itself! The self-respect, the power of command, the hospitality, the chivalry of the Virginians were not borrowed from England, but sprang into life on the soil of the Old Dominion.

The cavalier thesis, therefore, simply needed adjustment. The Virginia planters, Wertenbaker contended, were no less cavaliers for having descended from merchants rather than from English nobility. "The Colonial Cavaliers," he gave reassurance, "were little kings."[42]

Taken at his word, Wertenbaker seemed only to be doing in a modified and updated way what Bruce, Tyler, and other Virginia historians had been doing for years—weaving together two strands of Virginia tradition, that which drew its appeal from the ancient, the English, and the aristocratic, and that which claimed priority in American liberty, enterprise, and democracy. Wertenbaker's was a self-made cavalier, the product of American freedom and opportunity. But this version slighted the importance of distinguished or at least "gentle" English lineage and thus foreshortened genealogical continuity—a more serious challenge to Virginia tradition than Alexander Brown's excess of historical continuity. The initial temperate response of Bruce and Tyler to Wertenbaker's scholarship suggests that they were capable of accepting his chastening of Virginia shibboleths with professional grace, but the Princeton professor became a symbol of all challenge to tradition. His work was usable "in disparagement of the social origin of the people of colonial Virginia—the enemies of our state are only too happy to give publicity to his criticisms and insinuations," Bruce complained.[43]

Although Bruce, and even romantic writers like John Esten Cooke and Thomas Nelson Page, had questioned the excesses of the "cavalier myth," they were acceptable—to themselves and others—as traditionists willing to acknowledge the facts of history. Wertenbaker seemed in contrast a revisionist willing to make amends to tradition. The amends carried less weight than the revisions. To be right with tradition consisted less in subscription to a narrow orthodoxy of belief or unquestioning devotion to the past than in the perception that one actually belonged to the tradition and was decently respectful of its precepts.

The tradition was easier to respect than to define. It was complex, but it depended especially on a double balance: first between particularism and identification with the nation, and secondly between aristocratic and democratic elements. Virginians' commitment to the "defense of the inner circle," as Thomas Nelson Page put it, was not in doubt. But the social and political composition of the inner circle, and its relationship to the rest of the country, were problematical.

Particularism, whether expressed in the idealization of the isolated farm or plantation, the Jeffersonian precepts of states' rights, distinctive Old Dominion envisionments of the cavalier and the gentleman, or even a broad southern sectionalism, could not by itself define Virginia tradition. To be true to itself this tradition had also to embrace the national and even universal values of which such native sons as Washington and Jefferson and Madison were icons. Genuine loyalty to the tradition could never limit itself to such regionally distinct manifestations as the Lost Cause; it had also to embrace, in all their national significance, Monticello and Yorktown and the first American legislative assembly at Jamestown. After all, as Page exclaimed, "the Old South made this people. One hundred years ago this nation, like Athene, sprang full panoplied from her brain." And the Old South, as Virginians made clear, meant primarily Virginia.[44]

Page, although ever ready to rally to the defense of the Old Dominion, was also temperamentally conciliatory. In a more contentious spirit, the contradictory impulses of particularism and nationalism could issue in a dilemma which was never truly resolved. Lyon Gardiner Tyler, unsure whether his native state was the soul of America or merely of the South, most sharply illustrates this predicament. "As I go along I am more and more impressed with the impossible character of the Union," Tyler wrote to Philip Bruce in 1923; North and South, he thought, had really been two nations from the start. And yet, arguing their state's exceptional importance to the same correspondent two years later, Tyler contended that for a time in the early national history, Virginia "was not one of many states in a nation, but the nation itself." Drawing the logical conclusion from this conceit elsewhere, Tyler suggested that the entire United States should rightfully bear the name of "Virginia." But whether Tyler's state patriotism led him to contemplate the United States as Virginia writ large or to dream of the Old Dominion's separation from Yankees who had another vision of the common country, his identification of the Commonwealth with authentic American principles was unyielding.[45]

The proprietorial attitude of Virginians toward American history reflected a turn-of-the-century southern desire "to reconcile and converge with the rest of the country," as Edward L. Ayers puts it, which seemed to outweigh the kind of antagonism Tyler evinced toward sections which could advance rival claims. If the leaders of the New South dealt in myth, as is so often pointed out, it should be remembered that they found it as natural to speak the language of national myth as of sectional. Consequently not even Abraham Lincoln was necessarily beyond the pale. Page, less squeamish about the Great Emancipator than fellow Virginians like Tyler and Bruce, did not hesitate to invoke Lincoln's "government of the people, by the people, and for the people" in token of the destiny summoned forth on the banks of the James in 1607.[46]

The tercentenary of the founding of the first permanent English settlement in America provided the perfect occasion for celebrating Virginia's role in establishing American liberty and nationhood. At the Jamestown observances local tradition could be invoked unequivocally in support of the triumphant progress of a reunited country. This was especially so as the decision to base the Tercentenary Exposition in Norfolk rather than Richmond gave the celebration a forward-looking, New South tone which might have been less accentuated in the former Confederate capital.[47]

In preparing for the tercentenary, the executive committee of the Virginia Historical Society ascribed to the anniversary a significance far transcending the filiopietistic. The little colony on the James, it reported, had marked not only "the birthday of a great nation" but the inauguration of a "new civilization. . . . It meant, in some ways the revolutionizing of human thought, and the development of the human mind in entirely new directions." It was no wonder that a history published in 1907 should compare Jamestown to Bethlehem as an "insignificant village" which proved an "influence for the world's betterment and emancipation."[48]

Thomas Nelson Page's tercentenary address was only slightly more modest. For Page the founding of Jamestown was not only the great revolutionary event proclaimed by the Society, but the culmination of a European awakening which had produced new technologies, the Protestant Reformation, and the rise of England as the champion of Saxon liberties against Latin ecclesiasticism and prerogative. The Virginia settlers had brought with them the rights of Englishmen, had tenaciously defended them against encroachments by the Crown, and had nurtured the growth of liberty and popular government.[49]

Page gave the occasion a strong national emphasis. Alluding obliquely to the Civil War, he characterized Jamestown as an emblem of patriotism transcending all differences—"the cradle not only of the Commonwealth of Virginia, but of the Republic." Although he could not resist reminding his audience of the priority of the *Susan Constant* over the *Mayflower*, his address muted, as did the remarks of other dignitaries, the recognition of sectional differences. By 1907 national symbols were commonly mixed with sectional, even at Confederate reunions, but the tercentenary was a decidedly national occasion. There seems to have been little talk of cavaliers or other emblems of southern distinctiveness and contention. The published remarks of participants focused overwhelmingly on themes of national genesis, the blessings of American liberty, and sectional reconciliation. Given the nature of the celebration, this was not surprising, but Jamestown was important as a constant marker of that stratum of Virginia tradition which identified the state with the nation.[50]

Occasions of similar significance called forth like sentiments. Advising the Virginia Historical Pageant Association in 1922, when his bellicose championship of the Old Dominion was at full flood, Tyler insisted that the contemplated pageantry "should visualize the future" as well as salute the past. In depicting the first legislative assembly of 1619, in particular, "there should be a vision of democracy, . . . not democracy in Virginia alone, but as the ruling spirit of the American continent." In short, he urged, the Jamestown landing "should represent the founding of the republic of the United States."[51]

Given the history of the Commonwealth, linking Virginia to the nation was easy enough; reconciling aristocracy with democracy was a more complex problem. Adding to its complexity was looseness of definition. "Aristocracy" could retain its original political meaning of government by a select few ("the best"), or it could apply in a more modern way to a social elite. Conversely, "democracy" usually meant more than popular government; it carried connotations also of social egalitarianism. Sometimes historians distinguished between political and social meanings, but often usage was general and ambiguous.

Libertarian values, commonly conflated with democracy but with a root also in the aristocratic principle, offered one medium of reconciliation. Although less natural to Americans generally than the democratic connection, the association of aristocracy with liberty was a venerable one, on which the early-nineteenth-century Virginia statesman John Randolph had relied when he proclaimed that as an aristocrat he loved liberty though he loathed equality. This was of course a kind of liberty which left the aristocrat free to rule his lands, dependents, and servants as he saw fit. Describing the southern plantation tradition in 1925, Francis Pendleton Gaines pointed out that it exalted "a 'splendid isolation' resulting in a conservatism of delightfully archaic flavor," and associated with "the flaming love of liberty which Burke emphasized." David Hackett Fischer in a more modern analysis distinguishes the "conception of hegemonic freedom" as part of the cavalier mentality, and notes that in Virginia it "permitted and even required the growth of race slavery for its support." But, pace John Randolph, even a species of egalitarianism could subsist in this kind of freedom. "The Virginia idea of equality," Moncure Conway observed of his native state in the antebellum period, "was not that of individual men, but of representatives; and each planter represented his subjects, black and white"— a description of master-class attitudes to which recent scholarship gives support.[52]

In general, however, historians of the late nineteenth and early twentieth centuries shied away from qualifying their forefathers' devotion to libertarian or democratic ideals with any such term as "hegemonic liberty." The centrality of Virginia tradition to that of the United States seemed rather to require some means of juxtaposing distinct social and political realities. Writers labored in consequence to fashion a plausible account of Virginia, especially in colonial times, as a "democratic aristocracy." One approach was to posit a distinction between political and social ranks and spheres, but historians differed on the significance of these categories. Despite class distinctions, republican principles lay "at the very foundation of the Virginia character," John Esten Cooke argued, and the planter, although a "feudal patriarch," was "among the first to proclaim that 'all men are created equal.'" This meant in practice, he elaborated, that the colony had been socially aristocratic but politically republican. Virginians had recognized "the great truth that the gold lace is only the guinea stamp,—the manhood of the free citizen is the real gold." Opportunity for upward mobility resolved any residual contradiction, Cooke suggested.[53]

Thomas Nelson Page agreed. Page acknowledged the Virginia colony's reputation as "an aristocratic country," which he thought had made it an attractive haven for royalist refugees. "Yet there was that in the Virginians which distinguished them, for all their aristocratic pretensions, from their British cousins," he added. "Grafted on the aristocratic instinct was a jealous watchfulness of their liberties, . . . which developed into a sterling republicanism, notwithstanding the aristocratic instinct." It had not been chivalry alone, but "chivalry and love of the rights of freemen" which (along with religious devotion) had given early Virginia life its "fibre," he concluded.[54]

In Page's rendering of early Virginia, American self-reliance had been gilded by the charm of aristocracy and guided by its values. Despite its hierarchical form, Virginia society "contained the essential principle of Republicanism," he maintained. "Every freeholder had a vote." Personal force outweighed family position in the new land, but having proved his individual worth, a man was eager to establish "his claim to honorable lineage, which was still held at high value." There were echoes from the age of chivalry as well as from the American wilderness: "the great landlord must be as hardy as his hunter; the mistress of the plantation must be as brave as her ancestress who defended her castle or her grange."[55]

Philip Bruce, in somewhat more muted tones, reached similar conclusions. But Lyon Gardiner Tyler, in *The Cradle of the Republic: Jamestown and James River* (1906), solved the problem in precisely the opposite way: for Tyler political aristocracy masked social democracy. The "great cavalier emigration" of the Commonwealth period had contributed to the rise of an "aristocratic class," he thought. Yet although this class had controlled the chief offices of government, its political dominance had been "a mere veneering" on the more egalitarian social life of the colony. Two factors had fostered "the spirit of democracy in Virginia," as he had previously contended in a review of Fiske's *Old Virginia and Her Neighbours*. Physical isolation "promoted self-confidence and self-reliance, and negro slavery made race and not class the real distinction in society." Thus, it might seem, Ralph Waldo Emerson went partners with John C. Calhoun.[56]

In treating with nineteenth-century Virginia, distinctions between aristocracy and democracy could be more easily collapsed. Historians and memorialists often downplayed the gaudier claims of an aristocratic past in favor of a defense—which could be no less romantic—of a rural republican gentry. In his biography of Thomas Nelson Page, the reputed dean of the "moonlight and magnolias" school of southern literature, his brother Rosewell noted the influence on the novelist of George W. Bagby, author of *The Old Virginia Gentleman and Other Sketches* (1884). In the wake of earlier writers who had viewed the Old South through lenses ground by Sir Walter Scott, Rosewell pointed out, Bagby had been the first to discover that "in the simple plantation homes was a life more beautiful and charming than any that the gorgeous palaces could reveal." Similarly Arthur Granville Bradley, in *Sketches from Old Virginia* (1897), observed that "the Virginia gentry of slavery days lived simply," and regretted that "so much florid nonsense about 'Barons' and 'lavish splendour' and the like" should have obscured this truth. Even Philip Bruce, who was not inclined to underestimate the importance of the planter class, insisted that "there was in that old society practically no ostentation, no pretension, no imitation of alien habits and customs." Bruce attributed this modesty precisely to the traditionalism of a relatively isolated society, the inherited usages of which were little subject to northern or European fancies.[57]

Lyon Gardiner Tyler sought more emphatically to emphasize the democratic strands in Virginia tradition. At the same time Tyler illustrates perhaps better than anyone else the social and political tensions which that tradition contained. Born in 1853, he was the son of President John Tyler (who was later elected to the Confederate Congress) and of Julia Gardiner Tyler, of a prominent Connecticut family. Outliving his own first wife, Lyon at seventy married Sue Ruffin, great-granddaughter of Edmund Ruffin, said to have fired the first shot against Fort Sumter. Like his contemporary and fellow Virginian Woodrow Wilson, Tyler trained for the law but was drawn into an academic career. As a legislator in 1887, he helped to obtain state support for the College of William and Mary, which was foundering in the aftermath of the Civil War. He was elected president of the college the following year, and held the post for the next thirty-one years. He was not too busy with his administrative duties to establish a reputation as a historian of his state; the *New York Times* in its obituary called him "one of the foremost scholars of his day." He remained active as historian, civic leader, and sectional controversialist until his death on, ironically, Lincoln's birthday, in 1935. As "distinctly branded" by birth as another historian and presidential descendant, Henry Adams, Tyler struggled with a more complicated legacy—at once single and divided in its precepts of devotion to state and nation. The Virginian's life-long quest for vindication was accordingly hard and uncertain.[58]

The terms of vindication required Tyler to render the Virginia cavalier as Jeffersonian democrat. In *The Letters and Times of the Tylers* (1884–1885), the young scholar made much of the ancient association of his family with the cause of "popular rights." Descent from the fourteenth-century English rebel Wat Tyler was a matter of particular pride, he noted. President John Tyler's brother had been christened Wat Henry Tyler after "the two greatest British rebels—Wat Tyler and Patrick Henry," as the child's mother was said to have explained. Both the president and his son Lyon admired still another rebel, Nathaniel Bacon, whom the historian characterized as "this new Wat Tyler." Yet the family also honored the seventeenth-century immigrant Henry Tyler, whom Lyon described as "a cavalier and a gentleman." This was the precise term the president had used in a popular address to characterize Bacon's adversary, Governor William Berkeley—although noting the governor's late lapse into high-handedness and despotism. Loyalty to tradition was hardly a narrow virtue in Virginia, for tradition was spacious enough to accommodate at the same time Cavalier devotion to the Stuarts, rebellion against the Stuarts' chosen governor, and a medieval uprising against the Stuarts' royal predecessors.[59]

Yet whatever the seeming inconsistencies, there is no doubt that the Tylers took pride in a family tradition of being on the side of the people. The historian described his Jeffersonian grandfather, John Tyler, Sr., as "a democrat in every thought of his head and every feeling of his heart." Lyon devoted his most careful attention to the vindication of the career of his father, however, defending the tenth president as the true champion of the people against northern "ultra democracy" and plutocracy, Andrew Jackson's "unrestricted" majoritarianism, and even southern "zealots" who defended slavery as a positive good. (John Tyler's democracy had recognized slavery as "a standing denial of the political equality of man," but rested on a strict interpretation of the constitution and a conception of states' rights as the basis for an equitable and therefore genuine nationalism, Lyon explained.)[60]

Virginia's identification with this authentic democracy was confirmed in succeeding generations. Lyon began his family tome with the text of his father's address at Jamestown on the occasion of the settlement's 250th anniversary in 1857. The ex-president had traced Virginia's history from Captain John Smith's installation as "president" in the early colony—"the first instance of popular revolt against tyrannical misrule . . . in our annals"—to Bacon's championship of "popular rights," and finally to the American Revolution. It was appropriate, the speaker thought, that in the Revolution "the first impulse to independence was given at Williamsburg, and the last battle for liberty was fought at Yorktown." In similar spirit the speaker's son, some quarter of a century later, described the Jamestown settlement as "the mustard seed from which the great tree of the Union had sprung," though it seemed clear in retrospect that by 1857 the "sweet birds" which had once nested there had been replaced by "vultures, with their bills and talons red with blood."[61]

The image of vultures in a mustard tree gave an odd twist to the popular arboreal figure of the Union, but was graphic enough in conveying the anguish of those for whom Virginian and American were almost equivalent terms. In the more conciliatory climate of 1900, Lyon G. Tyler offered perhaps the first public proposal of a national tercentenary celebration. Where his father had invoked Jamestown in token of common traditions which he hoped might still preserve the federal union, Lyon invoked the same traditions to proclaim Virginia's fidelity to the principles of true Americanism in the union restored.[62]

These principles were, above all, democratic. Always a defender of the relatively egalitarian character of early Virginia society, Tyler gave in his later writings, if anything, increased emphasis to the democratic aspects of Virginia life and history. He never tired of turning the tables on the Yankees. "Long before any New England Colony was on this Continent, democracy was born at Jamestown," he insisted. Indeed, he confided in a private letter, "for two centuries the South had cherished democracy when New England hardly knew the word." If the town and town meeting seemed to give the northern section a more plausible claim to democratic genesis than the rural society to the South, Tyler neatly transformed the sow's ear of slavery into the silk purse of equality. Virginia "aristocrats . . . had nothing like the political influence that the aristocrats had in New England, where power rested on white people," he argued.[63]

This analysis reflected a shift in Tyler's position from his former contention that Virginia's early aristocracy had been mainly of political significance. It seemed to Bruce that his friend's eagerness to establish the democratic roots of the Commonwealth had led him to underestimate the aristocratic role, however defined. Antebellum class divisions were distinct and clearly recognized, Bruce argued. "Political equality was entirely practicable in a slave community," he granted, but it seemed clear to him that "social equality was not." Tyler was confusing "political ideas with social," his friend advised him. Bruce found particularly unpersuasive Tyler's effort to contrast an aristocratic New England with a more democratic Virginia. "That sounds topsy-turvy to me," Bruce remarked, given the Puritan beginnings of the northern colonies and the cavalier roots of the southern, with class tendencies in the latter accentuated by slavery. "I fear that on the question of aristocracy and democracy we must agree to differ," Tyler responded. Invoking his experience as a genealogist, Tyler characterized Virginia aristocracy as "domestic and chiefly spectacular"— meaning, apparently, one of social custom and prestige rather than of substantive power. Intermarriage and social mobility had prevented the formation of fixed classes, he argued, and the social character of Virginia had been confirmed by its becoming "the headquarters of the Democratic Republican party." Yet Tyler finally conceded that the tradition was broad enough for those loyal to it to have it both ways. "I think Virginia presented the spectacle of the most spectacular aristocracy side by side with a haughty and independent democracy," he assured Bruce.[64]

Tyler acknowledged the aristocratic strain in Virginia tradition from a democratic vantage point; with Bruce it was more nearly the reverse. With such shades of difference Tyler, Bruce, John Esten Cooke, Thomas Nelson Page, and others struggled to bring the terms of this duality into an ultimate coherence, but no formula quite sufficed to order the vagaries of human life. Where history failed to reduce tradition to order, however, legend offered an archetype which unified far more effectively. Historically rooted and yet larger than history, the cavalier seemed effortlessly to bind together aristocrat and democrat, and to do so throughout the successive ages of the Commonwealth.

Often taken as a mere myth to provide a false pedigree for colonial Virginia's planter class, the cavalier theme in fact took on considerable complexity on several levels. In early usage, to be sure, the term applied rather simply to the notion that royalist refugees of the English Civil War were the "first founders of the aristocracy which prevails in Virginia to this day," as William Alexander Caruthers explained in his novel *The Cavaliers of Virginia* in 1834. It quickly became conventional to extend the term to the descendants as well as the ancestors, and twenty years later another novelist, John Esten Cooke, found it natural to invoke the "beautiful dames and gallant cavaliers" of Virginia society in the period of the American Revolution.[65]

By the time of the Civil War the cavalier had become an adversarial figure. Often contrasted with the mean and churlish Yankee, he imputed a romantic legitimacy to southern society generally, ennobling its still rough-hewn features and increasingly deprecated system of labor. It was the cavalier spirit which would vindicate southern honor on the battlefield. To northerners, the cavalier became a symbol of southern arrogance. In a Civil War tract entitled *The Cavalier Dismounted*, for instance, a Massachusetts polemicist sought to deflate southern aristocratic pretensions by contrasting the South's "ignorant and vicious" colonial immigrants with the gentle English settlers of New England.[66]

After the war, however, the cavalier served as a figure of both consolation and reconciliation. For southerners the cavalier ennobled and vindicated the "Lost Cause," and gave reassurance of continuity amidst the violent disruptions of the postwar period. Heralding the "New South" of industry and progress, and promising southern loyalty to the Union, such sectional spokesmen as Henry Grady were careful also to honor the traditions of the Old South. The Virginia cavalier was the most evocative emblem of those traditions. With the South no longer a political or a military menace, on the other hand, the northern public could accept the cavalier in a spirit of romantic escape from the regnant materialism and corruption of the time. As a model of gallantry in defeat from an earlier civil war, further, the cavalier could help effect the conciliation which most white people considered of primary importance: not that between the races but that among Americans of "Anglo-Saxon" and kindred extraction. Even further, the adaptive, evolving character of English political traditions suggested a way in which the putatively aristocratic southern cavalier might plausibly be brought to serve American democratic pieties.[67]

Quite naturally the cavalier flourished with least restraint in works of fiction. With historians who came to history by way of belles-lettres, such as John Esten Cooke and Thomas Nelson Page, and among a host of amateur and popular historians, ancestral pride and romantic sentiment were apt still to outweigh empirical evidence. The professionalization of historical studies encouraged more exacting standards, even among those without professional training, and helped to bring the cavalier under more careful scrutiny—although without entirely divesting him of the accoutrements of myth and tradition.

Even writers like Cooke and Page show the cavalier theme to have been more complicated than generally conceived. Its essential doubleness, in imparting an idealized aristocracy to the founders of the Old Dominion while supporting at the same time an equally idealized view of early Virginia as the cradle of American democracy, is well established in Cooke's *Virginia: A History of the People* (1883). Cooke was primarily a poet and novelist, and his forays into historical writing have not well withstood critical scrutiny. Thomas J. Wertenbaker in 1910 found Cooke's *Virginia* already "quite antiquated," full of inexcusable errors, and popular "out of proportion to its historical worth." More recently Ritchie Devon Watson has justly enough described it as a work which "served to preserve romantic legend behind the shield of scholarship."[68]

Yet as William Edward Walker has shown, Cooke did not blindly glorify the Old South. He became more defensive about his section and its chivalric totem in the aftermath of defeat, but even then did not purvey an entirely simple version of the cavalier myth. Cooke, who claimed no love for the upper class, gave his romance a democratic as well as an aristocratic edge. Recognizing with quotation marks the problematical nature of the term, he denied that "cavaliers" were necessarily dashing gentlemen on horseback or "butterflies of aristocracy." Rather, he identified them as the great majority of the people of Virginia during the English Civil War period—"always taking the word to mean friendly to Church and King." It appeared that these sympathies were not unconditional, furthermore, for Cooke also described these early Virginians as "simply English people living in America, who were resolved to have their rights," and who would have taken arms against either king or Commonwealth to protect them.[69]

Cooke's imagination was captured by the romantic image of the cavalier, but he did not lose all sense of perspective. In his "military biography" of Stonewall Jackson, he paid glancing tribute to Robert E. Lee as "a truthful type of the old Virginia cavalier," and in considerably more detail developed a portrait of the Confederate cavalryman Turner Ashby as a representative figure. Ashby was to Cooke "the ideal-type of the Southern cavalier, pure-hearted, stainless in morals, and of heroic courage and constancy." The usual historical references applied: Ashby fought with "the ardor of a knight setting out on a crusade"; even more, seeing Ashby in combat, "it was impossible to imagine a more perfect picture of the cavaliers of Prince Rupert in the days of Charles I."[70]

And yet, Cooke seemed almost to ask: it was magnificent, but was it war? Ashby was "a knight rather than a soldier," he pointed out, making up in daring what he lacked in military science. Cooke's main subject, on the other hand, was a man who could effectively channel the knightly ardor of such as Ashby, who could "compel the respect, arouse the enthusiasm, and control and direct the chivalric impulses of the men." And Stonewall Jackson represented another tradition altogether—not that of "the class of planters, living in luxury and elegance on the seaboard," but of "that energetic, intelligent, and thrifty population which settled in Western Virginia." Orphaned, toiling to overcome his early educational deficiencies to succeed at West Point, a stern Presbyterian rather than a liberal Anglican, awkward rather than graceful in carriage, more ruthless than gallant in war, Jackson was more recognizable as a nineteenth-century American than as a medieval knight or a comrade-in-arms of Prince Rupert. Yet Cooke's admiration for Jackson was unstinting; Stonewall for him "combined the loftiest virtues of the gentleman, the soldier, and the Christian." For all of Jackson's implacability as a warrior, moreover, he was in a way a reconciling figure, bringing together the tradition which Virginia and the South had appropriated as their own with the tradition of the Puritan, which southerners ordinarily identified with the North and feared was gaining national ascendancy. Recalling Jackson at a prayer service for his troops, Cooke suggested that "the reader may fancy his erect figure either that of some pious cavalier, or devout Roundhead, performing his devotions on the field of battle."[71]

In this proffered ambiguity, the cavalier seemed capable even of subsuming his historical adversary. Other writers kept the types distinct, but used them similarly to show the largeness of Virginia tradition. In an address in 1909, Philip Bruce invoked the Civil War archetypes: "England in her most fertile and affluent hour never gave birth to a nobler pattern of the Cavalier than Robert Edward Lee, or of the Roundhead than Stonewall Jackson. These men were but the flower of a people who, as a whole, belonged to one or the other of these transmitted types of English character, unmodified by nearly a century of independence, or by the intervention of thousands of miles of sea." This was another way of establishing the encompassing Americanness of the Old Dominion, as if to appropriate a figure identified with Puritans in order to stake out New England as what students of Elizabethan geography liked to call "North Virginia." The impulse to tradition here was anything but narrow or separatist.[72]

Thomas Nelson Page placed the cavalier in an even more inclusive context. In *The Old South* (1896), Page noted that the southern colonies had furnished asylum not only for "many hard-pressed Cavaliers" during the Commonwealth period, but also for Cromwellian refugees. He found it unnecessary to dwell on the cavalier element. In what would seem a non sequitur but for the long genealogical reach of the issue, he commented that it made no difference whether the ancestors of early Virginians had "fought with the Norman conqueror on Senlac Hill or whether they were among the 'villains' who followed the standards of Harold's earls." Although he acknowledged that a "gentle blood and high connections" had been potent assets in Virginia society, he balanced this assertion with the "prouder claim" of a colonial melting pot: the American settlers "were the strongest strains of many stocks—Saxon, Celt, and Teuton; Cavalier and Puritan."[73]

The cavalier controversy has been especially confused because the term itself has had no fixed meaning. Even nineteenth-century writers were apt at some point to cover themselves by defining "cavalier" as a party term, regardless of social class. Yet it was never able to divest itself of the dashing, aristocratic imagery imparted to it by nineteenth-century fiction. Years of indiscriminate fictional, historical, and popular usage left it a seemingly hopeless muddle. Maud Wilder Goodwin's assertion in 1895 that the southern colonists "were Cavaliers; not necessarily in blood, or even in loyalty to the Stuart cause, but Cavalier in sympathies, in the general view of life, in virtues and vices," renders a fair impression of the elasticity of the term.[74]

An almost insurmountable difficulty for the employment of the cavalier as a meaningful category in American history, this very elasticity gave the figure its extraordinary usefulness as archetype. Its reach and force was well exemplified in Lyon Gardiner Tyler's 1913 pamphlet "The Cavalier in America." Tyler's little production was intended as "A New Year Greeting," and therefore under less obligation of tight argument than a scholarly piece would have been. But it was consistent with Tyler's scholarly work, and there is no reason to doubt its sincerity. "Cavaliers" for Tyler embraced the early would-be colonizers Sir Humphrey Gilbert and Sir Walter Raleigh as well as hundreds of royalists who had taken refuge in Virginia during the English Civil War period. Jefferson, "whose ancestors on both sides were cavaliers," had written the Declaration of Independence; the "immortal cavalier" George Washington had commanded the Continental Army while another cavalier, George Rogers Clark, conquered the Northwest Territory. With a typical Tyler twist, the author noted that the Old Dominion's "cavalier representatives" at the Constitutional Convention had opposed the provision supported "by the Puritan delegates from New England, permitting the slave trade for twenty years." The Virginians Robert E. Lee and George H. Thomas had represented cavalier virtues on opposite sides during the Civil War, and Tyler looked to the impending inauguration of Woodrow Wilson to restore the "Cavalier spirit" to the counsels of the federal government.[75]

For those who might wonder what a term stretched so far could possibly mean, Tyler supplied only a brief definition, misleadingly specific even as a guide to his own usage. "The term 'cavalier,'" he stipulated, "is a generic one, and included all who supported the just prerogatives of the Crown under Queen Elizabeth and the Stuarts." The category could evidently be extended to include the descendants of those who had upheld the crown's rightful claims as well as those who would have done so if they had had the chance. It required a bit of finagling to bring Woodrow Wilson under the sacred rubric, as the Presbyterians had fought against Charles I, but Tyler noted that they had done so "in defence of the liberty of the subject," and that after the king's execution Presbyterians had joined with Anglicans to oppose the Puritans and restore Charles II.[76]

This effort to join the specificities of history to the inclusive strategies of tradition was in the end a feckless endeavor, not really pursued seriously by Tyler or other historians. History was window dressing for a hero capable of representing at once the antiquity and English roots of Virginia, pride of ancestry and of the virtues of honor, gallantry, and loyalty associated with it, and the increasing democratic benisons of liberty and equality of rights. The American cavalier accordingly cut a somewhat different figure from that of his reputed English original—a dashing but quixotic defender of hoary tradition. The maverick Virginia literary critic and historian William Peterfield Trent depicted the American version as a rearguard feudalist whose assumption of the right to "overlordship" eased the way to the institution of slavery, but this was not the cavalier celebrated by the keepers of Virginia tradition. As depicted by writers like Cooke, Page, and Tyler, even the original seventeenth-century model was a proto-freedom-fighter, the worthy progenitor, as Cooke suggested, of such revolutionaries as Washington, Jefferson, and Patrick

Henry. If he was an aristocrat, he was ennobled by nature as well as by birth, and was as dedicated to the liberties of the people as to his own.[77]

Perceived as a liberator, the cavalier became more than one of history's romantic losers, despite the setback at Appomattox, and thus assimilable to the faith in progress shared by Americans of both sections. Progress had once for Americans suggested discontinuity, a clean break with an oppressive and corrupt past. But at the turn of the century progress sought a pedigree, and the cavalier powerfully urged that the values Americans held dear might be reached by the alternative route of continuity and tradition. For Virginians seeking to reaffirm their priority as Americans, the cavalier showed the way.

He did so most persuasively when personified. Indeterminate and shifting as an abstraction, the cavalier gained force when he was embodied in historical figures—even though these figures tended to be sorted out with renewed abstraction into types and antitypes. One such embodiment was Nathaniel Bacon, leader of the 1676 rebellion against Royal Governor Sir William Berkeley. Long denigrated as a troublemaker and subversive, Bacon may have owed his rehabilitation during the nineteenth century to southern hostility to governmental authority and to the need of an alternative to the Pilgrim legend, as James Lindgren suggests. But Bacon also met some of the internal and structural requirements of the cavalier tradition, even while illustrating certain of its oddities. Although he was one of the few of its leading personal exemplars who actually lived during the time of the authentic cavaliers of history, he played the role of a proto-cavalier, the forerunner of men who brought the tradition to fruition. Bacon's status as a rebel against the governor of Charles I and Charles II, further, made him in a party sense an unlikely cavalier hero. Berkeley himself, who had maintained his loyalty to the Stuarts and welcomed genuine Cavalier refugees to the colony, would have been the more logical choice.[78]

Bacon, however, fitted an image of the cavalier which was more in demand in nineteenth- and twentieth-century Virginia. A young English immigrant of gentle birth, he represented the cavalier as popular leader much as George Washington did with pleasing symmetry exactly a century later. The two even appeared to have fought the same fight, for the events of 1676 and 1776 were said to have shared the same root cause:

"the inalienable right of British subjects to have self-government," as Page put it. Tyler perceived simply "democracy proclaimed a hundred years in advance of Thomas Jefferson." As late as 1957 Thomas Jefferson Wertenbaker—citing Philip Bruce in support—still regarded Bacon as "the torchbearer of the Revolution."[79]

While cavalier qualities were ascribed to many later figures, embodiments of truly myth-satisfying proportions were few. Even Washington, although often awarded the title of cavalier, did not really fire the imagination in that role. He was perhaps too much a man of the Enlightenment to bear with him the requisite whiff of romance. But there was one man whose entitlement to the name few white southerners questioned, and by the early twentieth century perhaps few northerners. Although Robert E. Lee lived in the age of the railroad and the telegraph, and not in that of the pike and the musket, it was agreed that—transcending history, more substantial than myth—the Confederate chieftain epitomized the cavalier tradition. In America he could do so only by gathering into himself its polarities and complexities.

More than a sectional figure, Lee was an established American hero by the early 1900s, praised for his "national spirit" by Philip Bruce and many others. In the South Lee had of course a more particular significance, and there it became a matter of almost ritual observance that the figure of the general joined the traditions of colonial Virginia, the American Revolution, and the Confederacy in a seamless whole. And interwoven with these, indeed, were the traditions of medieval chivalry.[80]

Cooke and Page were representative in presenting Lee as "essentially the type of the cavalier of the Old Dominion," in Page's words, steeped in the traditions of an ancient and distinguished lineage. His genealogy was found to include not only Lionel Lee, who had raised a company of crusaders for the Coeur de Lion, but Launcelot Lee, a comrade-in-arms of William the Conqueror. Cooke was particularly struck by the parallel between Launcelot and a later immigrant, Richard Lee, who had reestablished the family again in seventeenth-century Virginia—two "cavaliers," as he might have said, who had carried the home outward. Richard indeed had been ardently cavalier in sentiment, according to

Cooke, and eager to proclaim Charles II in the colony—"the Lees seem always to have been Cavalier."[81]

In Virginia a cavalier heritage was perfectly in keeping with rebellion against George III, and the war for American independence was readily identified with the war for southern independence. Southerners of Civil War days were highly conscious of the Revolutionary precedent, and because of the relative unchangingness of the provincial life of the section, as Bruce contended, the Revolution seemed less remote in time than it was. Many southerners were of Scots-Irish descent, the historian added, and these had family traditions which "went back, not only to King's Mountain, Guilford Court-House, and Yorktown, but also to Bothwell Bridge, the Battle of the Boyne and the Siege of Londonderry." These were traditions which gave them a fierce will to resist the tyrant and the intruder.[82]

English Cavalier rather than Scots-Irish Covenanter, General Lee nevertheless had impeccable ties to the American Revolution. His father, "Lighthorse Harry" Lee, had been a hero of the war, and Robert himself married Mary Custis, great-granddaughter of Martha Washington and a distant cousin. Claiming both his birthplace, Stratford, and Mount Vernon as ancestral homes, "the boy from his cradle found an atmosphere redolent at once of the greatness of Virginia's past and of the memory of the preserver of his country," Page remarked. It seemed clear to his biographer that Lee had taken the first president as his model, and as clear that the character and values of the two men demonstrated "an absolute parallel." As Page understood the issues and sentiments of the Civil War, furthermore, Lee's Army of Northern Virginia had been as much animated by the "love of liberty" as had Washington's rebels of 1775. Cooke also compared Lee to Washington, and the Confederates generally to Revolutionary War patriots.[83]

In this way traditions were knit together. If Lee recapitulated the type of the Virginia cavalier, it was a type which embraced ideals of liberation as well as those of chivalry, which reflected democratic as well as aristocratic myth, and for which the break with the past, by emigration or revolution, was hallowed by ancient precedent. All of this seemed to demonstrate that Virginians were the truest of Americans, whose cavalier traditions had provided only the richest nourishment for the national ideals. That this might be misleading or illusory in certain respects, that it might cover dreadful contradictions on matters of race, especially, can hardly be denied. But Old Dominion traditionists characteristically sought to show that Virginians had pursued the accepted national ideals—only by a truer path than that followed in other parts of the country. This argument is most clearly seen in Virginia's premier historian of the turn-of-the-century period.

If any modern man's values and principles were more securely rooted in personal and family background than Lyon G. Tyler's, perhaps it was those of Philip Alexander Bruce (1856–1933). Bruce was born on one of the largest tobacco plantations in Virginia, early enough to retain some recollections of the Civil War. He was as much an insider to Virginia tradition as it was possible to be. The first Bruce had come to Virginia about 1630, as he noted in a brief autobiographical account. His father and uncles "were among the largest slaveholders in Virginia, and their lives were those of the typical great slaveholders and land-owners of the old South," he recalled. His father, Charles Bruce, had married a sister of Confederate Secretary of War James A. Seddon, and had raised and captained a Confederate artillery company.[84]

Tutored by a great-grandson of Thomas Jefferson, Bruce went on to two years at a private school, and another two at the University of Virginia. One of his close friends in Charlottesville was Thomas Nelson Page, and Page married Bruce's sister, Anna Seddon Bruce. After graduating from Harvard Law School, and with some supplemental legal studies at the University of Virginia, he set up a law practice in Baltimore, but eventually found that he was more interested in literature and history than in the law. (His brother, William Cabell Bruce, resolved differently a similar division of interests: a biographer of Benjamin Franklin and John Randolph of Roanoke, he nevertheless took the main course of his life through the law into politics and served a term as U.S. senator from Maryland.) Bruce wrote editorials for the *Richmond Times-Dispatch* for a period in the early 1890s. He became corresponding secretary of the Virginia Historical Society in 1892, and the following year initiated the publication of the *Virginia Magazine of History and Biography*, of which he served as the first editor. A distinguished career as historian followed. After his *Economic History of Virginia in the Seventeenth Century* won favorable notice in 1896, he engaged in extended periods of research in England between 1898 and 1907, which helped him to complete the trilogy on early Virginia history which was his chief accomplishment in his field. *The Social Life of Virginia in the Seventeenth Century* (1907) and the *Institutional History of Virginia in the Seventeenth Century* (1910) brought this project to fruition.[85]

Always the champion of Virginia tradition, Bruce struggled between understanding the tradition through authentic historical methodology and sheltering it in the recesses of myth. Although he was not professionally trained as a historian and remained largely aloof from the academic and institutional sides of the discipline, Bruce has been nominated as "the father of scientific history in Virginia." His trilogy is criticized for an overemphasis on the plantation class, but much of it has held up well, the *Social Life* perhaps less well than the other two volumes. Bruce was a careful researcher and made extensive use of original sources. His attention called to the importance of county court records by Lyon G. Tyler, he took particular advantage of those documents in his works on colonial history.[86]

Bruce made no radical departure from the cavalier thesis, and critics of iconoclasts like Wertenbaker sometimes rallied to him on the issue, but his judicious handling of the available evidence helped to bring about a serious reconsideration of the question by historians. His main contention was that the early Virginia settlers had represented a cross-section of the English society of the time, and indeed had been hardly distinguishable from it in composition. This cross-section included a liberal representation of the "English gentler classes." Many of the prominent colonial families, Bruce noted, came from the "English squirearchy" which furnished vestrymen and magistrates, resided in manor houses, and sat in Parliament. To this class Bruce appended "the numerous cavalier military officers who took refuge in Virginia when the Puritans obtained their supremacy in England." He was careful to add that many other families which became prominent in Virginia were descended from traders and merchants.[87]

Bruce's best work preserved a due degree of scholarly detachment and muted the sentiments natural to one of his experience in life. In later years, however, such sentiments crept with too little restraint into his history. Such a book as *Brave Deeds of Confederate Soldiers* (1916) "unmistakably reflected Bruce's allegiance to the mythology and symbolism of the Old South and the Lost Cause," as a biographer justifiably remarks, and Henry Steele Commager, while acknowledging the worth of Bruce's major works, observed that his *Virginia Plutarch* (1929) showed him to be "one of those filiopietistic historians that Charles Francis Adams misthought the peculiar possession of New England."[88]

"Filiopietism" was the mot juste, though in a broader sense than that of mere ancestor veneration. Bruce was no less animated by domestic felicities than was John Fiske. His most intense emotions were engaged by memories of family and of the circles of kinship and acquaintance which had surrounded him as a boy. The society into which he had been born, Bruce recalled, had been made up of a set of families which he had never seen surpassed. "And the women of those refined families!" he exclaimed. "Well, a lump rises in my throat when I think of them—and those beautiful old homes,—beautiful even when most unpretentious." The lump could not always be contained. He responded tearfully to Thomas Nelson Page's *Social Life in Old Virginia* in 1897: "First, I read it and got so choked in the throat that I was afraid to say a word; then my wife read it, and was soon entirely overcome with blubbering. I have not read anything so fine and beautiful for many a day. You have drawn a picture of the old times that goes right straight to the heart." Page helped to convince him, he added, "that after all we are not far wrong in being so proud of that rural gentry to whom Virginia owes all her fame in the past."[89]

What gave particular poignancy to such sentiments was the failure of Bruce's own family to remain rooted in the land. "Like *Brer Rabbit* in *Uncle Remus*," Bruce remarked, "I was born in the Briar Patch down South, and the smell of the soil will stick to me as long as I live—God be praised!" Yet the smell of the soil did not pay the bills, nor was it always as refreshing to Bruce's kin as to Bruce himself. Lamenting the sale of the old family home at Staunton Hill in 1919, Bruce noted that his brother and sister-in-law could easily have afforded to keep it in the family—not to mention a nephew who had "accumulated one of the largest fortunes in Baltimore—But there is no sentiment in these times—It is all acquisition of money," he complained.[90]

Much to his regret, Bruce himself was not able to purchase Staunton Hill. He struggled for years, however, to maintain a farm which, although he was an absentee owner, at least preserved a sense of continuity with the traditions of his family and past. But the dissonance of tradition with modern social and economic realities was nearly insupportable. Even if he were to build a house on the property, he realized, he would not be able to induce his wife and daughter to live there—"they know nothing of the country except what they have heard of its isolation and its inconveniences." As the farm was too expensive and too distant from his home in Norfolk to enjoy as a "plaything," he decided, he must "put aside all sentiment . . . and deal with this property in a practical business spirit."[91]

That Bruce made these comments in a letter which, like many other such letters of the World War I period, was dispatched from London, seems to underscore the tenuousness of the tradition he sought to preserve—the more so in the case of letters Bruce feared had gone down on the *Lusitania* and the *Arabic*. Such symbolism aside, not even a "practical business spirit" sufficed to maintain the farm on a sound basis. "There are more different sorts of vicissitudes in farming than in any business I ever knew of," he wrote to his farm manager, Joseph Edmunds Gaines, in 1915. "Every kind of misfortune hits it." Taxes were too high; sharecroppers working the land were unreliable and at times dissatisfied with the terms offered them; tobacco prices were not high enough to bring in a decent profit even in relatively good years. Despairing of ever making the farm pay, Bruce was forced like so many other twentieth-century landowners to contemplate subdivision and sale.[92]

Besieged tradition easily becomes embittered, and it was perhaps personal disappointments with his farm, fed by the pervasive hysteria of the war and postwar period, which moved Bruce to unusual expressions of anxiety. He resented Yankee interlopers who he was afraid were trying to take financial advantage of him. Anticipating the escalation of labor conflicts in the North and racial "clashes" in the South in 1919, he wrote Gaines that he was glad that the Ku Klux Klan had been revived in Richmond. "I look for great Bolshevik commotions at the North before Xmas," he warned his manager in the same year. "If they want a Bolshevik government there, we in the South will set up the Confederacy again," he joked.[93]

At best, however, Bruce rose above both nostalgia and bitterness and achieved something approaching a philosophy of life. He articulated the foundations of his traditionism in a letter to Lyon G. Tyler in 1928:

> I consider it to be one of the most fortunate features of my youth that my life then was passed on one of the large plantations, where still lingered the glow of the past, and where all my associations were with people who had been born under the old system, and who carried to their graves the ideas which they had inherited from the society which prevailed in the greatest period of Virginia's history. . . . Their descendants may be shrewder and more alert in a practical way, but where can you find today their counterparts in ripe English classical culture; in serenity and mellowness of general outlook on life; in strength and purity of family affections; in disinterestedness of patriotism; in dignity and impressiveness of personal bearing?[94]

Bruce was aware that younger Virginians regarded men like him and Tyler as "mummies, mossbacks, and Bourbons," but he reassured his friend that they were not "sulkers in the tent, without spirit to participate in the march of mankind in our own age." He was disturbed by the breach of continuity which modernity seemed to effect, and most of all by a failure to accord the "profoundest reverence" to the heroes of Virginia's past and to preserve the "noble principles" for which they stood. He perceived no necessary inconsistency between "progress and conservatism"; European experience showed that the "growth of conviction" could take the form of a "broadening down from precedent to precedent." But the lapse of tradition which he observed in his later years seemed rather to signify "a thoroughly radical revolution."[95]

In Bruce, more than in Tyler or other leading Virginia historians, there was the germ of an Old World, Burkean traditionism. Based on a conception of society as organic, slow to change, and constrained by the general limitations of mortal existence, yet dedicated to liberties as they broadened "from precedent to precedent," in Bruce's words, a Burkean vision seemed capable of embracing even the contradictions of Virginia history. The British Whig had after all denounced the constitutional abuses which had driven Virginians like Washington and Jefferson into rebellion; on the other hand (although Burke himself had had no sympathy with slavery) a too precipitate solicitude for the denied liberties of the slave could be censured in the same tones with which Burke had indicted the French Revolution. Integral to the customs and traditions of Virginia society, Bruce contended, slavery could only with the greatest difficulty have been torn from the social fabric.

Yet the Burkean model of society has never quite worked in America, even in Virginia. In *The Southern Tradition at Bay* (1968), Richard Weaver cited the British Whig as the proper political philosopher for the South, in opposition to the North's Tom Paine, but admitted with some perplexity that southerners had taken little note of this. "It is a wonder that the South did not draw more freely from Burke," he remarked. Clearly one reason for this was that a favorable social context was lacking, as Bruce himself was aware. "An Englishman sees on every side the roots that bind the modern social life of his country to its farthest past," he pointed out; "we . . . can detect hardly a single root that pumps the sap of our social past into the spreading branches of our social present." He did not exempt Virginia from this assessment, and for all his emphasis on the perpetuation of English ways in the Commonwealth, his mutual commiserations with Tyler and others show him to have been uncomfortably aware of their vulnerability to the American flight from the past. And for that matter the Virginians, who embraced Thomas Jefferson as a hero of their tradition, were themselves too American to reject utterly the notions that time meant progress and that each generation could freely determine its fate. Those of this period, at least, seldom invoked Edmund Burke.[96]

There emerged among the Virginians a sort of hybrid traditionism, however. In some respects "Burkean" and "American" elements were easily resolved: particularism, suspicion of overly centralized authority, and devotion to home and family, especially, were as congruent with American as with Burkean precepts. Virginians evidently remained more respectful of social hierarchy and of tradition itself than most Americans, while retaining a more robust faith in human possibilities than Old World conservatives. Yet Bruce discovered in the broadest reaches of English experience a warrant for this ambivalence. Visible above all in Anglo-American history, he found, was a duality inherent in the English nature. "No people were more devoted to their own country than they," as he put it, "and yet no people were quicker to abandon it when the prospect of adventure, novelty, or gain was held out before them." In a poem, "Cape Henry," Bruce rendered the insight in succinct if not immortal verse:

> Staunch hearts of oak are they on land or foam.
> Along Adventure's way they burn to roam,
> Their feet, when most astray,
> Still most at home.[97]

In this variation on a theme, the home did not even need to be carried outward; the "wandering spirit of the Angles" never left it. The journey of colonial immigrants across the Atlantic simply followed earlier migrations of the race from the forests of northern Europe to Britain, and anticipated later English emigration to Australia, New Zealand, Africa, and India. The pertinent implication, of course, was that the early Virginian, as both adventurer and traditionalist, had been the best of Englishmen.

In Bruce's world, this made him as well the best of Americans, embarked on a less-traveled path to the realization of American ideals. Bruce offered an interpretation of American development directly antithetical to the contemporaneous "frontier thesis" of Frederick Jackson Turner, which appealed so strongly to the national belief that the past could be left behind. Bruce's very adventurers represented a tradition-infused continuity with the past. His observation that the early Virginia settlements "resembled more the long established communities of England than the communities of a new country as conceived of by us in the light of our knowledge of the modern American frontier" appeared directly to challenge Turner. Yet tradition, for Bruce, nurtured some of the very qualities of American individualism which Turner believed to be evoked by the discontinuities of frontier life. The pioneer planters of Virginia "were possessed of an unusual degree of self-reliance, energy, and enterprise," he believed, but were not for that reason inclined to break with the past. "Men of that character," indeed, "were the very ones who were least likely to be disloyal to the impressions of their formative years."[98]

Modern readers are apt to perceive an odd incongruity in Bruce's analysis of early Virginia society. The community at large was simply a "series of plantations," he wrote, none differing from the others in essentials, and each a "small principality," largely self-sufficient and self-governing. "Completely permeated with love of home," southerners lived under "roofs . . . made sacred by the long family story, and by the accumulated traditions of many generations." The master-slave relationship, Bruce briefly acknowledged, even gave "a certain barbaric aspect to the condition of the great Southern landed proprietor," as "distinguished" as was the social life it made possible. We are ready with little hesitation to contrast this premodern, tradition-bound plantation society with the individualism of the northern town, even of the northern farm.[99]

And yet Bruce—and other defenders of old Virginia—saw the matter completely reversed. The large plantation "fostered habits of self-reliance in individual men," Bruce wrote. It "promoted the aristocratic spirit," to be sure, but this served simply to foster the planter's "individuality" and "devotion to liberty." Thus, he concluded, "individualism was the most conspicuous feature of old Southern life. The extraordinary development of that quality was the direct result of plantation seclusion and plantation traditions in slavery times." This was not the milieu of the modern solitary and freely moving individual, clearly. Bruce was describing here—although without any clear conceptualization of it—something akin to "hegemonic liberty," or to the mind-set described by Barry Shain, which identified individualism with familial or local autonomy.[100]

In Bruce's rendering, certainly, the Virginia version had little to do with the kind of innovating, enterprising individualism conventionally celebrated in this country, but was indicative rather of "an abnormal conservatism of spirit, an extremely haughty and impatient independence of character" which only confirmed the planter's "loyalty to inherited points of view" and strengthened "his passionate desire to preserve the existing social system precisely as it stood." Like Tyler, Bruce admitted that this independent spirit "weakened the impulse of cooperation,—which is the main-stay of modern society." What Bruce conceded with one hand he took back with the other, however, for his description of "the civilization which governed the communities of the North, in which individual man sank into insignificance as the community rose in importance," was hardly an endorsement.[101]

Whatever the case in the North, the frontier in Virginia marked no breach of social continuity, as Bruce saw it; it simply gave fuller scope to an English character that was at once traditionalist and liberty loving. The country gentleman on his isolated plantation "became only more jealous of his personal and political freedom; only more intense in his love of home and family; only more scrupulous in his recognition of the claims of hospitality, and if religiously disposed, only more obedient to the authority of the church, and more submissive to the dictates of his early religious training." The effect of the plantation, in sum, was "to foster and strengthen in these transplanted Englishmen all those traits which had been a part of their moral and intellectual growth before they emigrated to Virginia."[102]

It could be said that Bruce and, less clearly, Page, Tyler, and others, offered at once a reaffirmation of the dominant American tradition and an alternative to it. In simplest form that tradition enshrined a faith in the power of a new social environment, frontier conditions, and institutions promoting "liberty and justice for all" to liberate the individual from the constraints and oppressions of tradition itself, with all of its institutional appurtenances. In the Virginia version, tradition and liberation conducted an oddly dialectical pas de deux, deriving from an ambivalence in English character but most fully played out in the Old Dominion. The quest for adventure or gain, seemingly overriding the love of home, led Englishmen to the frontier and the isolated plantation which intensified their self-reliance and love of freedom even to the point of jeopardizing the cohesion of the larger society. Yet the concomitant strengthening of domestic virtues and loyalties led also to an intensified respect for authority and devotion to tradition. So, as it turned out, they had never really left home at all.

Bruce thus formulated an Anglo-Virginian tradition in which Virginia particularism and Virginia's identification with America might be reconciled. It was fundamental to his understanding of history that America—or at least the Chesapeake region of it—gave freer scope to the development of the English virtues. He must have been gratified when an English friend confirmed this. "It seems to me that you Virginians, judging from those whom I have met, are in many ways more English than the English," wrote Gerald Smythe, to whom Bruce had dedicated *Brave Deeds of Confederate Soldiers*. Not only did Virginians share in the incomparable traditions of Old England, Smythe added, but they had produced Robert E. Lee, "the grandest gentleman this world has ever seen." But Bruce was also, in effect, concurring with Tyler that the Virginian was more American than the American—the American not so fortunate as to be a child of the Old Dominion, that is. America was properly an enlargement and intensification of the English tradition.[103]

No merely political or military event, such as the American Revolution, could sever this tradition. Yet Bruce was not saying that nothing changed; even continuity contained the achievement of gain and the pathos of loss. As he wrote,

> The history of Virginia resembles a calm and sluggish river, whose flow at two long intervals is suddenly and unexpectedly broken by a tumultuous fall, which dashes the waters to a much lower but far broader channel. The first precipice was Yorktown; the second, Appomattox. Socially, each was a leap, not upward, but downward. First, the abolition of kingship, and secondly, the abolition of Slavery roughly jolted us down to the monotonous and unpicturesque level of democracy, which, in its pursuit of social equality, admits no distinctions in birth, and discards all the aristocratic traditions of the past.[104]

Placed alongside John Fiske's image of the loom, Bruce's stream suggests some of the differences between the two defenders of tradition and between the sections that they represented. The bucolic watercourse furnished as fitting an emblem of continuity for Virginia as the mechanism of domestic industry did for New England, and perhaps bore as well a suggestion of resignation to the ways of nature in contrast to active engagement in a providential process. Most notably, the stream follows its ineluctable and melancholy course of declension, in sharp distinction from the loom's progressive rendering of the "garment of God." The course of the stream, moreover, is at intervals cataclysmic, plunging over the precipices representing the two great scenes of surrender enacted on Virginia soil—that Virginians were victors in the one and the vanquished in the other seems hardly to matter here. There is no parallel to these shocks in the smooth motion of the loom. (Ironically it is Herder's gently broadening "stream of history" which is adapted to represent revolutionary change in a conservative agrarian society, while the machine which could stand for Yankee get-up-and-go is linked to a placid gradualism.) Yet discontinuity only reaffirms a deeper continuity, as the waterfall reaffirms the continuity of the stream. And considering Bruce's entire body of work, we may suppose the stream to be more than a provincial tributary; it must be in some part or aspect the mainstream of American tradition.

Pride and resentment never completely obscured the yearning for confluence. It was the vindication of tradition, and not the abandonment of it, which for Bruce and other Virginia historians offered the surest path to sectional reconciliation. Virginia tradition stood vindicated, in their eyes, as at once the purest expression of English social and political genius and as the primary source of regnant American ideals. It was important, as it is for all peoples, to show that the travails of history had not been without meaning or consequence—that the gallant, presumptively aristocratic cavalier had been a torchbearer for modern liberties, that the "defense of the Inner Circle" was the first duty of the patriot, that the plantation home had been the nursery of American individualism and self-reliance. If tradition could not provide victory on the battlefield, it could perhaps provide vindication in values negotiable in the modern world.

CHAPTER 3
Tradition and Transcendence:
Ralph Adams Cram and the Tradition
of the Gothic

Advocacy of tradition in shallow, ever-innovating America runs easily to the quixotic. It can hardly be denied that the country has successfully carried on or invented traditions, but the defense of those which have been decisively quenched by modernity seems even less profitable an enterprise in the New World than in the Old. Even the Confederate cause, within a few years of being lost after the expenditure of enormous quantities of blood and treasure in its behalf, became a tradition which was almost as safely and mistily assigned to the past as the knights of King Arthur. The Confederacy was devoutly remembered by Philip Bruce, Lyon G. Tyler, and legions of other white southerners, but the idea that southern independence might be a cause actually to maintain or revive became a joke—"save your Confederate money, boys, the South will rise again." The South produced not even a Bonnie Prince Charlie.

How much more outlandish, then, were lost causes truly remote in time and space. Few would seem of less urgency in modern America than the Jacobite, and few would attract American adherents more likely to impress the majority of their countrymen as just plain silly. Yet the distinguished architect Ralph Adams Cram, in the maturity of his mid-thirties, invested considerable energy in the effort to transplant the Order of the White Rose, founded in England in devotion to the House of Stuart, to American shores. In a manifesto dated St. George's Day, 1899, and co-signed "Ralph von Cram" and "Alfred John Rodwaye," the authors proclaimed the order's devotion to "loyalty, chivalry, honour, . . . denial of the heresy of popular sovereignty, the upholding of the Divine source of power," and the memory of the martyred King Charles I.[1]

This was somewhat more than anachronistic whimsy. It was clearly important to Cram to show that the White Rose was congruent with American traditions and prospects—a vastly less plausible undertaking than the effort of the Virginians to establish the southern roots of Americanism. American Jacobites, he was obliged to acknowledge, owed "allegiance to no foreign Prince," and were "citizens of a State that we must hold to be independent and legally constituted, even though its basis be false in theory and unchristian in principle." Sensibly concluding that monarchy was not feasible in the United States, Cram could only offer Alexander Hamilton as a stand-in for the Stuarts. (This combined traditions of the Cram family, which had received a land grant in New Hampshire from Charles I and had later espoused staunchly Federalist politics.) Perhaps, the memorialists suggested, Hamiltonian principles could rescue American government from "the democratic follies of Jefferson" and "the dark ages of the eighteenth century." Dismissing political reunion with Britain as "neither possible nor desirable," they hoped for a strong alliance between "the two great Anglo-Saxon states" in the interests of liberty, righteousness, and "world dominion."[2]

Despite Cram's concessions to reality, his good friend and fellow Jacobite Louise Imogen Guiney failed to be persuaded of the practicality of his project. "Poor old R. Cram has been making a DONK of himself," she confided. "All our gang is howling with laughter. 'Loyal Americans' is a master touch. The thread of the argument seems to be that we're 'loyal Americans' because, to save our lives, we can't be loyal English!" Presumably unaware of being skewered so mercilessly behind his back, Cram was nevertheless shocked by his friend's rebuffs. "What a bitter disappointment!" he wrote her; "and I fondly trusted that my attempts to Americanize the OWR would meet with your approval." But Guiney, who shared Cram's traditionalist sentiments and had expatriated to England for the feel of the past underfoot, as she said, was without illusions that tradition could so readily bridge the Atlantic. Perhaps thinking of Cram, she observed that "good Americans 'desire and worship' what cannot exist in their own country until another thousand years have slipped through Time's hourglass, if even then."[3]

Cram *was* a good American, although perennially disgusted with his country's political and cultural inadequacies and more than once tempted to his own expatriation. While on one early trip abroad he wrote to Guiney that he was "always happy in this glorious old world, it is so real, so true, so vital. You *know* I am a good and patriotic American, and so I can say to you that over here I think of my own land only with a shudder, as of a vile prison that cages the dear people I love. How crude and brutal it all seems. . . . Dear Lou, between you and me I am coming back here to live and die. I love everything here and nothing there—but the people, some of them." Impatient with American hesitancy to come to Britain's aid during World War I, he again contemplated moving to England—feeling "in, . . . not of" a nation so pusillanimous as his own. In this, at least, Cram finally hewed to the path of Henry Adams rather than to that of Henry James, and lived out his life as an American. But that life was devoted to an effort to prove his friend wrong about the prospects of the past in his native country. It was not the past of the Stuarts that he finally determined to restore, however, but that of the Plantagenets and Capetians.[4]

"Quixotic" would always be a plausible verdict upon a life and career quickened by such labors as this. A cover story on Cram in *Time* magazine in 1926 seemed to render such a verdict in making fun of the "woe-begone forebodings and prophecies as fearsome as they were mystical" which had "settled upon his sensitive soul" after the World War. Least deserving of such condescending judgments were Cram's achievements in architecture. Through his buildings Cram made himself a pervasive presence in American consciousness, as one critic notes; he "revolutionized the visual image of American Christianity," in the decidedly positive judgment of another. His social and political criticism had no such results. But there was always serious thought and purpose behind even the most eccentric of his causes. Failing to "Americanize" the Order of the White Rose and so to provide a platform for ideals and traditions he believed of transcending value, he was driven to the more ambitious project of Americanizing the Middle Ages— and of medievalizing America.[5]

Cram carried on this extraordinary program beyond the lifetimes of any of the other figures of this study, with the exception of Edward A.

Ross. He survived to see the issues of his generation played out more fully than Fiske, Bruce, or Cooley: in world wars, economic crises, the growth of mass society and totalitarianism, in the development of Modernist sensibility in art and life. As an interpreter of society and history he could work with a time scale extending from what he called "Neolithic Man" almost to the middle of the twentieth century. The vantage point provided by his generation and relative longevity moved him more vociferously than any of the others to repudiate chauvinism both spatial and temporal. He set himself with almost obsessive determination against the "imperial modernism" which destroyed life on a "human scale," and equally against the dogma of "progressive evolution"—fatal alike, he was convinced, to transcendent values and humane society.

In defense of those values and that society Cram was unable fully to invoke tradition as ordinarily conceived, with an emphasis on its continuity. In the first place, as Fiske had shown, such tradition was all too congruent with the very idol of the linearly progressive which Cram was determined to reject; secondly, the traditions in which he wished to work had long been interrupted. Cram was consequently obliged to reinvent tradition. In doing so it often seemed that he was looking for progress in reaction. More thoroughly than the Virginians he was impelled to vindicate the past—not the near past of the Confederacy but the more distant past of feudalism and the guild. Yet he sought as hopefully as so progressive a thinker as Charles Horton Cooley an organic society which would be informed by useful traditions commensurate with modernity. The result, in Cram's case, was a conception of tradition which was part Platonic ideal and part Modernist collage, a device of discontinuities, juxtapositions, and epiphanies.

Ralph Adams Cram was born in Hampton Falls, New Hampshire, in 1863, in a family setting in which the main themes of his life and thought were already present. His father was a Unitarian minister, but one of Transcendentalist leanings which foreshadowed his son's idealism. Tradition was represented by his maternal grandfather, Ira Blake, whose standing in rural New York society entitled him to be known as "Squire," and also by a paternal genealogy tracing family origins to a Teutonic knight of the Middle Ages, Ludolf von Cram (the derivation of Cram's Order of the White Rose sobriquet). The sources of Cram's given names,

Ralph Waldo Emerson and the Squire's hero, practical John Adams, underscored elements of this varied heritage.[6]

Graduating from Exeter High School, Cram was unable to attend college for want of money, but he showed an early passion and aptitude for architecture and was dispatched to Boston in 1881 to begin an apprenticeship in the profession. After a period of uncertainty about the direction of his career, during which time he served as art critic for the *Boston Transcript* and traveled in Europe, Cram entered into his first architectural partnership in 1889, with Charles Francis Wentworth. The firm was expanded with the addition as partner in 1892 of Bertram Grosvenor Goodhue, whose skills admirably complemented those of Cram. Cram designed on his own All Saints' Church at Ashmont, Massachusetts (1892–94), which gave the firm new standing and which Douglass Shand-Tucci calls the "first masterwork" of the Gothic Revival in the United States.[7]

"To us it was a golden age, with the promise of high fulfillment," Cram recalled of his formative years in the 1880s and 1890s. Although he concluded the time to have been a "false dawn," at least in terms of the reigning faith in progressive evolution, it clearly provided enormous intellectual and aesthetic stimulation. Cram was revolted by the social environment of the late nineteenth century, and his revulsion only deepened in that of the twentieth. Industrial civilization provided a milieu of "dirt, meanness, ugliness everywhere,—in the people no less than in their surroundings." But against this dismal backdrop constellations of thinkers and artists who promised something better shone all the more brilliantly. Among others Cram cited in his autobiography Charles Eliot Norton, George Santayana, and Walt Whitman in the United States; a cluster of Englishmen including Cardinal Newman, Matthew Arnold, Walter Pater, William Morris, and the Pre-Raphaelites; Flaubert and de Maupassant; even Pope Leo XIII. Cram was particularly entranced by Richard Wagner, making his first trip to Europe, in 1886, chiefly to attend the Wagner Festival at Bayreuth. Experimenting rather promiscuously with other cultural offerings, he for a time "wallowed" in "Oriental occultism of the Madame Blavatsky type," as he recalled. His *Black Spirits and White* (1895) was a pioneering effort in the genre of horror stories, with a pronounced fin de siècle ambience.[8]

Cram may have been part of an "aesthetic-Anglo-Catholic-gay net-work in Boston," as Douglass Shand-Tucci argues. Patterns in his personal relations and associations, especially among the "Aesthetes" of the eighteen eighties and the "Decadents" of the nineties, provide plausible evidence for some manner of involvement in such a network. Further inferences about Cram's own sexuality are more speculative, as Shand-Tucci acknowledges. Modern conceptions of homosexuality were just beginning to emerge at the turn of the century and yet any active homosexual behavior on Cram's part would have been closeted; both factors work against any definite conclusions. In any event, Cram eventually entered into an apparently successful marriage and traded in his "bohemian lifestyle for that of a proper Bostonian and . . . paterfamilias." More important in the present context than the precise nature of Cram's sexuality is the light which Shand-Tucci casts on the particular traditions to which the architect adhered. Clearly, as Mary W. Blanchard points out, "the conventional association of American gothic architecture with moral uplift, Protestant gentility, or European elitism" needs to be reexamined. In Cram's case, at least, traditionalism was bound up with revolt against tradition. Whether or not his attraction to the Gothic was colored by a homoerotic sensibility, certainly his Anglo-Catholicism combined aesthetic appeal with rebellion against the Puritan-derived cultural norms of New England.[9]

Cram's aesthetic and religious loyalties were effectively catalyzed by his early travels in Europe. His second visit, in 1887, culminated in a "revelation" of the absolute value of beauty and of the integral connection of the arts to each other and to life. A fellow student of architecture, a young Marylander named T. Henry Randall whom Cram fell in with in Rome, proved an effective guide both in art and religion. A side trip with Randall to Palermo, where Roman, Byzantine, Arab, and Renaissance traditions commingled, taught the possibilities of "organic synthesis." In the Italian spring, church architecture took on a new life and meaning for Cram, and the sight of Venice—"the most consistent and concentrated synthesis of beauty in the world"—confirmed him in his sense of vocation.[10]

Meanwhile his friend had steered him to a religious conversion. "Randall," Cram recalled, "was an Episcopalian of the sound Southern sort, vitalized by Catholic tendencies." His example suggested a more vibrant connection between aesthetics and faith than his inherited Unitarianism was able to offer. In fact, he discovered, art led to faith. Attending a Roman Catholic midnight mass on Christmas with Randall in Italy, Cram was overwhelmed. Other Americans of the period found themselves swept along emotionally by the sheer sensual and aesthetic impact of ecclesiastical beauty—Brooks Adams, whose nerves "tingled for hours in ecstasy" after a visit to a Gothic cathedral, for instance—but in Cram head did not war against heart in the fashion of the Adamses. If he did not entirely comprehend the mass with his mind, yet, as he said, he "*understood.*"[11]

Cram joined not the Roman Catholic Church, however, but, as he put it, the "Anglican Communion of the Catholic Church." Midnight mass was followed by Christmas Day attendance at an Anglican church in Rome, and shortly after his return to America he was baptized as an Episcopalian. Within his new church, however, he was decidedly of the Anglo-Catholic persuasion, Protestantism denoting for him the post-medieval assault on beauty, a beauty represented especially by the Gothic cathedral. Anglican affiliation was certainly more natural to one of his social background, although it is not difficult to imagine him following in the footsteps of Orestes Brownson and other American Protestants who went over to Rome. Indeed, in 1919, he hinted to his Roman Catholic friend Louise Imogen Guiney that he might be about ready to change "the small 'c' for a large 'C'." But with some theological doubts about post-Tridentine Romanism and a strong affinity for English culture, and undoubtedly influenced by his perception that the Oxford Movement had encouraged the Gothic Revival in contrast to the "artistic barbarism" of the nineteenth-century Roman Church, Cram was content to remain within the Anglican fold.[12]

This affiliation provided Cram with a church for which tradition was of central importance, as even tradition-minded Roman Catholics have acknowledged. According to the theologian Yves Congar, "the doctrine of Tradition is one of those few points . . . where Anglicanism would be able to play the role of 'bridge church' [between Catholic and Protestant] that it dreams of having." For the Anglo-Catholic wing of the church tradition was especially important. In England, as John Shelton Reed remarks, Anglo-Catholicism functioned as a "countercultural movement," but it offered a strongly traditionalist counterculture: its adherents "inclined to a sort of neo-feudalism" which reflected a Tory scorn for "trade" as well as a version of socialism which could be viewed as "'mediaeval Catholicism turned inside out.'" Artists, intellectuals, educated professionals, and members of the "urban gentry" were among those most attracted to the movement. In an American setting Cram fitted the pattern well, even down to the neo-feudalism and flirtation with socialism.[13]

By the turn of the century, Cram was set on the course which would carry him through the rest of his life. Committed in his religious faith, he committed himself also to marriage, uniting in 1900 with Elizabeth Carrington Reed, a Virginian, by whom he had three children. All Saints' Church marked the beginnings of a career which brought him fame for his work on St. John the Divine and St. Thomas Episcopal Church in New York, the Bryn Athyn Swedenborgian Church in Pennsylvania, buildings at Princeton and Rice Universities and at West Point, and many other sacred and secular structures. Although Cram worked in a variety of styles, he became identified in the public mind as a Gothic Revivalist, and by the time of World War I he had established his reputation as the leading Gothic architect in the United States. His *Church Building* (1901), which prescribed English Gothic as the most fitting of styles for American Christianity, had become "a kind of bible of church design for its era." More broadly, Cram was embarked upon his neo-medieval program, which sought to restore to society both humanly tolerable values and proportions and the corporate means to spiritual transcendence.[14]

As Cram fully realized, this project flew directly in the face of the modern world. In the inaugural issue of *The Knight Errant*, a short-lived but spirited "Review of the Liberal Arts" which Cram founded in 1892, he decried the degeneration of liberty to license and anarchy, and complained that life had "become a riot of individualism." He added to his indictment realism, materialism, rationalism, agnosticism, eclecticism, and a "social equality based on abstract theory." In opposition to those evils, *The Knight Errant* undertook to lower its lance in defense of idealism, imagination, spiritual and aesthetic values, and natural social hierarchy.[15]

In the recovery of these goods tradition could be instrumental, but only if it could somehow be detached from immediate experience. Convinced that the nineteenth century had sunk to lower architectural depths than the "Dark Ages," Cram sought a tradition more profound than the debased and haphazardly eclectic vestiges he perceived in his immediate aesthetic environment. He took professional inspiration from those who seemed able to reach this deep tradition by making creative use of the forms of the past. Chief among these was H. H. Richardson, whose untimely death he felt as a "body blow" when he heard of it in London in 1886. "Richardson's work was at once traditional, of the time, and forward looking," as James F. O'Gorman observes, and therefore influenced architects ranging from creators of "Romanesque pastiches" to those as innovating as Frank Lloyd Wright. Cram found in Richardson a formative influence because, as he recalled, the older architect "somehow linked us up with tradition and the great world of the past, giving us a new basis on which we could work."[16]

Cram thought highly enough of Richardson to describe him as "our Adam"—the first great genius of American architecture. This oxymoronic but seemingly instinctive association of Adam with tradition was entirely characteristic of Cram. Usable tradition was for him never really old; it retained in its essence an Adamic freshness, a capacity for unconditioned creative genesis even in being perpetuated for centuries. The "American Adam," for Cram, was a member in good standing of Burke's partnership of generations.[17]

The role of tradition in preparing the creative moment was a problem inherent in the Gothic, and Cram responded most eagerly to those, like Richardson, whose work suggested answers. Also congenial to Cram's purposes was William R. Lethaby, almost certainly an indirect if not a direct influence. In *Mediaeval Art* (1904), Lethaby placed the Gothic in a careful historical context. "Every school of art is the product of antecedent schools plus the national equation of the moment," he wrote. The Gothic was continuous with the Romanesque and preceding forms. At the same time it expressed in a particular way the "life of the Middle Ages," manifested also in chivalry, the literary romances, town communities and guilds, the Church, and the universities. Structurally as well, universal and "organic" principles of building combined with the "phenomenal" characteristics of a particular time and place. But Lethaby seemed also to acknowledge a transcending beauty not bound by tradition or social context. "In the building of the great cathedrals . . . there is an element that we do not understand," he allowed. "The old builders worked wonder into them; they had the ability which children have to call up enchantment. In these high vaults, and glistening windows, and peering figures, there was magic even to their makers."[18]

That the Gothic was historically the product of extended architectural traditions could hardly be disputed, and a respect for tradition informed all of Cram's judgments, whether positive or negative. Although he professed to welcome Modernist "eclecticism and opportunism" as a possible seedbed for a more stable future, he charged the modern artist with denying "beauty in any sense that permits of definition and maintains through the ages continuity and substantial identity." These were essential criteria of worth. In his later years he could still discern in the Empire State Building a strand of "the cord of continuity that reached unbroken from the art of 3000 B.C."; Radio City, on the other hand, struck him as an "apotheosis of megalomania" which defied all precedent and tradition. As in art, so in society at large. Cram endorsed the Burkean principle that those who would not look back to their ancestors would not look forward to their posterity. Good government, accordingly, was government which followed custom and the common law, preserving continuity and tradition.[19]

Cram's very respect for tradition kept him from being an unalloyed traditionalist, however. His rejection of his society's most immediate—Victorian—traditions, apart from sheer aesthetic distaste, reflected his sense that they were sterile. "All of the arts of the late nineteenth century except music were retrospective, archaeological," as he put it. Gothic architecture in the true tradition had expressed a fresh vigor of spirit in the High Middle Ages, and could hardly claim authenticity in the modern world unless it was able to capture a similar freshness then. Cram consequently made a point of eschewing the "archaeological" revival of the Gothic which he attributed to some of his predecessors; rather he sought to recover the tradition in order to build upon it creatively and in keeping with the modern spirit.[20]

This presented Cram with a serious dilemma, as he was determinedly at odds with the "modern spirit" as it might most plausibly be represented—either as the spirit of industry, rationalization, and progress, or as the aesthetic Modernism which reacted against those aspects of modernity. The architect's response demonstrates the inadequacy of labels, although he best fits T. J. Jackson Lears's definition of the "antimodernist." He shared with others of this disposition a revulsion against modern bourgeois civilization and a yearning for intense and authentic experience, but looked to the past for inspiration rather than seeking to cut loose from it. His attraction to hierarchy, monarchy, and monasticism clearly placed him in the antimodernist camp; even socialism appealed to him only so long as it reflected premodern communitarian values, and not when it came to him to represent the leveling and standardizing tendencies of mass society.[21]

Yet "modernism" and "antimodernism" are not mutually exclusive, and Cram is not necessarily to be confined to either category. Self-definition offers little help. Aside from his pejorative catch phrase "imperial modernism," the architect used the term "modernism" broadly and usually—though not always—disparagingly to denote new and untraditional styles in art and architecture. Historians have suggested clearer points of reference. In his younger days a countercultural figure and rebel against the Puritan tradition and the Victorian milieu within which it lingered, Cram can be seen, Shand-Tucci suggests, as a "fin-de-siècle modernist"—distinguishing this persuasion from the High Modernism which followed. Perhaps more useful, although derived from Central Europe rather than New England, is Carl Schorske's distinction between the young Wagnerians of the 1870s and the literati of the 1890s known as "Jung-Wien." The Wagnerians, Schorske points out, "rejected the immediate past, in the form of liberalism, but sought attachment to the remote past, both Greek and Germanic, to regenerate society in the present and to build for the future. . . . Jung-Wien espoused the 'modern' . . . as a form of existence and a sensibility different from all that had gone before, one detached from history." The time frame was retarded in America by almost a generation, and the "remote past" a different one, but Cram wanted like his fellow Wagnerians to recover a usable tradtion, and rejected later Modernism insofar as it seemed to want to cut itself loose from tradition altogether.[22]

Arthur Tappan North evidently echoed Cram's sentiments about his own profession in reporting in 1931 that the firm of Cram and Ferguson "has always maintained, and will continue to do so, that 'modernism' has had and can have in it no place whatever." In the cardinal institutions of home, school, and church, North explained, "the continuity of tradition and integrity of spirit must be preserved." Yet Cram's own views were a little more complex. He praised architectural Modernists for their honesty in the use of materials and for their sense of texture and color. He allowed to such figures as Cézanne, Matisse, and Picasso the accomplishment of useful demolition work upon the moribund Victorian traditions which he himself detested. But the concession was grudging, and he could lapse into philistine rhetoric in disdaining Marcel Duchamps's "Nude Descending a Staircase" as a "pile of shingles after a cyclone." His more serious complaint was that the Modernists—all too faithful here to the Zeitgeist—"were afflicted with an acute type of megalomania that rendered their universe entirely egocentric."[23]

The difficulty of bringing the spirit which produced an art such as this within the compass of the Gothic seemed clearly insuperable. Cram asked more of art than that it render the "spirit of the age." It must also express the constancy of human aspiration by transcending the purely local and immediate. The Modernist spirit denied "both continuity and unity to human development," he charged; Modernism was "a thing cut off completely from all past history." In fact this was to ignore an important aspect of Modernism; inspired by primitive, classical, and other forms, Modernist artists and writers often sought in past experience timeless expressions of truth or beauty. Indeed it was because they demanded a direct access to the past, rather as Protestants had demanded direct access to God, that they rejected the mediating, filtering effects of evolutionary and linear schemes of development, and of history and tradition insofar as they conformed to those schemes.[24]

Cram also sought the timeless, and was as much put off by Victorian conceptions of linear development ("progressive evolution") as were the Modernists. One must wonder whether a fully embraced Modernist sensibility might better have enabled him to achieve his goals. T. S. Eliot's sense that tradition, rather than receding into the past, impinges directly on the trained sensibility regardless of chronology, might have suggested an easier access to the Gothic than the makeshift theory of historical cycles which Cram developed.

But Cram was an Anglo-Catholic, for whom the mediation of time did not diminish the light of the timeless. He acknowledged the "severing gulf" which seemed to divide history somewhere between Martin Luther and James Watt, a gulf which, most poignantly, had marked the lapse of the Gothic tradition in architecture. Yet to Cram the Gothic was all too clearly a tradition marked by continuity and development; less plausibly than the glories of classical civilization could it be stipulated as an atemporal impingement on the modern consciousness. The art of eternity, as Cram characterized it, was not to be immediately possessed or replicated in a modern context; it was a tradition to be restored. It was in failing to grasp this that Modernists seemed to him unable to transcend their time.[25]

The danger in restoring a tradition such as that of the Gothic, of course, was that it would fail to transcend its past. This was a danger of which Cram was acutely aware. "All the art of every time is founded on some specific art of the past;" he pointed out; "without this there is no foundation save that of shifting sands." Yet if it remained "in bondage" to the art of the past or chained to "the rock of archaeology," it was not true art. Only if tradition were to be understood as something more than a sheer duration of ideas and modes would such a recovery as Cram envisioned be plausible. A lapsed style or craft might be imitated, but only if the spirit which animated the tradition transcended particularities of time and place, and was therefore itself recoverable, could there be true renewal.[26]

However much against the American grain, the faith in the congruence of tradition with transcendent goods upon which Cram relied was familiar enough in human experience. Robert M. Torrance, for example, cites the tribal African who possesses "the transcendent validation of his existence which continuity with the ancestors, and through them with the gods, unstintingly gives." The modern Navajo has similar recourse: "within his traditional religion, the past, made potentially variable by myth, is the future, and adherence to it his only transcendence." Such a past is not an abandoned or lost region of experience; it is "supertemporal" and ever accessible.[27]

So to the believer are the events of Christian tradition—not merely recorded and recalled, but relived in the cycle of the church calendar. Even more fundamental are the sacraments which make or mark the availability in time of God's timeless grace. For an Anglo-Catholic like Cram these meanings were fundamental. In distinction from Protestants who relied more single-mindedly on the authority of Scripture, Yves Congar observed, Catholics recognized that "Christianity lives basically on the principle of tradition." Conveying unchanging truths, this tradition was yet as creative and progressive as it was conservative. Not mere memory, it was "actual presence and experience," and represented finally "a victory over time and its transience, over space and the separation caused by distance." The Holy Ghost was its "transcendent subject."[28]

Cram embraced sacramentalism as the supreme expression of these principles. As John Fiske had freighted federalism with a meaning beyond that of mundane constitutional devices, so Cram carried the meaning of sacramentalism beyond the actual prescribed sacraments of Christian liturgy. As federalism mediated between locality and empire, its more exalted counterpart mediated between material and spiritual realms. The sacramental was the means of carrying the home upward.

Cram's sacramental vision was based, as he remarked of medieval Christianity, "on the immanence of God, and through this the apprehension, mystically and symbolically, of something of the incommunicable Absolute." The sacrament was the juncture of matter and spirit, time and eternity, tradition and renewal. Art was in the nature of a sacrament for Cram because it was "both a symbol and a medium between the finite, the conditioned, and the infinite, the unconditioned." But the universe itself was sacramental, Cram wrote his mother in 1906—"'the outward and visible sign of the inward and spiritual grace.' We can't get at ultimate truths, but the symbols are very valuable: that is why the Catholic Church is the only real thing." Always nimble at connecting the traditional with the up-to-date, Cram insisted that this view was entirely scientific and pragmatic. Citing *Varieties of Religious Experience*, he argued that the philosophy of William James justified "the Catholic Faith absolutely," and was "incomplete without it." James himself, he admitted, was not yet aware of the affinity.[29]

Sacramentalism "worked" for the pragmatist, presumably, in bringing into fruitful conjunction the otherwise barren realms of material goods and detached transcendence. At Reims, even in the ruins of war, Cram found "that transfiguring and redemption of material things through the infusion of pure spirit, and that bringing down to earth of spirit itself . . . , which are the very essence and divine breath of Christianity." The Incarnation supremely proclaimed the triumph of this infusion. "Materialism, on the one hand, and transcendentalism, on the other, are synonymous of mortality"; Cram explained that "only when they assemble in union, each playing its own part, each reacting creatively on the other, have we that just balance that is man at his best and society at its highest, in accordance with the will of God." Blasted by the shelling of World War I, Reims seemed to him "the latest martyr to that materialistic philosophy which is the eternal antithesis of sacramentalism."[30]

As revealed at Reims, art played a special role in making matter the vehicle of the spirit. The "manifestation of man's worship of beauty and idealism, the symbolical expression of those dreams and emotions which pass experience and transcend all ordinary modes of expression," art was for Cram "the only means whereby religion can fully express itself." Yet the transcendence of which he spoke had two distinct aspects, it appeared. As the "touchstone of history" art provided a timeless standard by which the aspirations and endeavors of humanity might be gauged; at the same time it was capable of transcending continuity itself, at certain privileged points breaking free of the past.[31]

Even the birth of civilization itself seemed to Cram the result of such a discontinuity. In early Egypt, when "man-made beauty" had first appeared on earth, Cram observed, "apparently it came from some process of parthenogenesis"—nothing, he thought, lay behind but "the crude dolmens and the rough artifacts of the Neolithic race." This was "the beginning of human history—the beginning of time so far as man himself is concerned." It was the beginning too of the marriage of art and religion; "imagination, transcending experience, made art the vehicle of the Ideal." And art and religion had remained leagued until "a few centuries ago, when for the first time in six thousand years the golden cord was snapped and the relationship forgotten."[32]

As Cram worked out his counterpoint of continuity and discontinuity, then, tradition ordinarily bore with it such enduring ideals as that represented by the beauty of the Gothic, but was subject at the same time to all the development which the arts and crafts might devise. In Cram's acerbic opinion the ugliness and anarchy of modern art provided evidence enough of the disastrous consequences when, as he reiterated his metaphor, "the cord of tradition is broken." But tradition was capable of repair or revival because it bore transcendent goods and was therefore, in one aspect, timeless. It could also at rare intervals give rise to the mutation or quantum leap (to borrow metaphors of later currency) such as that which had created the Gothic style in the twelfth century. Apparent breaks with the past, these episodes really affirmed a deeper continuity. In them, unlike the parthenogenesis to which Cram ascribed the beginnings of civilization, genetic connection remained unsevered, as in the relation of a mutated organism to its forebears. Further, the transcendent good to which the tradition pointed itself bound the whole together. But no such good, in Cram's view, bound the modern version of temporal continuity—a linear, progressive, evolutionary social science–validated version which failed to provide true connection precisely bcause it denied the timeless goods which linked humanity. Such false continuity as remained could hardly conceal a break with the past more akin to an extinction than to a mutation.[33]

Without the possibility of restoration, Cram would have been spiritually stranded in the Middle Ages, for he dated the lapse of the Gothic to the time of Henry VIII, and he blamed the Renaissance, in part, for its submergence. Not even the Order of the White Rose had looked far enough to the past. Yet in actuality, for an American of Cram's time, the Gothic quest was less eccentric than the Jacobite, and the Middle Ages might well seem closer in spirit, despite Pilgrims and Cavaliers, than the seventeenth century.

Neo-medievalism, of course, was one of the great intellectual and cultural projects of the Romantic and post-Romantic periods in Europe and America. Taking its rise in reaction to the Enlightenment modes of "the poor and pitiful little eighteenth century, so purblind, so self-sufficing," as Cram sneered, it grew from the stylistic novelties of the Gothic Revival into what was for some almost a religion in itself. The discovery of the brilliance of medieval civilization provided "a counterculture to be posited against modernity," as Carl Schorske puts it. The Middle Ages offered themselves as a preindustrial "paradise lost," or at least as a "paradigm" against which modernity could be measured and with the instruction of which perhaps corrected.[34]

The appeal of the movement was manifold; it drew on Romantic sentiment, serious historical and antiquarian interest, a felt need to deny or ennoble a modern civilization which was so often squalid and troubling, the aesthetic appeal of the Gothic, and the spiritual attraction of the "Age of Faith." Medievalism met the retrospective emotional needs of the nineteenth century perfectly: amidst rapid and confusing change it offered the long continuities of tradition; in a world increasingly defined by materialism and determinism it offered beauty, chivalry, transcendence. At most it promised a resacralization of life, a return of universal significance to the grubby particulars of existence.[35]

Celebration of the Middle Ages was natural enough in Europe, but at first sight anomalous in the United States. Americans could aspire to transcendence, but the Middle Ages viewed as the great era of traditional society seemed the antithesis of Americanism. They were Catholic and therefore anathema to good American Protestants. Allegedly backward and antiscientific, they affronted a people enamored of the progressive triumphs of applied science. Even as ancestors and predecessors, medieval people were often reluctantly acknowledged. Some American historians tirelessly traced their country's Old World roots, but Frederick Jackson Turner's "frontier thesis" more effectively captured the national imagination by lending scholarly support to the myth of America as a new beginning in the world. To be physically removed from the site of medieval civilization and its surviving monuments made it easy to feel historical experience sharply truncated, and for many the Middle Ages stood for all of the cultural baggage that American immigrants had happily left behind.

Yet many others, like Van Wyck Brooks's "sight-seers" attuned to the sentimental aura of crumbling castles, wholeheartedly succumbed to the appeal of the past. Cultural colonialism had much to do with the medieval destination of so much of this sentiment. Americans imitated Europeans who imitated the Gothic. It was a matter of course to follow European architectural authorities like Augustus Charles Pugin, John Ruskin, and Eugène Emmanuel Viollet-le-Duc, and to design college quadrangles in imitation of Oxford and Cambridge. The rebellion of certain patricians and intellectuals against the notorious flatness and shallowness of American life has received much attention as well. This rebellion expressed itself in diverse ways, but for those who were at once committed to Western civilization and appalled at what it had become in modern America, the Middle Ages were an obvious recourse.[36]

The appeal of the Middle Ages to Americans never rested entirely on their otherness, however. A completely alien medieval civilization could have appealed only to those completely alienated from America, and that condition was rare. Rather the earlier age provided a foreshadowing or type of American experience, or even a projection of America's highest possibilities. What Robin Fleming observes of American medieval historians of the nineteenth century applies more broadly among intellectuals and aesthetes: they "sought to discover in the Middle Ages an idealized and romantic version of their own puzzling world." Americanized in this way, the epoch could serve as a standing reproach to America's betrayal of her own brightest promise, but it might also (as for Cram) seem to offer a submerged but still recoverable tradition in which that promise might at last be fulfilled.[37]

Americans could relate to the Middle Ages in either of two ways. They could locate themselves in a process of historical development or "social evolution" in the manner of John Fiske. Perhaps America "had no medieval past," as was often pointed out, but the truth of that statement rested on arbitrary geographical and political distinctions. Americans, to the extent that they were the heirs, beneficiaries, or victims of customs and traditions rooted in the Middle Ages and brought across the ocean, certainly did have a medieval past. In this perspective they were as entitled to revive the Middle Ages as were Europeans. But Americans could also point to direct parallels between medieval civilization and their own—sometimes in ways that Europeans could not. In seeming paradox, American newness could be identified with the remote past. "Do the childlike qualities attributed to the Middle Ages bear a particular relevance to this youthful nation?" Kim Moreland asks; to many they clearly did. Not only the cavalier but the cowboy or even the private detective could seem a latter-day knight, and Ralph Adams Cram could contemplate "walled towns" in the raw American landscape with little sense of incongruity. Like Europeans, Americans could accentuate the contrasts between medieval and modern or they could seek to integrate medieval qualities into modern life. But if castles and cathedrals gave the earlier period a brooding presence in Europe that it could never have in America, it was possible to believe that the vitality characteristic of a civilization in the making survived better on this side of the Atlantic.[38]

In the country's best-known champion of the Middle Ages, Henry Adams, the Americanizing impulse furnished at least a strong undercurrent to his pessimistic account of degeneration from Virgin to Dynamo. Certainly the qualities Adams exalted in medieval life were not those most alien to his own society. The Middle Ages were not, in Adams's rendition, gloomy, monkish, otherworldly, or oppressed by the weight of tradition; they were rather a time of youth, passion, and dynamism. In some ways, despite Adams's antimodern stance, they were strikingly modern: "the nineteenth century moved fast and furious, so that one who moved in it felt sometimes giddy, watching it spin," he noted, "but the eleventh moved faster and more furiously still."[39]

Laced with such characteristic hyperbole, Adams's portrait of the Middle Ages articulated several pertinent themes: (1) an insistence on the radically innovative character of the High Middle Ages, as suggested by the historian's description of the twelfth century's "greed for novelty"; (2) a vision of the period as one of liberation, represented by Adams in the spiritual or psychological release offered by the Virgin Mary for "the whole unutterable fury of human nature beating itself against the walls of its prison house," but available to more mundane interpretations; and (3) a motif of popular enthusiasm and participation, demonstrated especially by the townspeople who took part in the building of the Gothic cathedrals.[40]

However arresting in Adams's presentation, these themes had long been mainstays of American commentary on the Middle Ages. Even

Ralph Waldo Emerson, the relentless foe of bondage to tradition, had perceived in the medieval world the youthful vigor and directness characteristic of his own country. In Emerson recourse to the Middle Ages cast no long shadows of disillusionment with modern America; rather, as Kathleen Verduin remarks, medieval life offered him "a model of the potential greatness of America" as well as "an iconography of the vigorous personal life."[41]

In his *Notes of Travel and Study in Italy* (1859), Charles Eliot Norton approached more closely the themes expressed by Adams half a century later, although with none of Adams's sympathy with Catholic faith. Norton showed the mixture of enthusiasm, repugnance, and perplexity with which Americans in Europe were apt to confront the visible evidences of the Middle Ages. His Protestant sensibility—the more austere in the Unitarian form in which he received it—was predictably repulsed by the traces of the medieval church, which he regarded as the antithesis of Americanism. Even nineteenth-century Romans still seemed in the Church's thrall; under ecclesiastical rule and worshippers chiefly of the Virgin Mary, they impressed Norton as "belong[ing] to the Dark Ages."[42]

At the same time, Norton's aesthetic sensibility thrilled to the great cathedrals. Unwilling to credit these monuments to the "ecclesiastics" or the "feudal barons," he found their true source in "a great impulse of popular energy, by a long combination of popular effort with trained skill." This enthusiasm was supported, he believed, by "a true fervor of religious faith" which had somehow escaped papist perversion. Norton even suggested that the cathedrals represented, "in a measure, the decline of feudalism, and the prevalence of the democratic element in society." Liberated from feudal rule, the people of a town began immediately to plan a cathedral wherein "the popular beliefs, hopes, fears, fancies, and aspirations found expression, and were perpetuated in a language intelligible to all."[43]

Norton could not quite put on these popular activities the imprimatur of enlightenment, however. The spiritual conditions of such phenomena as the cathedrals and the Crusades belonged to "periods of mental twilight," he thought, with the fear of hell at the foundation of the great medieval achievements. To be sure, it was a marvelously vitalizing fear, disciplined for a time by artistic craft and genius to unsurpassed architectural expression. But fear-driven intensity of feeling had had in time to give way to less creative but more rational modes. "Living was both easier and more civilized than before," Norton noted of the Renaissance—adding wistfully that "living is not life." He was left seemingly torn between admiration of popular vigor and scorn for popular benightedness. Characteristic of Americans determined to be true to American democratic tradition yet repelled by the failures of democracy in their own time, this ambivalence later issued in Ralph Adams Cram's more sharply distinguished images of a good people ("producers") and a bad people ("mass-man").[44]

The theme of popular participation in medieval creativity struck an especially responsive American chord. In 1864 James Jackson Jarves described the medieval cathedral as "a miniature commonwealth" constructed by the whole community for the benefit of all. It embodied, he thought, "the fundamental ideas of natural and spiritual freedom which are born of Christianity." Other writers, in the same vein, made of the Gothic cathedral an emblem of popular freedom from feudal and ecclesiastical oppression. Mariana Van Rensselaer, a leading critic, found the impulse behind the Gothic in the "fresh and vigorous" spirit of the people themselves, who in their communes "often—men, women, and children together—worked with passionate enthusiasm upon the structure which was at once the temple of their faith, the sign of their city's greatness, and the hearthstone of their liberties. Romanesque art—monkish art—was dead; Gothic art—national art, the architecture of laymen—had taken its place. Thus liberty and architecture drew a fresh breath of life together and developed hand in hand." Charles Herbert Moore similarly attributed the Gothic to popular enthusiasm, and found in its character as a municipal and communal project "a substantial expression of the growing freedom from feudal oppression."[45]

From the popular and liberating qualities of Gothic construction it was a short step to the contention that the High Middle Ages, far from being tradition bound, had been an era of innovation, even of discontinuity with the past. Those making this argument invariably seized upon the suddenness with which Gothic architecture had emerged in the twelfth century. Moore, for example, was careful to point out the Romanesque antecedents of Gothic, but he was most impressed by the "unparalleled impulse," generated by eleventh-century social changes and sheer French genius, which had issued in "a remarkably spontaneous and national movement. . . . There was no mere imitation, there was nothing of the kind elsewhere to imitate." In similar though more muted tones, A. L. Frothingham presented the Gothic as the result of a "natural evolution" from the earlier style, yet a rapid one which had been possible because the region of France where it first emerged had had no "tenacious traditions" to oppose it.[46]

More casual or popular writers were apt less judiciously to generalize from Gothic innovation, and to leap to modern lessons and parallels. An anonymous reviewer of Moore's *Development and Character of Gothic Architecture* provided an illustration of American ambivalence toward tradition nearly as striking as Augustine Jones's confusion about the Puritan fathers. The United States itself, he suggested, was "a nation without traditions and monuments," yet this merely enabled Americans to approach Old World achievements "from an unprejudiced point of view," to "make the best use of precedent, and to develop new forms." Gothic architecture itself was to be admired because it had freed Romanesque methods "from the incubus of ancient traditions," yet also, it appeared, because it had itself become a venerable tradition. Although they were not traditionalists, the reviewer implied, Americans could accept their proper role as the heirs of all the ages; they were uniquely fitted, he thought, to carry on the "progress" of the Gothic from the point of its interruption "towards the consummation of a style adequate to represent the complicated civilization of today."[47]

In another review of the same work, Robert S. Peabody sought more single-mindedly to make the Gothic presentable to progressive American Protestants. Eager to show that art could flourish in a "trading democracy" like the United States, he neatly combined the themes of Gothic as a popular movement and Gothic as a break with tradition. (For good measure, he invoked Athens as an example of "a free people ridding themselves of Egyptian traditions and dogmas.") The Gothic departure from "Romanesque and monastic methods," Peabody predictably stated, had been sharp and drastic. France had been "seized with a fury of energy and enterprise, and the royal power, joining itself with this demo-

cratic and episcopal movement, began to arise from its feeble state."
Citing the "democratic bodies" of craftsmen and laymen largely respon-
sible for the construction of the great cathedrals, the writer doubted that
there was ever a time "in which art emanated more surely from the
people as a class." Peabody even insinuated the favorite Victorian theme
of the war of science against religion, although "religion," which could
hardly be invoked against the Gothic cathedral, was here confined to
monasticism, and "science" referred to the mathematical and engineering techniques of the builders. In sum, the new style of architecture "was
the first popular protest against the power of the monks. It was the first
vigorous effort of science against tradition." Peabody demonstrated how
readily the term "Gothic," once a label for medieval barbarism and su-
perstition, might be converted into a talisman of democracy, progress,
innovation, and even science.[48]

The most tenacious Americanizer of the Middle Ages was Ralph
Adams Cram, although Cram yields to Henry Adams in originality and
depth of insight. To an extent the architect was a disciple of Adams. He
persuaded Adams to publish *Mont-Saint-Michel and Chartres* for sale to the
general public—an achievement he described at the time as "the greatest
victory of my life." He found the book itself, as he said in his preface to it,
a "revelation." Like Adams, Cram could make sense of history only by
tracing a six-hundred-year declension from medieval glories, and he lived
to append to Adams's sad tale an account of another generation of war
and depression.[49]

Yet Cram was not the ironist Adams was, nor the pessimist. In Cram
the Victorian faith in progress was never really extinguished, although
he was forced to pursue it down the most convoluted of paths. And Cram
believed in both tradition and transcendence in ways Adams could not.
Adams sought, as he said, a spool on which to wind the thread of history, but he had little use for tradition as a medium of continuity. Seeking
to reduce history to laws as close to those of physics as possible, he could
hardly be bothered with the slow, often practical, often haphazard ac-
cretiveness which is the soul of tradition. And while Adams could delight in the spontaneity which seemed to escape the grip of iron law—
whether found in the Virgin of Chartres or in South Sea Islanders—and
could sympathize with the soaring aspiration represented by the Gothic

spire, he was unable to deduce from either spontaneity or aspiration any transcendence beyond the subjective.

In Cram, unconstrained by Adams's skepticism, the theme of Gothic representation of innovation, liberation, and popular will reached its apogee. He was as impressed as other students of architectural history by the suddenness with which the Gothic had emerged in the twelfth century, but more than most, it seems, he wished to perceive this as the result of an immediate influx of inspiration. He realized that the Gothic church incorporated the "general scheme" of its Norman predecessor. He argued, however, that it worked a revolution in structure and decoration—effected, indeed, an "instantaneous change." He could describe the Gothic, in sum, as "utterly unlike anything that had gone before, confessing in its ancestry far less kinship with the Norman, Romanesque, and Lombard it had discomfited and destroyed, than was so easily traceable between Greek and Egyptian, Byzantine and Roman." The style, "when it had fully found itself, was utterly without psychological or structural antecedents," he concluded. Such statements must be placed alongside others in which he emphasized continuity or tried to have it both ways. (The "Gothic, while a quick evolution from Norman origins, was revolutionary in character and absolutely, in this essential quality, without precedent," he explained in *The Significance of Gothic Art*.) Yet however he qualified, Cram regarded the Gothic as a sudden, almost miraculous mutation from previous styles.[50]

This interpretation served as much a didactic as a descriptive purpose. Gothic was for Cram not merely a style of architecture but "the trumpet blast of an awakening world," signifying the triumph of Christianity and human self-knowledge. It was an "utter emancipation" from the paganism, heresy, and sheer darkness of the Dark Ages. At its most exalted it seemed to effect an even greater liberation, in fact. In such a masterwork as Reims Cathedral, Cram suggested, art "without premeditation or self-consciousness" achieved a perfection which negated all ordinary human limits. A monument of stone and glass, the cathedral somehow transcended the accumulated experience of generations of masons and glaziers which went into its building. Continuity made possible the moment of discontinuity which escaped all limitations of time and place. But as Cram remarked of a very different architectural tradition, it was finally "only the Divine spark, the Finger-touch of God, that stirred the waiting potentiality into activity."[51]

The innovating and liberating qualities of the Gothic were for Cram no mere foreshadowings of American values. Unlike the old theological pattern of type fulfilled in antitype, the sequence of medieval and modern was one of declension. The Middle Ages represented America's better self, offering a paradigm woefully dishonored in twentieth-century actuality. Had the twentieth century become "a riot of individualism," threatened by its antithesis of collectivism? The High Middle Ages had managed to foster the growth of true individuality within a spirit of "real communism": "never before or since was personality developed so completely, nor the community of human interests so largely realized." Had industrial-technological civilization become a "Frankenstein Monster" spreading death and devastation? The Middle Ages, Cram pointed out, had had their own less menacing industrial economy. Did modern labor unions array the masses of workers against the power of capital? The medieval guild combined the interests of capital and labor without exploitation, maintained high standards of craftsmanship, and promoted fellowship and mutual aid. Even feminism, Cram seconded Henry Adams, had had its better medieval counterpart. While men of the Middle Ages flaunted the "glitter and show" of power, women often retained its substance. The result was "a certain feminine dominance," based on nothing so mundane as the suffrage, but on superior spiritual qualities.[52]

Where Cram went most conspicuously beyond others who had pursued such themes was in his sustained claim for medieval democracy. True, historians of the school of Herbert Baxter Adams had traced the roots of liberty and democracy through the Middle Ages to the German forests. Of this "germ theory" of democratic contagion Cram barely took note, however, and when he did it was to argue that "the roots of liberty and free democratic government . . . are to be found far deeper in the old parish of the Mediaeval Church than in Parliament or folkthing or shiremote." But Cram was not really interested in "roots" or "germs" or any evidence of linear development; he was looking for a Platonic form. It was authentic democracy, he held, which had flourished in the Middle Ages, and what went by the name in the twentieth century was not even an imperfect copy but at best a shabby counterfeit. "The true democracy of St. Louis, Edward I and Washington is forgotten," he lamented in 1917, "and a false democracy has taken its place."[53]

This extraordinary distinction derived partly from a conflation of liberal and aesthetic values which made of beauty a personal right. Cram expressed his sense of this entitlement—undreamed of in American constitutional tradition—most clearly on the unexpected subject of housing standards. Although reputedly an elitist, the architect was not without concern for the lives of the less-favored. He had done some of his earliest professional work on working-class housing, and as Chairman of the Boston City Planning Board in 1918, he strongly promoted the elimination of slums. Addressing the National Conference of Housing in America two weeks after the Armistice, he presented the choice as one of building up a new civilization "from below," or sinking into a new Dark Ages. (That phase of medieval life threatened to become America's worst self.) In support of his plan for slum clearance he cited "the natural right of every man to live decently and in an environment that has some elements of attractiveness, if not actual beauty." He found it necessary to add the reassurance that he was "no Bolshevik," but he returned more forcefully to the theme in the calmer days of the mid-twenties. Whether or not life, liberty, and the pursuit of happiness were natural rights, he remarked, "I do know that to live beautifully and to live in beauty are natural rights." Ugliness, conversely, was "a crime against society."[54]

Unfortunately it was the "whole tendency" of modern civilization to obliterate this "right to beauty in life and thought and environment," Cram feared. And democracy decayed with art. He was struck by the "curious fact" that the year 1828 in America had marked not only "the moment when the last traces of real beauty disappeared from architecture and the other arts and the fifty years' interlude of excruciating ugliness began," but also the election to the presidency of Andrew Jackson, avatar of the new and false democracy. By counter-association, Chartres and Reims became temples of the authentic democratic faith.[55]

But if art was the emblem and expression of true democracy, the whole texture of medieval life—decentralized, communal, customary, in contradistinction to the massive aggregates of what Cram called "imperial modernism"—provided its seedbed. "The essence of democracy is differentiation, local autonomy, and a building up of authority from primary units," he explained. As for the Virginians, local patriotism was the fountainhead of all political virtue. Liberty was a communal phenomenon, and consequently "a mania amongst the Mediaevals . . . it was they who laid all the foundations of such liberty as men have possessed ever since, but they knew, as we do not, that liberty means obedience, precise and highly articulated society, communal action as opposed to individualism. Knowing this they produced the greatest unity, achieved by and expressed through liberty and individuality, history has thus far recorded."[56]

Cram could point easily enough to such documents as Magna Carta and Bracton's *De Legibus* in support of his contention that constitutional liberties had sprung from the medieval social context. It was considerably bolder to locate in feudalism the essence of democracy; it suggested indeed a Modernist willingness to juxtapose apparent opposites in affront to conventional categories. Yet he found in the feudal system principles of mutuality, subject to custom and the common law and ultimately to "divinely revealed moral principles," which had come closer to the democratic mark than the modern simulacrum. Feudalism, in sum, was "a scheme of reciprocal duties, privileges and obligations as between man and man that has never been excelled by any other system that society has developed as its own method of operation." Above all, Cram thought, feudal man had lived as a free man.[57]

If nothing else, Cram's argument challenged the widespread American assumption that liberty and democracy issued from negative conditions: from a society of essentially detached individuals, unconstrained by traditional or communal precepts and only minimally constrained by law. No less than John Dewey, Cram contended that democracy consisted in the substance of social and economic relationships rather than in mere procedure—"not in miscellaneous machinery and vicissitudinous panaceas, but in certain ends of right and justice," as the architect put it.[58]

Cram offered as well at least a defensible argument that meaningful democracy had been overwhelmed in his time by the massive scale of

political and economic organization. He was certainly not alone in realizing, for instance, that this gigantism made a mockery of any notion
of democratic give-and-take between the ordinary working person and
the large corporation. There was much to be said for his insistence that
the substance of the country's democratic hopes required a respect for
local self-determination and a real reciprocity of obligations and benefits. In all of this Cram, like Philip Bruce, was offering not so much
an alternative to the American creed as alternative means to realize
it. The weakness of his position, of course, lay in his too-ready identification of medieval society with the democratic virtues for which
he contended.

Leaving the historical evidence well behind, Cram argued summarily
that the feudalism of the High Middle Ages "came nearer a real democracy than any other of the manifold and optimistic experiments of man,
for it more nearly abolished privilege, established equal opportunity and
utilized ability, while it fixed the means of production in the hands of
the people, guaranteed a fairly even distribution of wealth, [and] organized workmen and craftsmen and artists on a just and equable basis
of labour and compensation." Cram acknowledged the existence
of a traditional aristocracy and a servile class, but in between, he
thought, was a large body of rural and urban "producers," themselves
"the proudest product of Christian civilization." There was even
scope for the self-made man. "As through the Church, the schools and
the cloister there was room for the son of a peasant to achieve the
Papacy," he pointed out, "so through the guilds, chivalry, war and the
court, the layman, if he possessed ability, might from an humble
beginning travel far."[59]

If this was an idealized picture of the Middle Ages, it was as much an
idealized picture of the American past projected onto the earlier period.
Cram believed both societies to have been based on cooperation and self-
sufficiency, production for use rather than profit, and life in a "human
scale" of small economic and social units. Personal and family experience reinforced the association. "Passionately attached to the land," according to his daughter, Cram recalled the "unity of place and character" at his grandfather's rural estate. He felt that he had glimpsed
in Squire Blake's community "a lingering episode out of the eighteenth

century," which in turn followed much older patterns of life. In nostalgic memory, indeed, the ancestral hearth became a "last phase of . . . feudalism."[60]

To explain the connection historically, however, Cram had to rescue the American Founding Fathers, post-medieval men as they so clearly were, from the taint of the intervening centuries. As the political absolutism born of the Renaissance had grown intolerable, he supposed, the ideals of medieval freedom had appeared in a new guise in the eighteenth and early nineteenth centuries. The Declaration of Independence, the Tennis Court Oath of the early French Revolution, and the British reform laws had held brief sway as expressions of true democracy. Like its medieval forerunner, this was a democracy underpinned by gentlemanly leadership and based on contract. (The same contractual principle operated, Cram believed, in the modern constitutional covenants as in the relationship of lord and vassal, king and people, even seigneur and serf.) Most fundamental of all was the quality of "spiritual liberty," derived from medieval political theory and issuing in the principle that "all men are free and equal before God and the Law."[61]

Unfortunately, the liberal revival of the eighteenth century had only briefly reversed the decline of medieval principles. Liberty had run to anarchy, natural hierarchy to a falsely conceived social equality, social graces to the pursuit of wealth. With the loss of a sense of spiritual liberty, society had become enslaved to the "quantitative," materialistic standards of "mass-man." Like Herbert Marcuse's later "one-dimensional man," mass-man was so in thrall to economic and political shibboleths as even to be "unconscious of his own enslavement." A false democracy, pinning its hopes on universal suffrage and majority rule as the means of human perfectibility in this world, naturally followed. The end result was a "reign of mediocrity" fatal to all "excellence in literature, arts, science, [or] statesmanship." That any prospects for the revival of the Gothic tradition, in its authentic transcending power, could have survived this devastation might have seemed absurd.[62]

The severance of the tradition was apparently fatal. Certainly the doctrine of "progressive evolution" would never bring it back. Art, in Cram's own credo, must be the product of its environment, and the modern environment seemed radically unpromising. But behind the transient environment of time and place, for the idealist, lay an ultimate environment of truth and beauty which was unbound to time, although approachable through tradition. This suggested the utility of a cyclical theory of history. There was of course nothing inherently odd about this. Before the modern age, cycles had been the most common way of making sense of mundane history, and the waning of the nineteenth-century faith in progress brought them back into fashion. Cram's fellow antimodernists Brooks and Henry Adams had proposed cyclical schemes in the hope that they would authorize a recrudescence of medieval qualities of life. Oswald Spengler offered his grander system not much later. Altogether Cram was in an ample company. He disdained the Renaissance and Reformation, but his effort to revive the Gothic was not more quixotic than the efforts of those movements to revive classical civilization or primitive Christianity. And American faith in progress aside, it was perhaps not less American than the national penchant for religious revivals and awakenings—especially as Cram had shown the Gothic to have arisen from a society which was American at heart.

Generalizing from the rapid emergence of the Gothic, and struck too by the "baffling fact" that the earliest human civilization seemed suddenly to have emerged as a completely articulated society rather than as a result of steady development, Cram worked out his own version of cyclical history. Evolution was balanced in the "cosmic process" by devolution, he hypothesized. But the cycle moved unevenly; its "upward drive" was swift, for each era of civilization began with a great burst of energy. The downside was more languid. Perhaps because of his central concern with the easily bisected millennium of the Middle Ages, Cram thought that he descried a law of history in a five-hundred-year cycle from one crest to the next. In company with the Adams brothers and others, he viewed the events of the early twentieth century as marking the exhaustion of one wave of creative energy and the gathering of the forces of the next.[63]

This philosophy of history lent itself to apocalyptic interpretation, most readily and literally during such a genuine disaster as the First World War. Events had vindicated his old prophecies of the breakup of civilization, Cram wrote to Louise Imogen Guiney in 1915. Condemning once again the destructive work of Protestantism, a degraded democracy, and evolutionary philosophy, he perceived in the war "the reign of Antichrist; and following this reign," he supposed, "can come only the wide ruin foretold from the beginning of the world." Three years later, with the United States at last fighting by Britain's side, as Cram had long urged, he was more hopeful. Apocalypse after all had happened before. "In every case," he observed, "two laws work with grim certainty, first, the complete, comprehensive and definite change every five centuries, second, the effecting of that change by a cataclysmic process." In the aftermath of the cataclysm of 1914–1918, accordingly, an "entirely new world" seemed in the offing.[64]

If the cyclical scheme provided Cram with an explanation of the dire events of his own time, it also allowed him to realize a kind of compromise between the continuity of tradition and the discontinuity of creative vigor. It was a natural solution for a Gothic Revivalist who as an American was also heir to an anti-traditionalist tradition which insisted upon the virtue of the fresh start. It accorded as well with Cram's conviction of the timeless, transcendent beauty of the Gothic by making this beauty perennially accessible. Cycles were doubly mediating: like types and antitypes they circumvented chronology to marry one age to another, and they juxtaposed a timeless ideal to time-bound representations of it. The tradition which recorded these representations might be suspended but could never really be outmoded. If the energy of one wave of history miscarried, its object could be recovered on the next. Although the Gothic had succumbed to the Renaissance and Reformation, it was not truly dead. In Cram's own figure it only slumbered at Avalon with King Arthur, and the architect believed that the moment of awakening was at hand.[65]

That the aesthetic and spiritual achievement of the Gothic was timeless did not mean that its architectural embodiments were unchanging. Despite himself, Cram was too much affected by nineteenth-century historicism and sense of development to suppose that medieval forms could or should simply be duplicated in the modern world. The Gothic was dynamic rather than static, and its expressions were manifold. Once regained, he acknowledged, the Gothic tradition could only be followed self-consciously until such time as it might burst "forth of its own impulse." We should return to the medieval Gothic, he emphasized, only "for the sake of getting a fresh start." A living Gothic would adapt to at least the more compatible aspects of the contemporary world, and, he speculated, become as different from the fifteenth-century style as the fifteenth was from the thirteenth.[66]

But if the Gothic spirit was to take new root, it must have congenial soil. Authentic art, in Cram's view, was spontaneous and popular, although borne by tradition. Above all, it was "a communal thing," expressing a vision transcending that of the individual. In the Middle Ages, he supposed, "everyone was more or less an artist, for . . . sense of beauty and real creative power ran in the blood." Thus art, in the loose terminology of Cram's day, was "racial"; it expressed the "soul" of a people or nation. The question, as he put it in 1905, was whether Americans were the spiritual successors of the Borgias and Medici, or did they "hark back to the mighty glories of Church and State in the thirteenth century in Italy, France, Germany, and England?" Could the American soul support a recovery of medieval tradition?[67]

It was a measure of Cram's idiosyncratic Yankee optimism, distilling progress from tradition and seeking forward-looking expression for what was conventionally termed reaction, that he never lost faith in his neo-medieval agenda. Seemingly deterministic, Cram's cyclical theory was certainly not fatalistic; its realization depended on practical effort. This Cram never ceased to supply. His career as an architect centered on the great project of recovering the sacramental beauties of medieval tradition, and in his role as a social commentator he tirelessly devised schemes to provide a social order capable of nourishing the soul of that tradition.

Cram had long hoped that "the enveloping clouds of ignorance and misapprehension engendered by the pagan Renaissance and the Protestant Revolution" would dissipate, and for a moment at the end of World War I this happy outcome seemed within reach. "Four years have ended the work of four centuries," he exclaimed, "and—there is no going back." But going back was, in a large sense, precisely what he supposed the war had made possible. So unquestionable an apocalypse must mean a turn in the cycles of history sufficient to explain the signs he professed to see of "a startling and anomalous return to Medievalism." In more measured terms, this would mean looking to the Middle Ages "in order to retrieve some of the things we have lost and so build up a new and better civilization." Cram moved away from his prophetic role during the flush times of the twenties, but returned to it quickly with the onset of the Great Depression. It again became important to interpret the portents of neo-medievalism and to plan for his own version of a "postmodern" world.[68]

In his sense of crisis during the thirties, Cram of course was in the company of virtually everyone else; even in his preferred solutions he was far from being a lonely crank. Still, he is not easily categorized, least of all on the neat left-right political scale of the Depression decade. He is most glibly labeled a reactionary, but his revulsion at the world made by capitalism and large measure of support for the New Deal make that stereotype difficult to sustain. (In fact he initially joined the left in attacking Franklin Roosevelt for trying to salvage the capitalist system.) Like many in the thirties he engaged in a "mild flirtation with fascism," initially perceiving in Mussolini's corporate state a modern version of medieval communitarianism, as Robert Muccigrosso notes. The attraction showed the dangers of cyclical and typological ways of thinking, but it did not survive the dose of reality administered by the Italian invasion of Ethiopia.[69]

Cram had most in common with decentralizers and back-to-economic-basics advocates like the English Distributists and Southern Agrarians, and with certain European writers who combined a lingering devotion to nineteenth-century liberalism with dismay at modern social dissolution and loss of traditional values. The Europeans typically rejected a "mass society," which they perceived to be most fully embodied in the United States, asserted an implied or explicit preference for an "organic" and hierarchical society, and made a sharp distinction between authentic democracy and the modern perversion of it. All struggled with the problem of "the people"—of what the people were or could be in an age of greatly expanded social and political units and broadly disseminated popular culture.

Cram was an assiduous compiler of reading lists, which he offered to correspondents and general readers eager to unravel the perplexities of modern history. In a specimen list from 1935, he recommended among social commentators and historians William Aylott Orton, José Ortega y Gasset, and Nicholas Berdyaev. Two years later, after the appearance of Salvador de Madariaga's *Anarchy or Hierarchy*, the Spaniard was added to Cram's roster of prophets. As much kindred spirits as "influences," these figures provide a context for the American architect's own long-incubated analysis of history.[70]

In *America in Search of Culture* (1933), Orton wrote as an Englishman who had lived in America and was sufficiently acquainted with American history and society to seem sympathetic and knowledgeable. Nevertheless, his impression of modern America was conventionally British: America lacked the depth of time necessary to nurture a true culture, and even promising beginnings had been unfulfilled. Almost precisely echoing Cram himself, Orton believed that the country had lapsed into a dark age with the coming of Jacksonian democracy, which had been as fatal to art as to spiritual values and to genuine community. For the past century, the Englishman lamented, American society had been driven by "the acquisitive instincts of traditionless people." Individualism denied "the corporate basis of society," at fatal cost to the individual himself. Losing the local and regional roots which fed his own substance, he lost as well the sense of continuity which gave meaning and scope to his "private destiny." In such a society, "the past itself was lost. The struggle for power (or loot) in purely financial terms left no room for tradition."[71]

Writing within a more spacious geographical and philosophical frame, Ortega y Gasset viewed the loss of the past as more a modern than an American problem. It was in the nature of mass society, he thought, that "any remains of the traditional spirit have evaporated," leaving problems to be solved "without any active collaboration of the past." Even cultured Europeans were ignorant of history, it seemed to him, and human beings needed history—"not to fall back into it, but to see if we can escape from it." Yet Ortega, with a strong underpinning of nineteenth-century liberalism, was less concerned to defend tradition per se than to defend a well-articulated civilization, founded on a traditional hierarchy of values, against the leveling-down pressures of "mass society."[72]

Mass society was nothing less, in Ortega's view, than the recrudescence of barbarism, defined as "the absence of standards to which appeal can be made." Even more ominously, he suggested that "the type of man dominant to-day is a primitive one, a Naturmensch rising up in the midst of a civilised world." Although Ortega did not blame this development on Americanization—internal European reasons, he thought, were quite sufficient to explain it—he regarded America as "in a fashion, the paradise of the masses," and Americans as a "primitive people camouflaged behind the latest inventions." Ortega, however, preserved a distinction which, important to the European social critic, was even more important to the American, and which certainly helped to shape Cram's analysis. "The old democracy was tempered by a generous dose of liberalism and of enthusiasm for law," the Spaniard acknowledged. "To-day we are witnessing the triumphs of a hyperdemocracy in which the mass acts directly, outside the law, imposing its aspirations and its desires by means of material pressure."[73]

Ortega's countryman Salvador de Madariaga enlarged on similar themes, which could only have confirmed Cram in his social precepts, well established when Madariaga published *Anarchy or Hierarchy* in 1937. Madariaga also defended the principle of tradition. "Historical continuity," he pointed out, "is the basis of culture." He feared that the principle of equality, once invoked against unjustified privilege, had become a "levelling down" oblivious to necessary social differences and "organic specialization." The healthy society, he contended, was built around a hierarchy of three natural orders: a people, rooted in the soil and the past, exercising a "chorus-like" social function; a bourgeoisie competent to administer the present; and an aristocracy of principle and vision to lead into the future. Not surprisingly, Madariaga found the United States lacking in such a hierarchy, without an adequate aristocracy or even a "robust popular basis" to compose an organic whole with its omnipresent bourgeois types. Madariaga's version of the familiar distinction between good and bad democracy opposed the "merely . . . statistical or numerical" to the "organic." His vision of an eventual "*organic unanimous democracy*" can now only suggest the corporate state of the fascists, although Madariaga emphasized that his version would evolve "gradually and spontaneously" and serve the higher ideals of peace and common humanity.[74]

In *The End of Our Time* (1933), Nicholas Berdyaev provided a headier offering to tradition and transcendence, served up with an apocalyptic urgency which was easily a match for Cram's own. The World War, Berdyaev thought, was the beginning of the end for the "atheistical and hypocritical" civilization inherited by the twentieth-century West. Europe found herself in "a condition very similar to that at the beginning of the middle ages," he thought, facing perhaps "a new chaos of peoples" and a new feudalism. Modern democracy, for Berdyaev, was incompatible with the authenticity of " the people," which he perceived as "a great historical whole which includes all its generations, not only of the living but also of the dead, of our fathers and forebears." No generation isolated in time could truly express the will of a people, he added, citing "the rooted falsehood in Democracy which entails a break between past, present, and future, the denial of eternity, and the worship of a destructive modernism."[75]

Like Cram, Berdyaev found the route to the timeless through the traditional. The things of highest worth were the things of eternity, as he put it, and such things "were to be found also in the past insofar as the past touched upon eternity and took its rise therefrom." Like Cram too, he looked hopefully to the advent of a new Middle Ages in which tradition might point the way to spiritual transcendence. The new medievalism would supplant modern social atomism with a new social hierarchy, in which unions, guilds, and corporations of all types would find their place. Above all it would reignite the blazing light of Christian faith, for "the image and likeness of man is revealed and maintained in Christianity alone." Modern rationalism would yield to "an irrationalism, or better to a super-rationalism, of the mediaeval type."[76]

Writers such as Orton, Ortega, Madariaga, and Berdyaev corroborated and shaped Cram's own perceptions of the plight of humanity. Like his European counterparts, Cram believed that progressive evolution had been an illusion, and that civilization was in decline as society disintegrated and "mass-man" replaced the self-sufficient citizen. For an American, however, the problem of the people was inherently more difficult. Commitment to the national ideal of democracy, even if filtered through a vision of the Middle Ages, somewhat inhibited Cram from a frankly class-based or hierarchical conception of society and left him in confusion. Like the European writers he admired, he called for a true aristocracy to set social standards, but it was unclear how such a body would be constituted. As an American, he could cite the impeccable authority of Thomas Jefferson, who had supported the leadership of a "natural aristocracy." Yet Cram muddied the waters by defining this as an aristocracy of birth, worth, and talents—Jefferson had emphatically excluded the "artificial" criterion of birth. The discrepancy confirms the very un-Jeffersonian value Cram set on tradition, of which bloodlines were conventionally regarded as a means of conveyance. It also suggests the heightened difficulty of fitting "the people" to a neo-medievalist program in a country like Cram's own, where tradition itself was largely and ineluctably rooted in the assumption of popular wisdom and sovereignty. Further, in America tradition and popular rule alike were linked to growth and expansion. But for Cram the carrying of the home outward, as William B. Weeden called it, had ended not in an apotheosis of domestic and local virtues, but in the grotesquery of "imperial modernism." In the United States even neo-medievalism, it was clear, had to be founded upon a theory of the people.[77]

Cram was deeply ambivalent on the subject. His devotion to democracy—rightly understood—collided with his disgust with what he perceived as the debased democracy of his own time, and his larger revulsion at the mass society which seemed its concomitant. He accordingly offered two theories, without bothering clearly to choose between them or to reconcile their inconsistencies. One expressed simply an undisguised and vitriolic disgust with "mass-man." The crucial distinction, Cram wrote in *The American Mercury* in 1932, was "not between Neolithic Man and the anthropoid ape, but between the glorified and triumphant human being and the Neolithic mass which was, is now and ever shall be." "Neolithic Man" supplied "an endless flood of basic raw material," which flowed on without change century after century, he argued. From this mass emerged those fine and exceptional personalities to whom Cram, in this mood, would have limited the claim to full humanity. If nothing else, this formulation enabled him to give scattershot vent to peeves and prejudices: "From the Australian 'blackfellow,' the writer of popular songs or the publisher of a tabloid newspaper to Akhnaton, Leonardo da Vinci, or Pope Leo XIII is a space that almost needs to be measured in astronomical terms," he mused. "The first law in the Book of Man is inequality."[78]

While affording polemical satisfaction, the thesis of radical inequality was too narrow to sustain Cram's rosy view of both medieval and traditional American society. His more considered solution postulated a medieval population of rural and urban "producers" as a healthy social base. "Mass-man," in this version, was not a historical constant but the result of the subversion of this society of producers. With the Renaissance, Cram wrote, power had become the chief object of life, and "a type of man emancipated from the restraints of religion, tradition and the sense of ethical and social responsibility" had consequently arisen. The "human scale" of the Middle Ages was supplanted by "imperial modernism," which from the fifteenth century on had worked to eliminate essential distinctions among human beings and break the ties of their traditional relationships, so that it could group and order them mechanically.[79]

"Mass-man," in this scheme, embraced both the highest and lowest orders of society, it is to be noted. "Imperial Modernism" had fostered two new classes: an aggressive bourgeoisie subsisting on trade, usury, and management, and a submerged proletariat—both "non-producers" according to Cram's rather arbitrary definition. Modern "financial-technological civilization" remained similarly bifurcated: "The nether millstone is that of organized, proletarian labour, the upper is that of organized financial, industrial and commercial power."[80]

Ground between was the "Forgotten Class." (If Cram was indebted to William Graham Sumner's "Forgotten Man" for the term, he did not acknowledge it.) Cram regarded this as essentially a middle class, but his definition of it was uncommonly broad, leaving one to wonder how such a large agglomeration could ever be forgotten. It included farmers, small businessmen, professionals, intellectuals, "small rentiers," even skilled and unskilled manual laborers, if nonunion. The class descended from the medieval "producers," but it served in its modern context as simply a benign representation of "the people," shorn of such disagreeable, "adventitious adjuncts" as organized labor and powerful capitalists. In this country it stood, Cram summarized, for "the old, original Americanism."[81]

This tenuous continuity of medieval "producers" with their modern counterparts supported Cram's hope that the Gothic tradition would be reestablished as the authentic embodiment of the American spirit. On the social plane this tradition might then foster what Cram supposed to be a neo-feudalism in personal relationships, based on mutual rights and obligations. Property rights in particular, he emphasized, were to be linked to obligation. Still perhaps Ralph von Cram at heart, he envisioned monarchy as an ideal eventuality, while stipulating that this would be a monarchy limited by other powers as in the Middle Ages and not a Renaissance-style absolutism. Such a monarchy, representing the whole people rather than a party, might make genuine democracy possible, he thought. Essential to the whole would be the acceptance of transcendent authority, of sanctions above the merely human.[82]

Yet tradition itself, Cram realized, inhered best within a limited compass. In the mundane order he came most of all to value "the small group of human scale," for which the family was the preeminent model. "Human scale" was a frequent refrain, thrown up by Cram in the face of the impersonal "Brobdingnagian scale" of modern life, and of the imperialism which he perceived to have brought on the World War. It had once been quite different. Medieval civilization had been "a great unity built up of groups organized on the basis of human association," he believed. "Decentralization was its strength and its virtue. Men lived and worked in manageable human units—feudal estates, parishes, guilds, communes, free cities, monasteries, orders of knighthood, colleges, principalities, small kingdoms."[83]

One of these units had special significance. While the great religious and aesthetic emblem of Cram's new medievalism was the Gothic cathedral—"the title-deed to our inheritance," as he put it—his model for society itself was the monastery. By monasticism Cram meant broadly the freely associated community, self-sufficient and cooperative, separated from "the world," and centered on a religious ideal. In an era when secular progress no longer seemed the ally of tradition, and tradition no longer seemed capable of perpetuation on an imperial scale, as they had to John Fiske, the monastery offered another way of rendering time—or timelessness—as space. It could also be another way of defending the "inner circle." As privileged space the monastery was the counterpart of Fiske's New England town, the Virginia plantation, and even, as we shall see, Charles H. Cooley's primary group in its family or local milieu. (The monastic ideal also inspired Cooley.) More intensely traditional and defensive than the other formulations—the least modern, it might appear, of any of them—monasticism was actually and portentously coming into conjunction with the historical cycle, Cram was convinced.[84]

Cram had entertained a monastic impulse for a long time. In *The Decadent* (1893) he had given fantasy expression to it, imagining a country estate called "Vita Nuova." Languid opium smokers, served by a slim Japanese girl in translucent silk, supply the trappings of fin de siècle mischief which justify the title, but these prove hardly more than decorative. (This may indicate the depth of Cram's "bohemian" proclivities.) "This is my monastery," the proprietor, Aurelian, proclaims in revealing the real purpose of Vita Nuova. He likens himself to "those of the old Faith that, during the night that came down on the world after the fall of Rome, treasured as in an ark the seeds of the new life. Here I gather my Children of Light and bar my doors against the Philistines without." The little community is at once the refuge of tradition and a realm of the timeless. "Within my walls . . . is the world of the past and of the future, of the fifteenth century and of the twentieth century," Aurelian proclaims. Amidst the trivial decadence of the sensualists at Vita Nuova and the more profound decadence of the ugly industrial civilization surrounding it, the proprietor adds a more temporal reassurance: "the law of evolution works by a system of waves advancing and retreating, yet . . . the tide goes forward always."[85]

During the 1890s Cram was serious enough about the possibilities of the monastery in the more traditional sense of the term to draft a proposal for "An American Congregation of the Canons Regular of St. Norbert," complete with more than thirty pages of rules for monks of the prospective order. For a thousand years monasteries had been central to the life of the Church, Cram pointed out, and he argued that they were as much needed as a haven from modern materialism as they had been from the "dying heathenism" of the sixth century. He felt the aspect of artificiality which necessarily colored such ventures in the modern world—all the more need to compensate with a heavy appropriation of tradition, he suggested. Moderns lived "in a time of salvage, not of revelation," he feared; they consequently labored " in self-consciousness, not in obedience to a heavenly vision." Yet he was hopeful that a monastic tradition so venerable and historically fruitful as the Christian might itself bequeath a measure of vitality to those united in spirit and commitment. Cram did not suppose that tradition could be a substitute for spiritual transcendence, but only that it could be its foundation and bearer: that was enough.[86]

Very much "in the world" himself in his professional and domestic life, Cram readily conceded the limits of a modern otherworldliness. Celibacy in particular seemed unlikely to play the role that it had in the monasticism of ages past. Along with the fantasy of *The Decadent*, therefore, the old-fashioned cloister yielded to the hope that monastic values and functions could be reconstituted in other ways. The university, always regarded as apart from the "real world," was an obvious possibility. As an architect of university buildings at Princeton and Rice, Cram sought to represent the college community as "a citadel of learning and culture and scholarship, at the same time inclusive and exclusive, . . . a walled city against materialism and all its works, with a 'way out' into the broadest and truest liberty; the heir of all the scholarship and culture of the past."[87]

The idea of the " walled city" was one that Cram later developed more fully in another direction. By the time of his work at Princeton in 1909, he was already mulling over the possibility of linking monasticism to family values. "My solemn conviction," he wrote Louise Imogen Guiney, "is that the great demand of the present century is for a monastic order which will take in married men with their wives and children!" Yet, he added, he was afraid that such a plan would not work. Spurred by his sense of crisis at the end of the First World War, convinced that civilization was at a crossroads, he was willing to entertain it more seriously.[88]

Accordingly, in *Walled Towns* (1919), Cram described a modern monasticism based on associations of families rather than communities of celibates. Entering into a communal although not "communistic" life, inhabitants of the towns (metaphorically rather than literally walled) would create islands of simple and joyful living in the midst of the larger world. Conceived as an alternative to a postwar restoration of imperial and materialistic modes of life on the one hand, and to a descent into a new dark age on the other, the new communities would make possible life on the human scale. Private property would be maintained, but self-sufficiency and cooperation would replace competition and profit as governing principles. Society would be organized on the guild system, with every man required to belong to "one guild or another." A true democracy would be established, based on a land-owning qualification for voting. The "walled town" was to be at once "individualist, cooperative and aristocratic," and would be held together by a common religious devotion. It was, in all, an idealized version of medieval society as it might be reconstituted in the modern world.[89]

"Communal life . . . in the human scale" was of course more easily conceived than realized, and Cram's difficulty in finding a practical embodiment for the "Walled Town" was a measure of the elusiveness of Gemeinschaft in the twentieth century. He was briefly encouraged by the New Deal's "subsistence homestead" program, but as that plan faltered he proposed a back-to-the-land movement based on a common religious faith. He envisioned "self-contained, self-supporting, self-sufficient Catholic communities" which would be "cities of refuge" from the woes of the Depression and the larger ills of modernity.[90]

These hopes rested on the odd faith that somehow the "Mediaeval Sequence" could be restored. This was in a sense a traditionism beyond tradition, for the continuity of the tradition, as Cram acknowledged, had long since been severed. But what traditionism was more appropriate to America, which proclaimed itself a product of such severances? Cram's version upheld a kind of tradition which was disjointed, discontinuous, and innovative, to be invoked not as something predetermined or even prescribed, but as something freely chosen. Despite his cyclical theory of history, Cram was no determinist, and even amidst the shock and horror of World War I held the shape of the future to lie within the compass of human will. American know-how was surely capable of constructing whatever the spirit of the nation might truly call forth. American too was Cram's emphasis on the usability of tradition. As dubious as his understanding of history often was, he never proposed to recover the Middle

Ages as such, but only a medieval tradition which he was convinced could be as instrumental in serving contemporary needs as one of his neo-Gothic churches was in housing Christian worship. Tradition so conceived represented neither the dead weight of the past nor an escapist nostalgia; in Cram's mind, at least, it was entirely pragmatic and even progressive. Society could go forward, he was confident, on the principles of the Middle Ages.[91]

American too, finally, was the search for transcendence which for Cram was the ultimate meaning and justification of tradition. An unleavened traditionalism yields no final or timeless answers; its authority is that of past experience and it looks only to future experience as a corrective. Such a traditionalism is alien to a country so largely defined by Jonathan Edwards and Ralph Waldo Emerson, where even practicality is linked in the public mind with idealism. And Cram, at bottom, was hardly more an intellectual than he was a physical expatriate; tradition was of dubiously American standing as means, but in Cram's world it led to very American ends. The monastery was a better model of the "group of human scale" than Brook Farm; even a broken aesthetic and cultural tradition was a more promising guide to human betterment than the doctrine of "progressive evolution"; the Gothic cathedral reached more truly to heaven than the skyscraper did to the empty sky. In his own way Cram was a seeker of liberty. In an age when most of the greatest artists and writers strained to escape tradition, Ralph Adams Cram pursued it as the only path of escape from the limitations of time and space: from the tyranny of the merely temporal and the spiritual cramping of the endlessly expansive.

His sense of tradition as opening up rather than restricting possibilities also kept Cram from some of the provincialism which limited both Fiske and the Virginia historians. Despite his Anglo-American bias, his intense devotion to the particular tradition of Gothic art and the contempt he sometimes showed for poor, everyday "Neolithic Man," he respected beauty and spiritual aspiration where he found them. His idealism permitted the appreciation of diverse forms. "All art meets and is judged on one common and indestructible basis," as he stated it, "but each manifestation possesses numberless other qualities, many of them of almost equal value, but peculiar, intimate, and personal."[92]

In 1898 Cram visited Japan. He was certainly prepared to be impressed with the country's art and architecture, given their modishness in the West during this period (reflected in some of his own writings). Further, as Margaret Ellen O'Shaughnessey points out, an interest in medieval and "Oriental" culture often went together in the late nineteenth century; admirers were apt to seek in Gothic and Eastern arts the same qualities of transcendence, mysticism, or repose. If his predisposition needed reinforcement, it must have been provided by the two best-known American students of Japanese culture, Lafcadio Hearn and Ernest Fenollosa, with whom he kept company during his visit. In his professional capacity Cram submitted plans for the proposed new houses of the Japanese parliament, although these were not ultimately accepted.[93]

Cram praised Japanese architecture in the highest terms, placing it in the same class as the "Greek, Medieval, and Early Renaissance" schools. Indeed it was "the perfect style in wood, as Gothic may be called the perfect style in stone," he thought. He was particularly captivated by its domestic sources. "The great temples are the apotheosis of this system of building," he observed, "but the private houses are its basis." In fact, compared to the taste and simplicity of the domestic architecture, providing a perfect setting for the courtesy and hospitality of Japanese home life, "the chaos of western houses" seemed "an ugly dream."[94]

A quarter of a century later, Cram felt more optimistic about American domestic architecture, but he retained the view that aesthetically as in other ways it was the home which had to be carried outward. Domestic architecture was "the foundation for vital art of all kinds," as he put it. "For no river can rise above its source, and if the springs of common life are polluted so will the well be poisoned." The Japanese, he thought, had long maintained their aesthetic purity.[95]

Enlarging upon the parallels between the Japanese and Western architectural traditions, Cram perceived in the one not an image or reverse image of the other, but an alternative line of development. (He believed that Greece was the common source of both.) In both societies long traditions had nurtured creativity, although Japan was more impressive for sheer continuity. Whereas Western countries had shown "dazzling flashes of transcendent genius," in Japan one civilization and one architectural tradition had held sway for some twelve hundred years, the architecture "essentially" unchanging, yet "adapting itself always with the most perfect aptitude" to successive phases of the country's history.[96]

This was not to deny to the Japanese achievement a dimension of transcendence. As the Gothic was the supreme aesthetic expression of Christianity, so it was clear to Cram that the architecture he saw in Japan was "the architecture of Buddhism, and . . . must be read in the light of this mystic and wonderful system." It was a system, he acknowledged, quite different from the Christian—representing a "religion of meditation, of spiritual enlightenment, of release from illusion . . . . separated from the art of the Western religion of action, of elaborate ethical systems, of practicality, by the diameter of being." Yet clearly the Buddhist way struck a powerful chord in the Western Anglo-Catholic, and he appears to have recognized in it the counterpart of his own reliance on past experience—on tradition—as well as of his willingness to disregard linear continuity in his quest for the ideal. In Eastern philosophy, he explained, art is "an absolute beauty" which is dual in nature. It is a selective manifestation of many lives; "also is it, in another aspect, mystical foreknowledge of the final Absolute to which we all are tending through incarnation and reincarnation; not only the subliminal composite of the good of all the past, but a leaping on by force of achievement to heights yet unachieved: Karma and Beatific Vision in one. So beauty is something that never was in the past, nor is now, but shall be hereafter, the last residuum from the winnowing of experience illuminated by the aura of Nirvana itself."[97]

Unfortunately, in Cram's view, Eastern art had suffered the same decline as Western, Japanese aesthetic traditions having been all but extinguished by the "Black Death" of "Occidentalism" and "the ignis fatuus of technological culture and industrial-commercial supremacy." Yet the parallel was not exact, as the artistic "cataclysm" in Japan had not been accompanied by a "crash of ethical and spiritual standards" such as had occurred in the West. Cram, ever watchful for a favorable turn of history's cycle, could therefore be all the more hopeful that "racial instinct" and reverence for ancestors would bring a quick "return to all that was good in the old Japan."[98]

Cram's hopes for both East and West of course went unfulfilled. By the time of his death in 1942 the Gothic Revival had run its course in the United States; more violently the Japanese version of "imperial modernism" would shortly bring down upon itself the destruction of a great many of the homes in which Cram had seen the perfection of "life on the human scale." On his own premises these developments did not rule out future renewal. But perhaps it was enough that in his own time and place Cram the architect had demonstrated that even a tradition dormant for centuries, revived in a country notorious for its scorn of tradition, could yield results capable of delighting the eye and turning the spirit to things of transcending meaning and value.

CHAPTER 4

The I and the We:
Charles H. Cooley and the Tradition
of the Sociologists

The emergence of the social sciences as professional fields of study
after the Civil War brought to conceptions of tradition both sharper
definition and greater confusion about its proper role in human life.
Leading American social scientists of the era—and leading sociologists
especially, with the signal exception of William Graham Sumner—
wanted characteristically not only to describe society but to change it. As
Americans they were inclined to identify their country with the rejection
of tradition for the purpose of making a fresh start in the world; as
trained professionals they little doubted the efficacy of scientific knowledge in disposing of the unexamined detritus of the past.

Further, as Thomas L. Haskell contends, social scientists of the late
nineteenth century sought to replace what appeared to be the fading assurance of traditional authorities—those of family, church, and village—
with a "community of the competent" which would provide a more enlightened, scientific basis for decision-making and, not coincidentally,
help to preserve the power of the "gentry class" from which the relevant
professions largely drew their members. In some ways the Progressive
movement of the early twentieth century gave broader expression to
this ideology, although with greater reliance on social and political
action as opposed to the autonomous individual. "Progressivism,"
as the term applies to the sociologists under consideration here,
refers especially to their reliance on the public and professional realms
to induce social progress, on the efficacy of scientific and social
scientific expertise brought to bear upon social problems, and on positive
government to implement social planning and establish rational social
control for humanistic ends. At first glance tradition had little place in
such a program.[1]

Yet sociology was among other things an effort to make sense of the past as a means of understanding the course of social development—a task which sociologists were fairly sure historians did not accomplish. The continuities which made such a study intelligible included inescapably those of custom and tradition. Evolutionary doctrine, which moved the matter of continuity through time from the realm of the providential or the merely fortuitous not only into biology but also into the social sciences, provided a scheme of compelling persuasion. And if from a certain perspective evolution might seem to replace tradition—at least as a usable explanation of social phenomena—it could also demonstrate its ineluctability. Social continuity might indefinitely elude progress, social scientists were obliged to admit; it was never without the traditional.[2]

Anthropologists, necessarily aware of the role of custom and tradition in primitive societies, recognized that not even modern society escaped these bonds. Franz Boas, while conceding that civilization tended to distance logical thought from considerations of tradition, believed that everyday activities were "controlled by custom almost as much among ourselves as they are among primitive man." But the importance of the traditional impressed itself just as forcefully on sociologists. A product of nineteenth-century concerns and conditions, sociology passed its formative years at the very time when the gap between "traditional" and "modern" ways of life seemed at its widest. The sense of a momentous passage from the one to the other acted as a strong stimulant to sociological thought. The classic expressions of traditional-modern polarity—Sir Henry Maine's distinction between status and contract societies and Ferdinand Tönnies's antinomy of gemeinschaft and gesellschaft—reflected this consciousness of transition. Max Weber was similarly prompted to his conception of "rationalization" as the distinctive, anti-traditional feature of modern life.[3]

In these formulations the notion of "community" figured with especial prominence. The "rediscovery" of community, as Robert A. Nisbet observes, was "unquestionably the most distinctive development in nineteenth-century social thought." But community, at least in the sense of gemeinschaft, was inseparable from tradition; "we find," Nisbet adds, "paralleling the rediscovery of community, the rediscovery of custom and tradition, of patriarchal and corporate authority." Community involved, necessarily, continuity in time. Continuity may have been in shorter supply in the United States, new society as it was, but the American small town furnished a usable analogue to the traditional European community. As academically adopted, the small town was less provincial than in John Fiske's New England version but similarly tailored to American values. In particular, as Jean B. Quandt points out, it was perceived as more nurturing of individualism than its European counterpart. The small town served as a model of community for a host of Progressive Age intellectuals, including such sociologists as Franklin Henry Giddings and Charles H. Cooley. In Cooley, unexpectedly, it provided a vantage point for the reconsideration of the role of tradition which went well beyond its local community associations.[4]

Acknowledging its inevitability, sociologists endeavored to reduce the subject, so little amenable to systematizing, to system. Giddings achieved at least a rough order of classification. He developed as the cornerstone of his sociological thinking the conception of "consciousness of kind," by which he meant "a state of consciousness in which any being, whether low or high in the scale of life, recognizes another conscious being as of like kind with itself." The basis of ethnic, class, political, and other sorts of groupings, consciousness of kind also made possible the customs and traditions which preserved the ways and practices of such social entities. Tradition was thus "social memory," in which "the relations, the ideas, and the usages that have sprung up unconsciously and because of their intrinsic usefulness have survived, are consciously defined and memorized. The garnered experience of the past has become the common possession of all individuals. Tradition is thus the integration of the public opinion of many generations." Giddings proceeded to differentiate among "primary" traditions, representing such "tangible" areas of experience as the economic, juridical, and political; "secondary" traditions, which included religious and aesthetic sensibilities; and "tertiary" traditions, which embraced such categories of conceptual thought as the theological, metaphysical, and scientific.[5]

Toward the role of tradition generally Giddings evinced the ambivalence which was so characteristic of the sociologists of his time. He was convinced of tradition's "tremendous hold over the human mind," and invoking Walter Bagehot, remarked that that hold could be the most terrible of tyrannies. Even Americans seemed to him all too prone to cling to ineffective and discredited ideas and practices. Yet, he acknowledged, "folkways, folklore, and tradition have been necessary." They served to "mediate between individual impulse and the conditions to which life must adapt itself," he agreed with William Graham Sumner. The communication of diverse cultural achievements to successive generations by means of tradition was clearly indispensable to the rise of civilization. Yet only when critical intelligence was brought to bear upon tradition could it be completely fertile, he concluded.[6]

Although Giddings cited Sumner's celebrated analysis of "folkways" and "mores," these categories did not add substantially to his evaluation of tradition. This should not be surprising. Sumner's *Folkways* contributed importantly to the general appreciation of the ways in which patterns of behavior persisted in human life, but it left the more specific notion of tradition in a curious limbo. Sumner seemed at times to relegate "tradition" to the role of disembodied conveyance for the folkways and mores. From the efforts of people to satisfy their needs, he explained, there arose "folkways," which had the force of habit for the individual and of custom for society. With the addition of "moral and reflective judgment," folkways became "mores." Folkways, developing unconsciously out of experience, were "handed down by tradition and admit of no exception or variation, yet change to meet new conditions, still within the same limited methods, and without rational reflection or purpose." Sumner was emphatic that the process survived modernity: "all the life of human beings, in all ages and stages of culture," he insisted, "is primarily controlled by a vast mass of folkways handed down from the earliest existence of the race," only slightly modified by "intelligent reflection."[7]

Sumner's point was to show human subservience to the inexorable processes of social evolution, however, not to praise folkways—or tradition—as the wisdom of accumulated experience or as a source of social enrichment. Although he had defended tradition as a young Episcopal priest, in his maturity he substituted science as a principle of authority, Robert Bannister notes. Sumner did not hold the legacy of the past to be an unmixed good or evil, and indeed pretended to a moral relativism. "In the folkways, whatever is, is right," he explained. "This is because they are traditional, and therefore contain in themselves the authority of the ancestral ghosts. . . . Therefore morals can never be intuitive. They are historical, institutional, and empirical."[8]

In practice, removed from his stricter attempts at objective analysis, Sumner fell readily into conventional American usage, commending such specific "traditions" as those of civil liberty, but perceiving tradition in the abstract as inertia. Seen in this way the mores could well be at odds with tradition, as in the case of religion. Modern mores tended toward "naturalistic views of life" which placed them in opposition to "traditional religion," he argued. "What the mores always represent is the struggle to live as well as possible under the conditions. Traditions, so far as they come out of other conditions and are accepted as independent authorities in the present conditions, are felt as hindrances."[9]

Sumner had complained in his "Forgotten Man" lecture of 1883 that "traditions and formulae have a dominion over us in legislation and social customs which we seem unable to break or even to modify," and he retained a strong sense of the tyranny which tradition could exercise. Least excusably, an unthinking adherence to tradition frustrated the natural selection of useful folkways. "Tradition, prejudice, fashion, habit, and other similar obstacles continually warp and deflect the social forces," he observed. Unlike John Fiske, for whom tradition was simply part of the process of social evolution, Sumner viewed tradition as an artificial vehicle capable of bearing useful folkways but acting frequently as an impediment to evolution.[10]

At bottom Sumner seems to have been animated by a very American suspicion of tradition, qualified by a sociologist's recognition of its inevitability and by the unexceptional realization that particular traditions could be benign. At least Americans in emigrating from the Old World had been empowered to choose their traditions, he argued, and he was impatient when, as in its 1898 imperialist venture, the country seemed to backslide into unhealthy European ways. "The men who came here were able to throw off all the trammels of tradition and established doctrine," he wrote in "The Conquest of the United States by Spain." "They could not, it is true, strip their minds of the ideas which they had inherited, but in time, as they lived on in the new world, they sifted and selected these ideas, retaining what they chose." This suggestion of choice, embedded in a grudging admission of social continuity, was curiously dissonant with the ineluctability of folkways and mores as they appeared in Sumner's most important work. However understood, the formulation left little room for a Burkean respect for traditional authority, and nearly as little for a more modern sense of tradition as means to the enrichment of life. Generally labeled a conservative, Sumner demonstrates how little conservatism, as understood in America, can have to do with tradition.[11]

The anti-traditionalism which vied uneasily with social scientific objectivity in William Graham Sumner appeared more or less prominently in other American sociologists of the time, the product of a native creed and a Progressive commitment to change. Lester Frank Ward (1841–1913) and Edward Alsworth Ross (1866–1951) illustrate in successive generations the degree to which anti-traditionalist premises could shape their discipline, as well as the limited utility of those premises.

Self-consciously hard-headed and rebellious against conventional pieties, Ward wrote appropriately for a Washington periodical called *The Iconoclast* during the 1870s. He struck a belligerent village atheist (or at least village agnostic) stance, less witty but not markedly different in tone from Mark Twain, or even from H. L. Mencken fifty years later. Ward enlisted enthusiastically in the great Victorian war of science and religion. "Science is the acknowledged enemy of Theology. Why?" he catechized his readers in a typical squib in 1870. "Because it teaches truth. Theology is error."[12]

Theology was emblematic of "certain great, pernicious, and iniquitous institutions, customs, laws, and social or political systems" to which Ward ascribed "nearly all the unhappiness and misery of the world." In support he offered a devil's litany of enormities, including divine-right monarchy, church-sanctioned slavery, religious wars, witchcraft persecutions, capital punishment, and intemperance. It seemed a simple thing for Ward as a young man to promise fearlessly to criticize everything which served "to keep the mind in bondage and thwart the aspirations of the human race, by holding up to the people as finalities effete systems of the past which are wholly inadequate to their present wants and demands."[13]

Much of this youthful ardor remained in the mature Ward. Making clear the bent of a lifetime toward the end of it, he recalled that he had never taken any interest in genealogy, regarding pride of ancestry as a "mark of degeneracy." "My mind," he perhaps needlessly explained, "has always been trimmed toward the future rather than the past." He never accepted the Burkean theory that tradition represents the ever more refined experience of the race. The history of the subjugation of women—Ward was an emphatic feminist—seemed a sufficient demonstration of the power of custom and tradition to enshrine any injustice. Standing the usual canons of traditionalism on their head, further, Ward argued that the worst customs were the oldest and most universal. Although arising with at least some "basis in reason and advantage," they tended to grow away from this, and frequently in time became mere "survivals," increasingly irrational and incomprehensible.[14]

This visceral anti-traditionalism was qualified by social values which at bottom were largely conservative, centering on order and self-discipline. Ward's later thought inclined to a neo-Hegelian idealism and he came to a more sympathetic view of the function of religion, even to a quasi-religious sensibility himself. A simplistic anti-traditionalist stance did not truly fit with such ways of thinking and the sense of social connectedness which they entailed; nor could it support Ward's sociology in its more technical aspects. And certainly a Reform Darwinist (or Social Lamarckian, as he has more accurately been styled) had to acknowledge in human culture the continuity of past and present of which custom and tradition were necessary parts. Ward represented this continuity quite graphically as a "social germ-plasm"—immortal "in the great trunk line of descent of civilization." Shifting metaphors, he characterized this "plasm" as "the Promethean fire" that must be maintained at all costs: "cut off any portion of mankind from the main stream of thought and it loses at once all that has been bequeathed to the civilized world at such enormous cost."[15]

Ward concluded finally that such phenomena as custom, tradition, religion, and conservatism represented in society simply the principle of heredity, essential to evolution but powerless alone to achieve development. Whatever the further mechanism required in biological evolution, in social evolution human rationality had to supply the principle of variation. This formulation did not take away Ward's contempt for outworn customs and traditions, but it did lead him to an appreciation that "nothing is ever wholly lost, and the accumulations of unnumbered generations continue to exist, albeit long latent, but liable, and perhaps in fact destined, ultimately to come forth and exert their due influence upon the world." Thus "the human polyp is perpetually building a coral reef, on the upper surface of which the last generation lives and builds."[16]

Ward came to see custom and tradition, then, as possible resources for progress. Ideas and social structures were ever in danger of "ossification," he emphasized, for human beings continue to revere the ideas and structures which have served them well, long after their usefulness has departed, and a "highly useful conservatism thus becomes a dangerous misoneism." In place of the "survival of the fittest," therefore, he proposed the "survival of the plastic"—of the adaptable. Ward the iconoclast seems to end merely by insisting upon the shaping of the social heritage progressively by intellect and conscious volition.[17]

Yet this was no negligible conclusion. The principle of Ward's "Reform Darwinism"—that "all true social progress is *artificial*," as he stated it in *Dynamic Sociology*—allowed in one way for a more authentic kind of tradition than thinkers like Fiske or Sumner provided for. With Fiske, tradition is effectively subsumed in a deterministic evolutionary process; it lacks autonomous existence as a social phenomenon. Although this might logically be the case with Sumner as well, Sumner was wont to present tradition as lying athwart the course of evolution— a troublesome if ultimately futile obstacle. Ward, starting from a bias against the past similar to that of Sumner, more emphatically allowed for custom and tradition as resources for "telic"—planned and purposeful—progress. He thus helped to free tradition, as well as progress, from the thrall of blind necessity. This liberation was not an end in itself; there could be neither equality nor justice, he wrote, "so long as society is composed of members, equally endowed by nature, a few of whom only possess the social heritage of truth and ideas resulting from the laborious investigations and profound meditations of all past ages." Tradition, which had once summed up for Ward all that obstructed human progress, appears here as its prerequisite, a treasure of which progress demands universal possession.[18]

Similar reconsiderations emerged in the thought of Edward Alsworth Ross. Ross deserves relatively extended notice here, most of all because he so strikingly illustrates an anti-traditional bias overcome at length by the realization that tradition was both inescapable and, in some measure, salutary. In both its positive and negative aspects, Ross's take on tradition provides as well a useful background for the more complex views of Charles H. Cooley.

Ross was Lester Frank Ward's nephew by marriage, and it was chiefly Ward's influence which drew the younger man from economics into sociology. Sharing "identical values," as it has been said, Ward and Ross nevertheless parted on generational lines in their assessment of human personality—Ward clinging to a long-lingering Enlightenment faith in rationality and Ross more impressed by the motivating force of "impulse and self-interest." Although less original a thinker than his uncle, Ross came also to be regarded as one of the founders of sociology in the United States, especially for his pioneering work in social psychology.[19]

Ross was a vehement Progressive, a proponent of a planned society making use of social institutions developed on a national scale. His outspoken views gave him prominence as a public intellectual, heightened by his opposition to Japanese immigration (strongly opposed by organized labor on the West Coast). His politics also put him at odds with Jane Lathrop Stanford and cost him his professorship at the university named for Stanford's husband. After this episode, which became a cause célèbre of academic freedom, Ross decamped for the University of Nebraska in 1901, and four years later began a long career at the University of Wisconsin. (He narrowly escaped losing another job after officially welcoming the anarchist Emma Goldman to campus on behalf of the Wisconsin Socialist Club in 1910.) At Wisconsin he was part of a distinguished group of Progressive scholars which included also Richard T. Ely, John R. Commons, and Frederick Jackson Turner. Ross's most significant contributions in his own field, *Social Control* and

Social Psychology, came early in his career, however, and in the years after World War I he came to be regarded by many as a popularizer and "academic entrepreneur."[20]

Like Ward, Ross had entered upon his career with an American horror of retrospection. In 1891 he published a short article in The Arena entitled "Turning Towards Nirvana." He was then not quite twenty-five years old. A midwesterner and graduate of Coe College in Iowa, Ross had just completed his Ph.D. in economics at the Johns Hopkins University. He had also recently spent a year and a half of study and travel in Europe, and his Arena article was based on his observations of the Old World.

"Turning Towards Nirvana" was a somewhat early but not particularly original diagnosis of fin de siècle malaise, most interesting for the frame of mind it indicates in the young social scientist. Ross reported a mood of despondency in Europe, conspicuous in art and literature but most completely expressed in the fear of international conflict. It seemed to the writer that the European found himself "aboard a train . . . speeding to sure destruction. . . . Nothing, it seems, can save Europe from the fatal plunge into the abyss of war." Afraid to face the future, the age yearned "to lose itself in the past"—or in the pleasures of the moment. "The forces of darkness are still strong," Ross warned, "and it seems sometimes as if the Middle Ages will swallow up everything won by modern struggles."[21]

Ross found the role of modern science to be particularly disturbing. Unlike most of those who kept him company on this score, Ross was entirely committed to a scientific point of view, and certainly entertained no theological scruples about biological evolution or other ideas which challenged traditional views. Science was the harbinger of progress. And yet, ironically, Ross was struck by the fact that science had been "most successful in studying the past." Social scientists traced the evolution of institutions as biologists traced the evolution of species. Neither group could find any vestige of a soul or ego which could "maintain itself against the past." Heredity had taken the place of "that supreme primeval necessity that stood above the Olympian gods." It seemed to the young American, in sum, that the age was "'possessed' not by demons but by the dead." The grip of determinism provided no comfort or security, but rather fostered a sense of homelessness and bottomlessness from which people fell into despair or sought refuge in "Hindoo pantheism."[22]

Ross appears here not so much as a young man fascinated by decadence but as an American of his countrymen's forward-looking instincts dismayed to find, as he remarked of contemporary drama and literature, that "anything optimistic falls flat." There is also a strong hint of religious loss in his plaint that in the modern scientific dispensation "nothing is found mysterious, nothing unique, nothing divine." The month after the publication of his article in The Arena, he wrote to Ward, "I am now so free from theology that I do not even feel resentment toward it." Yet Ross, who always maintained the social value of religion, fits the pattern of many of his generation who sought secular substitutes for spiritual values. "In a century of Götterdämmerung like ours . . . [the] apotheosis of society is especially marked," he commented later; he could have been talking about himself.[23]

In the United States, the apotheosis of society could pose special problems for the social scientist. Ross's disquiet about his perception that scientists had recently been most successful in studying the past suggested a tension between his incipient role as sociologist and his American inclination, as in the Arena article, to regard the past as dead weight. It had been an American conceit to suppose that this weight could be jettisoned, but Ross's professional training and experience led him to perceive custom as "a power—and an ally and reënforcement of the other powers that bind the individual," which could not be so easily escaped. Human institutions changed slowly and reluctantly, yet they were volatile compared to the ideas behind them. "It is the thoughts of dead men that enslave us," Ross observed, "not their social order."[24]

Appropriating Walter Bagehot's famous phrase, Ross lamented that even the most progressive peoples "suffer terribly from the cake of custom that forms so quickly, yet withal so quietly, and confines them ere they are aware of it." Even Americans were not immune, as "their idolatry of an undemocratic Federal Constitution" and reverence for an "irresponsible" Supreme Court demonstrated. Ross was a vivid stylist, and his language amply expressed his animus. In the ancient civilizations, he remarked, the young were "stung and paralyzed with tradition, thrown into a mental catalepsy by exclusive contact with sacred books and classics." Custom was a "cave" or a "prison"; at its most complete it constituted "the rule of the dead."[25]

Yet Ross, like other sociologists of the time, was obliged to recognize that progress and tradition were necessarily congruent as expressions of the continuity of human society in time. He perceived as clearly as did John Fiske that the invention of tradition had been a key moment in human development. The child could thenceforth do more than simply imitate its parents. It became possible "to organize the individual life, and to lay a solid basis for the social union, by organizing the lives of many individuals about the same ideas and habits." Like Ward, Ross accepted the analogy of tradition with heredity, suggesting that "the variations that break the current of heredity can be compared to the inventions and discoveries—the innovations—that break the otherwise peaceful descent of the stream of tradition." The analogy worked better on Lamarckian lines, and he noted that just as acquired characteristics were "probably" transmissible, so traditional beliefs and practices were likely to be modified during the lifetimes of their recipients, and passed on in an altered form.[26]

Ross added two important qualifications to the analogy. In company with Ward, he rejected the view that the fitness of a tradition or custom was demonstrated by its long survival; indeed, he thought, "the older an institution, practice, or dogma, the more hopelessly out of adjustment it may be presumed to be." Secondly, he pointed out that custom was, after all, much more elastic than heredity. Its force was "purely psychical," and therefore malleable by human will and reason. The two arguments were curiously at odds; the plasticity of custom and tradition (reinforced even on the biological analogy by Ross's Lamarckianism) clearly entailed an adaptability which undermined the notion that the oldest uses were presumptively the worst. Appearing within the compass of several pages of the same work, the incongruity suggested a hardly uncommon confusion between professional analysis and temperamental or political inclination.[27]

Subjectivity had freest rein when Ross projected his hopes and fears on foreign and especially on immigrant populations. His extensive travel accounts were often thoughtful and balanced, and argue against a too-hasty diagnosis of racism. It was social inertia that aroused his ire abroad. He attributed Latin American problems not to race but to "a paralyzing social tradition." The Spanish colonial legacy, although it included such positive values as a sense of honor, had also left habits of indolence and a tradition of "masculinism" oppressive of women, he pointed out. Ross returned from China in 1911 declaring that Asians were "Equal Mentally and Superior in Vitality to the White Race," as the *New York Times* headlined the story, and predicting "a Great Future for the Chinese." He was however dismayed by the "Mediaeval" torpor of contemporary Chinese society, and especially horrified by the ancient Chinese practice of female foot-binding. This seems to have been for him, indeed, the ultimate example of the cruelty and stupidity which custom could harbor.[28]

Ross was initially optimistic about the prospects of the Bolshevik revolution, largely because of "the freedom of the [Russian] masses from the guidance of tradition." There was, for example, little customary "chivalry" such as served to limit the role of women in the United States, and in consequence a remarkable number of Russian women in medicine and other professions. Ross was impressed enough with such evidences of personal liberation to suggest, in 1919, that there was a sounder basis for Russian-American friendship than there was for our "special relationship" with Great Britain. True, we shared with the British language and "a few common political traditions," but the similarities of the two vast frontier nations seemed more compelling. "Both [peoples] are easy-going, democratic, and familiar," he pointed out. "Neither has known feudalism and the caste sense it inspires. Neither has grown up amid historical buildings and monuments, nor feels much reverence for the past." Ross soon distanced himself from the Communist regime, however.[29]

Benign ethnocentricity in the sociologist abroad—the Chinese destiny was "that of the white race," he proclaimed encouragingly—took on a more xenophobic cast in the sociologist at home. Ross's Progressivism and his nativism had a common source, as Julius Weinberg pointed out—"the breakdown of the *Gemeinschaft* of his youth." Bathed in nostalgia, memories of an older, rural, and small-town America heightened resentment of the more alarming features of the modern nation, of the deluge of immigrants as well as of the rise of powerful and irresponsible corporations. A familiar enough reaction during the turn-of-the-century period, it enmeshed Ross in a typically American tangle: moved by an unacknowledged traditionalism of his own, he condemned tradition itself as the un-American gift of newcomers.[30]

Ross's discomfort with the immigrant populations in the United States, tinctured by racialism, given urgency by the fear of overpopulation, and reflecting deep concern for the coherence and established values of the country, fastened also on the ethnic traditionalism which he viewed as an intolerable drag upon social progress. It seemed to him in 1914 that "the Middle Ages are beginning to show among us." This was not the good news that it would have been for Ralph Adams Cram, needless to say. It meant, at a minimum, clerical domination, excessive breeding, dirt, and illiteracy—conditions which condemned much of the Polish immigrant community, in Ross's mind, as "a rancid bit of the Old World." Central to the problem were traditions which, he feared, "will no more blend with American traditions than oil will blend with water."[31]

As with William Graham Sumner, rejection of tradition in the abstract did not keep Ross from invoking the particular traditions of his country. But generalized tradition, it seemed, represented the full obdurate burden of the past; "American tradition," somewhat paradoxically, stood for values unlimited by space or time. The West remained the stronghold of traditional America, in Ross's view, because it was "a century nearer its frontier experiences" and—spared "the presence of great numbers of low grade, un-Americanized" immigrants—"still cherishes much of its pristine democracy." This seems precisely the "'back'-look on the past" which he argued that democrats must eschew in favor of the "'in'-look upon reason and conscience." But Ross entertained an essentially timeless vision of a society made up of people individually— and only individually—diversified. Members of such a society were supposed capable of acting together, but from a common loyalty to principle or ideal rather than "from clannishness or allegiance to a leader." The American genius, which came closest to realizing this ideal, was accordingly for "individuation"—defined as "the processes which pulverize social lumps and release the action of their members."[32]

Ross recurred frequently to this terminology: groups of people bound together by custom and tradition were "lumps" or "clots" in the social body, and the detachment of the individual from them was central to his purpose as a Progressive sociologist. Ethnic clots limited personal freedom and threatened cultural unity—not to Ross's way of thinking contradictory ideals or objectives. Democratic society suffered, he thought, "as it becomes more heterogeneous in composition." Fundamentals could no longer be taken for granted, and had to be decided all over again. Conversely, the effectiveness of democracy was "reinforced by the break-up of custom." But this was difficult to effect among the newer immigrants, who failed to disperse as had their predecessors. Concentrated in "a Ghetto, a Little Italy, or Little Hungary, or Little Armenia,—the later aliens form, as it were, insoluble clots," he fretted. And what a contrast to the sons of the pioneers, even in the early twentieth century visible in "the recesses of the Rocky Mountains"— "steady-eyed, eagle-faced men with tawny mustaches, whose masterful, unswerving will and fierce impatience of restraint remind you of their spiritual kinsmen, the heroes of the Icelandic sagas!"[33]

One effect of such rhetoric was to make Ross look more prejudiced than his certainly racially tinged xenophobia—moderated in his later years—might warrant. He was accused of having "no faith in Americanism to mould the characters of the descendants of other races than Teutons and Celts into true Americans," and more specifically of anti-Semitism. Ross himself denied such charges, condemning anti-Semitism as a "cruel prejudice." He was blind to any suggestion that hostility to the traditions of a people could be taken as hostility to the people themselves. To him there was nothing anti-Semitic in urging the dissolution of clots of ethnic identity, and he took satisfaction in thinking that "America is probably the strongest solvent Jewish separatism has ever encountered." After all, the "dogma" that the Jews were a peculiar people was "only a tradition," and therefore, he implied, worthy of no special respect.[34]

At times a harder note of Progressive efficiency crept into Ross's calculations. "As pulverizing a lump of lime hastens its slaking, as comminuting food aids digestion, as splintering wood accelerates its combustion, so there is a speedier termination of the conflict between the peculiar and the general when social lumps are broken up," he noted. Yet he had faith enough in the solvent powers of American society not to rely on coercion. Pleased to believe at the beginning of the century that "the reign of custom with its vague terrors is about over," he did not permit his youthful optimism to be entirely over-whelmed by later forebodings. The modern spirit had exterminated astrology, mesmerism, the hypothesis of special creations, even, he oddly supposed, the Christmas carol; clots of Old World tradition had surely to yield as well.[35]

Essentially Ross's confidence resided in his understanding of the nature of America itself. "No civilized people ever so belittled the past in the face of the future as we do," it seemed to him. "This is why tradition withers and dies in our air." Inevitably captivated by the American spirit of individualism and progress, the immigrant was braced to "defy the commands of priest, rabbi, and padrone, the natural upholders of tradition." It was not that Ross proposed to substitute Progressive edicts of his own for those authorities; that was unnecessary. As in the fable the hot sun caused the traveler to remove the cloak that the blasting wind could not blow off, so a policy of toleration and accommodation would lead most surely to assimilation, Ross believed. Despite his fears, he was encouraged to think that the bright American sun afforded "the most striking example in all history of a rapid assimilation of aliens of extremely diverse origin."[36]

Ross glimpsed the possibilities of a consumer society in effecting this assimilation, but his real faith—characteristically American and Progressive—was in education. Although he was aware that education could be used to perpetuate moribund traditions, he believed that it served most effectively in the United States to detach the young alien from his ancestral past. Tolerance of exotic ways ended with education. "On one point only is America inflexible," he explained. "'Dress as you please, speak as you please, worship as you please, but you must let us teach your children.'" The effects, he thought, extended beyond the classroom: "The moulding influences that can be brought to bear in the school not only detach the young from the parental traditions, but actually inspire them to become accomplices in the Americanizing of their parents."[37]

The Progressive penchant for social engineering, overlying the breezy American scorn for the past, was here at its apogee. Yet Ross was too sophisticated a thinker not to have second thoughts. After Darwin, some form of social continuity could not be left out of account, and the social scientist had to be aware that it could shape society in positive as well as negative ways. The very aspiration to management held by the "community of the competent" suggested the utility of tradition, in certain of its forms, for "social control." Secondly, and more weakly, there was a glimmering in Ross of the more characteristically post-Progressive notion that tradition could enhance the quality of individual life, giving it a bearing and richness denied by the conditions of mass society.

The urge to social control, to be sure, worked very largely against respect for tradition, which was apt to stand in the way of the controllers. There is some justification for charges that Ross and his sociological contemporaries "espoused a form of democratic elitism." A "spirit of self-reliance" was natural for a frontier people, Ross thought, but in a more complex society, it was "foolish and dangerous not to follow the lead of superior men." Such an elite would be little constrained by custom and tradition; on the contrary it would necessarily pull against the weight of the past. It was the function of the expert "to command the ordering of one's life according to ideas and principles, rather than according to precedent and tradition." And yet even such lofty leadership could not do entirely without the supports which tradition provided for the social structure.[38]

Ross's 1901 work Social Control helped to make its subject for a time a central "paradigm for American sociology"—perhaps more in the sense of "supervision" or "guidance" than of domination, as Georges Gurvitch contends. Fears that industrialization and urbanization would fragment American society and threaten its continuity and stability gave the problem an appearance of urgency. Yet Ross evinced little apprehension of unrest among the classes which had fared worst in the processes of modernization. On the contrary, he pointed out that reformers had had historically to struggle against their inertia—"the brutish ignorance, the crass stupidity, the rhinoceros-hide bigotry of the unenlightened masses." Even members of the modern wage-earning class, he feared, were often "slaves to tradition."[39]

If this impatience concealed any anxiety about the masses awakened, Ross projected it onto those whom he considered the most active members of society. It was advanced and individualistic Occidentals who stood most in need of an ordering hand. The "small gregariousness of the Westering Teuton" had rendered community life problematical at best, he thought. "Social order, even among the passive, unambitious Hindoos, presents a problem," it seemed to him in 1901. "But it is a much more serious problem among the dolichocephalic blonds of the West." His countrymen, moreover, represented a further distillation of this unruly strain. "The same selective migrations that made the Teuton more self-assertive than the docile Slav or the quiescent Hindoo, have made the American more strong-willed and unmanageable than even the West European," he concluded.[40]

The high-flying racialism of this analysis seemed hardly to veil the determination of an academic-managerial elitist to bring under control a rival, entrepreneurial elite. Ross stated the problem, however, as one of unchecked individualism. In counterpoise he postulated—and designated as the theme of his *Social Control*—"a kind of collective mind" emerging from "the interactions of individuals and generations" to safeguard "the collective welfare from the ravages of egoism." The collective mind might have to rely on "institutions of control" which he elsewhere described as "fossiliferous"—legal, political, religious, and other institutions which necessarily partook much of the customary and traditional. There were "cases in which the discrediting of tradition is like picking out the mortar that holds together the fabric of society," he conceded. "The withering interrogation of all maxims, doctrines, and ideals by men without a sense of the past may lead to a denial of everything save one's own will."[41]

It was an almost tragic realization for Ross that social control was based, more than anything else, on the "domination of the living by the dead." While resisting their sway, he was willing to concede the deceased a vote. "The dead count as a social element," he believed, "for their recorded experience and transmitted institutions may be stalwart factors in the life of their descendants. When the living acknowledge an initial presumption in favor of whatever has survived from the past, yet preserve toward it a scrutinizing critical attitude, the generations are in proper balance." He consequently proposed "rational imitation" as a solution to the problem, based on the unexceptionable proposition that it is best to keep that which is inherited from the past until something better is found.[42]

If tradition could, in this qualified fashion, serve the purposes of rational social control, it could also, Ross discovered, preserve and nurture the life of the individual. Despite his strictures upon unrestrained individualism, this was a crucial point. "In blood and bone," Ross was certain, "the Western man is *individualist*, and most so is the American, the product of the last, most Westerly decanting of the Germanic race." Tradition would be hard to justify unless it could be shown to offer support to the individual and an alternative to the limitations of what Ross called a "canned life." As with so many others, misgivings about the plight of the individual in conditions of modernity led to a more receptive view of the traditional.[43]

Ross was greatly indebted, as he acknowledged, to the French sociologist Gabriel de Tarde, especially in the writing of *Social Psychology*. He followed the argument of Tarde's "incomparable" *Lois de l'imitation* that "everything which is social and non-vital or non-physical in the phenomena of societies is caused by imitation." Social imitation took the two great forms of custom and convention, which alternated dominance according to a cyclical pattern, as Ross put it, of *"outlook and backlook."* Despite agreement on these basic points, differences of nuance and emphasis between the Frenchman and the American were revealing.[44]

With little of Ross's reluctance, Tarde viewed the role of tradition as largely benign. Innovations were rooted in customs and traditions, he pointed out, and conversely "any invention or novelty . . . would perish still-born" without the force of tradition to conserve and propagate it. It would be too much to characterize this as a European viewpoint, but it was perhaps indicative of transatlantic differences. European social scientists who were so disposed seemed better equipped to defend the customary and traditional than their American counterparts. Aside from Tarde's rather mechanical linkage of novelty and tradition,

European society provided a context within the thickness of which custom and tradition appeared as more complex phenomena than they did to Ross. For instance, like Ross, Ferdinand Tönnies decried Chinese foot-binding as an absurd and cruel custom, but he attributed it largely to the effort of the upper class to distinguish itself rather than to a simple effort to subjugate women. And despite such admitted enormities, Tönnies characterized custom (*Sitte*) as in the main a humane institution, a natural support of community life which provided particular protection for those lacking in the resources of power: for the old, for women and children, for strangers and the poor. It provided a "counterpoise" especially to the legal privileges of males, he elaborated, giving women their "unique rank."[45]

Ross had no interest in promoting custom and tradition as mainstays of gemeinschaft, which he assumed in the proper scheme of things would steadily succumb to progress. Nor did he recognize in them the special defenses of the weak. Yet they could appeal in a roundabout way to his basic American individualism. "Backlook" as well as "outlook" threatened the imagined autonomy of the individual. It was backlook which more readily drew his scorn. Not even progressive America could avoid such retrospective currents as those he observed in the "revival of historical studies, in the formation of hereditary patriotic societies, and in the dread of 'drifting away from the ancient landmarks.'" On the other hand, he was uncomfortably aware that insofar as traditionalist "obscurantism" had faded in modern society, the result had been largely "to put one kind of imitation in place of another. Instead of aping their forefathers, people now ape the many." Conversely, "when it is not Mrs. Grundy that coerces, it is tradition."[46]

Other-directedness, as David Riesman would later call it, was clearly as fatal to individuality as a surfeit of custom and tradition. It was not without a strong undercurrent of regret, therefore, that Ross observed that tradition no longer served so effectively to give meaning to life. When in this mood he recurred repeatedly to images of drift. Although traditionalism could impede socialization, he pointed out, "traditions of friendship and mutual aid may perpetuate good feeling when living currents of interest are bearing people in opposite directions." But, he feared, "we moderns are like mariners on a ship sailing an uncharted sea. We cannot lay our course in the light of the experience of our ancestors." Again, there were too many modern minds "that, broken from the old moorings of custom, drift without helm or anchor at the mercy of wind and tide, . . . social derelicts."[47]

Even more in the vein of twentieth-century anxiety was the fear, to which Ross gave occasional clear expression, that the weakening sway of tradition reduced the individual in some crippling fashion. "The main prop of custom is not the fear of the ancestral gods," he wrote in 1901, "but the dread of self-mutilation. For to give up the customary is to alienate portions of one's self, to tear away the sheath that protects our substance." This bleak prospect suggested the need for a larger conception of personality. Socialization, Ross realized, could be understood as an expansion of the individual, producing in one dimension "the linear self, which keeps to the family line, ranging back among one's ancestors—particularly the illustrious—and forward among one's anticipated descendants." From one so frequently hostile to tradition, this was a striking acknowledgment of how ineluctably the individual lived in it.[48]

None of his misgivings about the detachment or mutilation of the modern individual made Ross a traditionalist, but they contributed to a modern re-envisioning of tradition—a sense that the past is not authoritative but is inescapably present, or re-created, in our conscious lives. The nineteenth century had become more fully aware of the processes of time than any previous age, in the forms of evolution, history, and tradition; it thereby discovered the full weight of the past on the individual. The instinct of liberals and Progressives was to seek escape from this crushing burden. The twentieth century seemed to an unprecedented degree, and for both better and worse, to escape it, but discovered anomie, alienation, self-mutilation. Ross was one of those who glimpsed the possibility that tradition, accepted selectively and provisionally, could strengthen a society of free individuals—that the past might be not merely the danger to the soul which he had feared in 1891, but also a source of the soul's sustenance.

Others perceived this more clearly. In September of 1904 another midwestern sociologist, Charles Horton Cooley, visited the New York

"Ghetto"—a term Cooley took from contemporary usage to denote the Jewish section on the Lower East Side of the city. Cooley's reaction to the Ghetto dwellers, which combined fascination with respect and admiration, contrasted sharply with Ross's response to immigrant populations during the same period. Cooley, further, was capable of making the Ghetto a counterpart of Fiske's New England Town, Cram's monastic community, and the Virginians' plantation: a model or type of an idealized larger society.

Cooley was not entirely unprepared to like what he saw; his Protestant background had bred in him a rather romantic attraction to the people whose history was the subject of the Old Testament. Professional interest reinforced biblical inspiration. The Jews seemed able to combine individual integrity and prophecy with cultural unity, originality with tradition, in ways that Cooley had been searching for since beginning his career as a sociologist. He wrote his fiancée in 1889 of the strong appeal the Old Testament prophets had for him:

> Here is a vigorous priesthood, half-democratic, half-hereditary, holding a wayward people for unknown centuries to political unity and a noble conception of God. The prophets are ascetic but, not like the Roman Catholic priests, cut off from wholesome sympathy with the people. They have wives and families. . . . They are the head and conscience of the nation. They mediate among the traditions and laws of the people and are charged with a half-fanatical, hierarchical patriotism. . . . I admire them intensely. . . . Such passionate visions come to men who contemn common ambitions and live for years in contemplation of some great and *living* truth.

Cooley's added comment that the world was awaiting such exceptional men in his own day contained an unconscious and sinister irony, coming just two months after the birth of Adolf Hitler. But his encomium on the prophets also suggested, with greater felicity, themes he would pursue throughout his career—above all the theme of the "I" and the "We," as Cooley termed it, and of their conciliation in society and the world.[49]

For most American Protestants, biblical prophets were one thing, Jewish and other immigrant groups in twentieth-century American cities quite another. Cooley himself admitted to being saddened by the diminution of the "English sentiment" in American life, but unlike those of Ross's mind-set he recognized in polyglot immigrant traditionalism a source of enrichment compensating for the fading of cultural strains older to America. In place of Ross's "lumps" and "clots" awaiting pulverization, Cooley offered a different metaphor. Many immigrant traditions, he noted with regret, were left behind or quickly lost. Yet "how poor American life would be without the immigrants," he exclaimed, "—strangely colored threads from the fabric of the old world come to enliven our texture!"[50]

This enthusiasm was evident in Cooley's East Side visit of 1904. "The Russian Jews are fascinating beyond anything I could have imagined," he reported—eager, clever, "many of the girls pretty and the children delightful." Yet he brought to the Ghetto something more than a tourist's readiness to be dazzled. Guided by his friend Jacob Billikopf and the social worker Florence Kelley, he observed with a professional eye and found much that confirmed both personal and scholarly predilections. He was pleased to discover that Ralph Waldo Emerson, a strong formative influence on his own thinking, had been translated into both Yiddish and Hebrew, and was much read. His perception of Jewish loyalty to family life could only have reinforced his sense of the family as the basic paradigm of social relationships, the most important of "primary groups."[51]

Cooley's enthusiasm fastened especially on the Jewish immigrants' sense of themselves as a people, which, combined with their intelligence and ambition, placed them above other immigrant groups in his estimation. After going with Billikopf to see the Yiddish play Die Wahrheit, Cooley provided his wife with a detailed summary of the plot. He was much moved, not only by the power of the play itself but by the "passionate interest" of the audience: "It was right out of their deepest experiences, those of an intellectual and sensitive but homeless race, struggling for a footing in an alien land. I never felt so strongly the meaning of the phrase 'a people' as I have here. . . . And they have the most intense national consciousness, right along with a great eagerness to become good Americans."[52]

The Jews' apparent determination to cherish their traditional life, even as they joined the American struggle to get ahead, resonated strongly with Cooley. This traditionism, he thought, provided a necessary matrix for a productive and creative life. Above all the Jews seemed to Cooley to conduct out of their tradition an uncompromising pursuit of truth—just as had the prophets. He generalized to himself about these phenomena with almost cryptic readiness; they clearly touched deep personal needs of his own. In musings occasioned by his visit to the East Side, Cooley wrote in his journal that "some tradition, some habit of thought, some organized system of suggestions and symbols there must be to keep one up to the clearer, higher, happier life. With me the need of truth, of mental reality, is the most persistent higher need. It lasts when love and fear fail."[53]

The discordant responses of Cooley and Ross to immigrant traditions provide an index to their differences as sociologists and human beings. Most to the point, Cooley expanded Ross's grudging recognition of the positive uses of tradition into a much more fully articulated vision. This implies no direct influence; of this there was little or none, although relations between the two men seem to have been cordial. Ross praised Cooley's first important work, *The Theory of Transportation* (1894), and assigned it to his students at Stanford. Cooley, who was inclined to view even the most brilliant of his contemporaries with a sharply critical eye, was less enthusiastic about his colleague. Conceding to him an "honest, noble and magnanimous" character, Cooley privately taxed Ross's work with a lack of unity and continuity,and concluded that he was not "a sane and weighty thinker." He perceived in Ross something of "the intellectual athlete playing with principles and similes; some lack of intimate human sympathy of a certain kind."[54]

Whatever the justice of Cooley's assessment, it pointed up a marked difference of temperament. Ross's personal style, at once witty and managerial, contrasted sharply with Cooley's earnest sympathy for the multitudinous expressions of human life as they ramified through space and time. And contrasting personalities were reflected in contrasting sociologies. Thomas Bender calls attention to a key difference between Ross and Cooley. Ross claimed to have formulated a distinction between "community" and "society" independently of Ferdinand Tönnies' far more celebrated dichotomy of gemeinschaft and gesellschaft. But whereas Tönnies believed that both forms of interaction would persist, Ross argued simply that in modern conditions community was progressively transformed into the less personal, more bureaucratized forms of society. Thus, as Bender concludes, "we find in Ross no sense of communal and associational patterns of social relations coexisting in modern society." Cooley, on the other hand, was one of a number of social thinkers who "maintained the dual perspective of Tönnies"—a position with much recent scholarly support.[55]

Believing in the paramount role of the "primary groups" of family and locality in shaping social consciousness, Cooley accordingly placed a higher valuation on the customary and traditionary qualities which such groups typically harbored. Ross found it difficult to recognize in tradition more than a hindrance to progress or a device for social control; Cooley more readily perceived in it a means to the reconciliation of individual and society within their modern arena. He accepted the loss of the authority of tradition in an unstable and pluralistic age, but insisted upon its power to guide, to enrich, and finally to make possible a transcendence of its own particularities.

This side of Cooley has been too little appreciated. To the extent that the sociologist's attitude toward tradition has been considered at all, it has usually been regarded as hostile. He was less inclined than some of his colleagues to view the human being as "a creature of tradition and habit," Ellsworth R. Fuhrman maintains, and Cooley himself advised against ultimate reliance on established usages. "It is well always to avoid that choice which is urged by custom or worldly interest," he observed late in life. "It is surely the choice you will repent in better moods, that will weigh down your character."[56]

Certainly Cooley was no traditionalist in the usual sense, not only because he was a Progressive social scientist interested in benign social change, but because of his strong Emersonian faith in the individual conscience in the greatest amplification of its sensibility. "Only our highest self; only God, if you please, should make important choices," he cautioned. From this quasi-Transcendentalist perspective society seen through Burkean spectacles was only a realm of illusion. "There is a world of tradition," he wrote in 1898—explaining the term with the emendations "appearance," "custom," and "as we are taught to see it"—

and a world of reality, the one bright but transient like the clouds at sunset, the other obscure, substantial, mysteriously real, like the dark earth beneath. One tells us of things as men have imagined them; a sharp line between right and wrong, definite commands with heaven for those who follow them and hell for those who disobey. The other is distinct in its near details, but vague and terrible in the distance. We are only a little part of it: its vast and inconceivably diverse life moves on with apparent indifference to us. It is unknown, yet apparently knowable and its unexplored modes of power draw us strongly while they humble and appall us. The more we look upon this the more trivial seems the other.

In this vision tradition was oddly ephemeral, capable in its persistence only of obscuring a reality too deep and mysterious to be more than glimpsed, perhaps, by the solitary seer.[57]

In less rarified contexts, however, Cooley fully appreciated the uses of tradition in informing this seer. If Ross was appalled by the thrall of the past which he found in Europe in the 1890s, Cooley, studying abroad not long before, rejoiced that the French had not "lost the past to anything like the degree that we have." He evinced a conventional enough appreciation of the Gothic cathedrals as a chief glory of that past, embodying as no comparable modern work a "communal idealism." They were "truly organic" in their incorporation of the "self-expression of the common man," he believed. The cathedrals represented for him a marvelously fertile combination of an ideal vision and a progressive architectural tradition. "Now the chain of practice is broken and the vision gone," he lamented—he did not entertain the hope, with Ralph Adams Cram, that either could truly be restored.[58]

Despite the extinction of the Gothic tradition, Cooley felt a personal connection to it that would have been foreign to Ross. "The men who built and carved the cathedrals were like me," he thought, "—I have their passion when I carve at my oaken table." His medieval predecessors were more skilled, he acknowledged, and were better supported by custom and institutions; yet he had "the same native feeling" and in different social conditions might have been a master builder or sculptor rather than an amateur carpenter. But what failed as modern career plan succeeded as metaphor. "Life should be as single in design and as rich in detail as a great cathedral," Cooley wrote his fiancée, Elsie Jones, in 1890. "Every act should be a necessary part of the whole." Cooley recurred to the image often, using it to express the "organic" unity which honored the integrity of particulars in the continuity of time. It had a special application to his profession. "How closely are sociology and architecture connected!" he exclaimed. "Scarcely a social tradition powerful and enduring but is in some way embodied in architecture." He aspired to the architectonic in his life as in his work.[59]

In this endeavor Cooley succeeded better than most who seek to make of practical existence a work of art. He grew up in the university town of Ann Arbor, where his father, Thomas McIntyre Cooley, was on the faculty of the University of Michigan Law School. His father was appointed to the Michigan Supreme Court in 1864, the year of his son's birth. In later life father and son struggled with a relationship which was "sympathetic but strained." Charles reacted against his father's laissez-faire individualism, which was highly principled—as a judge he had ordered a black student admitted to a theretofore all-white school—but in his son's view too narrow. Perhaps most significant for the son's professional development was Charles's conception of the family as a nursery of fellow-feeling in contrast to Thomas's sense that it represented individual independence and success.[60]

Rather sickly in his youth, Charles sought in the manner of Theodore Roosevelt to build himself up through rugged summers of outdoor life and physical labor in Colorado and North Carolina. He passed a year of travel and study in Europe in 1884, which included a mountain-climbing expedition in Switzerland. Cooley graduated from the University of Michigan in 1887 with a degree in engineering, worked for a time as a draughtsman, and was later employed by the Interstate Commerce Commission and the Census Bureau in Washington, D.C. He married Elsie Jones in 1891.[61]

His interest in sociology stimulated by a systematic reading of the works of Herbert Spencer, Cooley took a doctorate in that field in 1894, studying under such eminent scholars as Franklin Henry Giddings and John Dewey. He subsequently embarked upon a career of teaching and writing at the University of Michigan, which ended only with his death in 1929. Although by present standards he was more of an armchair analyst than a scientific researcher, Cooley's distinguished trilogy, *Human Nature and the Social Order* (1902), *Social Organization* (1909), and *Social Process* (1918) established him as one of the founders of American sociology. His conceptions of the "primary group" and the "looking-glass self," especially, gave him a significant and enduring influence in the social sciences. More broadly, as Edward Shils concludes, Cooley contributed (along with Robert Park, W. I. Thomas, John Dewey, and George Herbert Mead) to a "conception of society as an anonymous moral order, of institutions bearing traditions and changing them, of a perpetual strain towards and away from consensus, of conflicts among individuals and groups for a better standing and a larger share . . . [which] still persists."[62]

Cooley's groundbreaking sociology issued, in large measure, from the exigencies of his personal life, and life was for him a constant problem of the "I" and the "We." His personality was grounded in a distinctly Victorian tangle of tortured but resolute individualism, a strong emotional need to belong to a social whole, and a mediating and urgent sense of social duty. In some ways, indeed, the young Cooley seems the quintessential Victorian. His journals voluminously and repetitively record his acute awareness of duty as well as his aspirations to a higher, more spiritual life. In his earlier entries, especially, he evinced a concern for "purity" and distrust of "sensuality" which would seem strange to people born after the turn of the century. His struggles to subdue his vanity and ambition— "ambition to me is suicide," he noted grimly—seem even to reach back through the Victorian milieu to earlier times, to the introspective agonies of Puritan diarists. Certainly his scruples over whether or not he really deserved pay raises and promotions placed him closer to the Saints of New England than to most twentieth-century academics. He sensed the affinity: "Surely my forefathers were Pilgrims and I must have some of their virility in me," he urged himself. Whatever its precise provenance, Cooley's moralism suffused his work. "I want to be a scholar in righteousness, to be taught all the ways of strength and truth," he wrote while still a student. As a professor of thirty-eight he observed with all indications of accuracy that "when I think most largely nothing satisfies me that does not have a moral outcome."[63]

Like many Victorians of the upper and middle classes, Cooley fell into a pattern of isolated infirmity, although with him it occurred early, and he was strong-willed enough largely to master his difficulties. The exact mixture of physical and psychological causes can probably not be known, but his exaggerated dutifulness seems at least symptomatic. He himself reflected late in life that "my principal mistake as a boy and a young man was that I tried too hard intellectually and morally," with consequences which he thought had been deleterious to his health. His illness received at one time a dubious diagnosis of malaria; on the mental side he recalled years of "chronic neurasthenia." Constipation, which was also chronic in his youth, seems to have been especially demoralizing and psychologically isolating. Prescriptions of arsenic did nothing to alleviate his misery, unsurprisingly, and Turkish baths proved of less avail than the strenuous life in the Rockies and Smokies.[64]

His ailments helped to throw Cooley into an early and intense introversion. His constipation was aggravated by "an almost incredible shyness," he remembered in maturity. "It made me unlike other boys, so that my inner life proceeded with an intensity and apartness hardly normal." He eventually achieved an adequate social competence. Yet the "passion for introspection," as he called it, remained with him for the rest of his life. "I look upon myself as having a peculiar call to stand apart from the world," reads a representative journal entry; "society is not for me," wrote the student of the social self on another occasion. He was aware of the paradox, characterizing himself in his innovative work in sociology as an "isolated adventurer." The term was a dramatic one for an often cloistered intellectual, but not too dramatic for Cooley's I in pursuit of its We.[65]

Yet on a deeper level Cooley found in his psychological inwardness the very means to breaking out of his isolation. Introspection, he concluded late in his career, was "a normal and common process, without which we could know very little about life." Awareness of one's own thoughts and feelings, he argued, was indispensable for insight into the minds of others. He believed that this applied in the new technique of psychoanalysis, but equally it gave him the sense that he could "relate" (in today's lingo) to men and women of the past, as they appeared in history or tradition. As a younger man he had discovered his empathy with the medieval cathedral-builders, and later he cited the even more remote subjects of Herodotus as figures accessible through likenesses of their inner life to that of moderns. Introspection was thus a key to the wealth of past human experience. The dinosaur may have left behind her eggs, Cooley remarked; "man deposits a fossil mind"—a mind, however, which was anything but dead to one who knew his own.[66]

In the religious sphere as well, Cooley recognized that inwardness could feed a deeper sympathy. He often described his search for a "We" in religious language, and this is not misleading as to its ultimate character. His life and work demonstrate how attenuated a theology is compatible with an intensely religious temperament. Virtually an agnostic in doctrinal terms, he identified God with the highest human ideals and aspirations without quite denying to Him a dimension of transcendence. Retaining a facility in religious modes of expression, he retained as well a Protestant confidence in the invincibility of the individual alone with his God. Even the society of which the individual was a part yielded to the sanctity of this bond. "I would do everything I do in the inmost spirit of truth, as God manifests it through me, so that no work of mine could be the work of another," he wrote at fifty. "I avoid with disgust whatever has no individual flavor. To be true is to be unique."[67]

The culminating American expression of such views had been the Protestantism above Protestantism known as Transcendentalism, and Cooley wholeheartedly embraced the leading exponents of this school. He recognized in Henry David Thoreau a paragon of withdrawal, integrity, and purity, but Ralph Waldo Emerson, if a shade "too clever and hortatory," was the more useful guide for a sociologist obliged to make his way in the American world. Like others who left their marks on the Progressive Age, Cooley early found in Emerson an uplifting alternative to religious orthodoxy, and the attraction never entirely faded. "I think his influence has been stronger and better over me than that of any other one mind," Cooley wrote his fiancée in 1888, and near the end of his life he cited Emerson, Goethe, and Darwin, rather than colleagues in his immediate field, as those who had most influenced him as a sociologist. He admired Emerson for his "intellectual unconstraint," faith in the individual, and the supremely high and pure expression which he believed the Sage of Concord had given to the spiritual impulses of his age. He loved Emerson, in sum, for the soundest of Emersonian reasons: "This is his bottom fact; if this is not true nothing is. A man's first duty is to live, not according to the world but according to himself. If there still linger, in this generation, the notion that the divine light is in some way outside of man and not within him; at that Emerson strikes as at the root of all evil." Cooley later expressed this lesson in authenticity more succinctly in a letter to his fiancée: "I think the first duty of a man or woman is to be himself, or herself," he wrote.[68]

Cooley saw clearly, however, that the self was not entirely of self-manufacture, even if it might be of self-definition. Introspection summoned forth its antithesis: the need, which Cooley felt keenly, to plumb his relationship with others, through society, through tradition, ultimately through the communion of ideals and aspirations which he knew as "God." This was not of course only a personal problem, and it resonated more strongly in Cooley's professional work because he perceived it to belong with particular acuteness to his time and place. The several decades bisected by the turn of the century seemed clearly an age of the disintegration and reconstruction of social institutions. American cities especially seemed full of the detritus "of the old order looking for a place in the new: men without trades, immigrants with alien habits and traditions, country boys and girls who have broken loose from their families and from early ties and beliefs." He was aware that new customs and traditions, institutions and standards, could not be "created in a moment." Yet he could not but contrast the impersonal business corporation or labor union unfavorably with the medieval guild in its rich social, aesthetic, and religious dimensions.[69]

This was not a random example. Cooley joined Ralph Adams Cram, Henry Adams, and many others for whom the Middle Ages signified an "organic" or unified social ideal as an alternative to modern "multiplicity." But the strength of Cooley's insistence on individual vision, juxtaposed with his equally strong insistence on community, gave to his medievalist strain its own flavor. He found an irresistible appeal in Thomas à Kempis, to whose *Imitation of Christ* he repaired frequently throughout his adult life. The fifteenth-century mystic represented a soaring spiritual aspiration, combined with an "intensified fellow-feeling," which struck the deepest chords in him. Thomas seemed a late-medieval Thoreau, but a Thoreau whose spirituality flourished within a community.[70]

Thomas's Brethren of the Common Life appealed to Cooley for the same reason as did the Ghetto: the brotherhood seemed to combine the gemeinschaft of the "primary group" with an uncompromising individual pursuit of the highest truths. But Cooley drew back from the monastic ideal, which even more than the Ghetto required a separation from society at large. He must do his work in the world, he regretfully concluded, even at the cost of moral purity. Nevertheless his sociology was a quest to realize the vision of the Brethren by scientific means. Thomas had sought God by withdrawing from the world and achieving harmony within the limited and simplified life of the monastery. "If we are to find God and harmony in the world must it not be by reducing the world to law?" Cooley asked, recurring to the subject years later.[71]

This was the project of Cooley's sociology, in which an element of religious exaltation was retained. "Can I see our ideal of democracy as a joyous whole and make my readers see it so?" he quizzed himself of a work in progress in 1915. "Nothing less will do." Like many Americans, Cooley understood the "ideal of democracy" to encompass far more than popular government and such associated benefits as equal opportunity and civil rights. In its larger connotations—intellectually vague but emotionally compelling—it signified as well a community life of mutual respect and neighborliness, happiness not only pursued but achieved, "home" truly become "homeland." The ideal, he was obliged to admit, was far from the reality. As a young traveler not overly impressed with Germans in other ways, he had been entranced by Munich gemütlichkeit, for which there seemed no counterpart in busy America. "Our American life, promising in many ways, is hurried, superficial and common," he lamented in 1901; twenty-seven years later, shortly before his death, he remained disappointed that it had "not matured its forms, it is crude, riotous, wasteful." And escapist—in an unusually acerbic comment he compared a movie theater to an opium joint: "people pay and give themselves to sensuous dreaming."[72]

To realize the "ideal of democracy as a joyous whole" the conventional American prescription would once have started with liberation from the past. For Cooley, on the contrary, the problem was American newness, compounded by an excess of social mobility. Without yielding any of his faith in democracy, he concluded that his country simply lacked the store of tradition adequate to support its ideal expression. "Our life is, in general, so shifting, that little moss grows on it," he observed. "We lack traditionary character, culture and depth." Without "monuments of the past," Americans had, indeed, no real culture—"only a jangle of more or less creditable aspirations."[73]

Unlike those inclined to measure progress by the standardizing tendencies of modern life, Cooley discerned in diverse traditions an abundance capable of contributing to the richness of a common society. He was therefore dismayed to observe a creeping sameness in what passed for a national culture. Almost everything, he complained, suffered from "*panmixia*, like the flavors of a boarding-house dinner." He attributed this dispiriting uniformity to the circumstances of history—"Europe being a complex of ancient and settled divisions, while America is a new and assimilative region"—and could only hope that time might supply his country with its own kinds of diversities and traditions.[74]

Cooley's strictures upon American culture were not those of a reactionary or spiritual expatriate. "There is nothing more myself than America," he wrote in his journal in November of 1918, and the claim was more than post-Armistice patriotism. He was American enough to welcome the demise of traditions which stood in the way of progress. But the general thinness of culture which he observed in the United States entailed a cost, he realized, to his "social self." Without the nurturing of tradition, people were thrown back upon "immediate human nature," and although this could stimulate such frontier virtues as plain dealing, hospitality, and courage, it could also encourage sensual excess, pride, and caprice—none of which was a virtue in Cooley's scale of values.[75]

Cooley's sense of the importance of tradition helped to shape his sociology from the beginning, contributing to his crucial break with Herbert Spencer. As a young scholar whose interests were shifting toward sociology, Cooley had assiduously studied the great British autodidact, more attracted by "his general conception of the progressive organization of life" than by his specific views, as he recalled, and instructed by his systematic methodology. Yet even while explaining to his fiancée the need to master Spencerian fundamentals, he characterized Spencer as "a very cramped and one-sided man," and within a year had concluded with youthful self-confidence that "soon I must find somebody deeper or write my own books." Defections from Spencer were common enough, but Cooley described his as "one of the earliest and most complete." It was also influential. Cooley's objection that Spencer treated individual and society as different and irreconcilable aspects of reality—contrary to the younger man's germinating conception of the "social self"—helped to lead American sociology away from Spencerian precepts.[76]

Cooley's criticism of Spencer hardened as he settled into his career. He coupled Spencer's system with Tarde's in appealing to "the passion for simplification and to the mechanizing impulse," he wrote in 1909. "It is not human, not sociology in any intimate sense." Spencer could "see things in the large," he conceded, but the Englishman was oblivious to the detail without which genuine society vanished into abstraction. He suggested a uniformity which was false to life, and Cooley, in consequence, began to find him simply tedious. "He is so consistent that his works are but an elaboration of certain chapters in his 'First Principles,'" the young sociologist complained in 1895. "You go on and on in his road, but the climate and the scenery never change." Such monotony could never accommodate the vagaries and idiosyncrasies of tradition, which Cooley observed as a sociologist and cherished as a human being. At bottom, perhaps, his revulsion was aesthetic. The "human mind working through tradition is an artist," he remarked, "and creates types which go beyond nature."[77]

Lacking a feel for "the traditional, social, and personal elements" of culture, Spencer tried to explain too much by a sharp dichotomy between egoism and altruism. A true sociological view, Cooley thought, would be that "the higher sentiments are in general neither egotistic nor altruistic as regards their source, but just social, derived, that is, from the stream of an organic common life." The proof, he added, lay in the often-observed fact that group customs and mores could make almost anything appear to the individual as right or wrong. Spencer's position seemed tantamount to maintaining that such ideas as that of justice were "created anew in each generation," while failing to see that they also represented "the accumulated wisdom of the past." The English philosopher dealt well enough with the biological and individual terms of evolution but, as Cooley summed it up, had "little perception of a social organism continuous with the past."[78]

Spencer's failure to define any clear social plane of development meant that for him, as for his American follower John Fiske, tradition tended to be subsumed as a phase of human evolution, removed from the strictly biological but part of the same grand process. For Cooley, the evolutionary and the traditional were not only distinct but even opposed. The child at birth, he pointed out, "represents the race stock or hereditary factor in life in antithesis to the factor of tradition, communication and social organization." Tradition was no blind genetic phenomenon, but the product—although fallible and often obscure—of human intelligence and will. The distinction was a key one, for it brought tradition into the realm of public goods. It was not an unfortunate or merely necessary legacy of an earlier stage of social evolution, but a part of the life which Cooley described as "one great whole, a kinship, unified by a common descent and by common principles of existence." Further, it was passed on not by "animal transmission" but by "communication or social transmission," and hence subject to a normal public scrutiny.[79]

Influenced by John Dewey and the German sociologist and economist A. E. F. Schaffle (who helped his American colleague to see the social importance of communications), Cooley constructed a sociology at sharp variance with what seemed to him the rigidities of Herbert Spencer. He became a pioneer of the "interactionist" school of social psychology—further developed by Dewey, George Herbert Mead, and others—which deemphasized biological givens in favor of "the actual field of interpersonal interaction as the primary source of social organization."[80] Not set over against society as Americans often imagined, the "individual" self was in reality a social self. "We get our self-consciousness, our confidence and poise, from interaction with other people, from the continuous experience of social self-expression," Cooley explained. In one aspect, indeed, the social self was a "looking-glass self": consciousness of oneself directly reflected the perceptions of oneself which one attributed to others. (Here the dialectic was between the "I" and the "Me," as John Patrick Diggins notes—between the self as subject and the self as object.)[81]

Especially influential in his field was Cooley's idea of the "primary group," according to which the self was shaped through face-to-face association and cooperation. Among such groups the family was pre-eminent as the taproot of human relationships, the rightful type of all larger societies. "Perhaps we may characterize all social development as a striving to extend to all relations the felt joy of child-love and mother-love," he suggested as early as 1895. He developed this insight into a conception of the family as the model for the "sympathetic, christian [sic] organization of life," which it was the work of progress to elaborate in the larger social order. "We must demand of all social relationships that they be such, in spirit, as prevail in a good family, in a loyal fellowship. There is nothing to which this is not applicable," he concluded.[82]

Cooley grounded his quest for a nexus of "I" and "We" in a sociology which provided for "carrying the home outward" in a new way. No longer a celebration of pioneering or imperial expansion, this vision in Cooley's rendering relied upon modern means of transportation and communication to enlarge the sphere of domestic goods. These goods proliferated on the temporal plane as well. Human evolution was distinguished from that of animals, Cooley pointed out, by "its cumulative character. Through language and other symbols we preserve the results of the past in a continuous and growing social heritage upon which all our progress rests. Conservation, then, is at the root of everything: we must cherish and preserve the good already achieved, and there is a presumption that whatever has been preserved in the past has in it something of value for the future."[83]

This analysis diverged sharply from the presumption of Ward and Ross that the older a custom or tradition, the less value it retained. The difference is ascribable partly to the character of Cooley's idealism; he conceived of the social organism above all as a mental construct, and accorded tradition a prominent role within it. "The great institutions are the outcome of that organization which human thought naturally takes on when it is directed for age after age upon a particular subject," as he put it, "and so gradually crystallizes in definite forms—enduring sentiments, beliefs, customs and symbols." The last was no negligible category; in an idealist perspective the community might well embrace personages of divine or otherwise symbolic character. Thus Henry Adams had shown the Virgin Mary to be a most important member of the medieval social order, Cooley pointed out, and he appeared to sympathize with Adams's regret that the modern world lacked its own such representation of psychic unity.[84]

Yet Cooley did not permit an idealist pull toward unity to procure a closed system. His social organism composed neither the "block universe" abhorred by William James nor the blind flow of energy represented by Adams's anti-Virgin, the Dynamo. He could say, as he did in *Human Nature and the Social Order*, that the individual derived his very life "from the whole through social and hereditary transmission as truly as if men were literally one body." But individuals in his thinking were not after all only cells in an organism; the integrity of the parts was as important as the unity of the whole. Holding the question of freedom and determinism to be strictly "meaningless in an organic system of thought," he nevertheless regarded a practical indeterminacy as integral to it. Freedom itself was "organic," he concluded—it consisted, that is, not in an ability to act independently of society, but in the opportunity to accomplish "a fresh organization of life." Although there could be no break with history and environment, determinism need not be inferred from continuity. Rather, he postulated "a plastic heredity prepared to submit itself to the guidance of environment as interpreted by intelligence." Freedom consequently required "an orderly process of growth," and flourished best within a well-articulated social order. Yet no less than William James, he believed that "life would be intolerable . . . without something original and venturesome at the heart of it."[85]

From the interplay of venture and continuity emerged the "social process," multiform yet indivisible. Central to Cooley's idea of the social process was the notion that human beings, with their congeries of associations, traditions, institutions, and ideals, were radically interdependent, the growth of each individual or collectivity taking place "in contact and interaction with that of others." The process was often obscure. "There is something rank and vague about human life," Cooley wrote, "like the growth of plants in the dark"—adding, however, that the growth was toward the light. But Cooley preferred vagueness to doctrines he viewed as one-sided or reductionist. He allowed that psychoanalysis was "immensely suggestive and stimulating: the human mind is indeed a cave swarming with strange life," but he felt that it had been worked out without appreciation that "the individual mind is part of a social process." Similarly, he was willing to entertain a "moderate behaviorism" and perceived a pragmatic value in behaviorist methods, but observed that by themselves they issued in "particularism, the isolation of an aspect of life."[86]

The intent of Cooley's sociology was to achieve precisely the opposite: to combine apparent antinomies and create a scheme encompassing all human social phenomena. Cooley retained the Victorian penchant for universal system building without the Victorian insistence on absolutes, hierarchies, and bipolarities. He was impatient, for instance, with the perennial heredity-environment debate. More promising than this "quasi-metaphysical antithesis," he thought, would be a hypothesis postulating "human life as a single organic process in which the germ-plasm, the social process and the various phases of individual development have complementary functions." Just as our bodies, although the products of heredity, also form part of our environment, so conversely do phenomena of our environment like movies and automobiles serve as expressions of our organic life, he suggested.[87]

Corollary reasoning led Cooley to deny an opposition between environment and tradition—so often cited as the social counterpart of heredity. Taking a broad view of environment, he established the basis for an equally broad view of tradition as a perennial force in human affairs. In the case of "imaginative persons," he argued, environment might "extend itself to almost any ideas that the past or present life of the race has brought into being." In this view the traditional became increasingly part of the intellectual environment with the passage of time. He cited as example the Gothic architecture of northern France, so "splendid" and "dramatic" an innovation in twelfth-century culture, but hardly appreciated for its distinctive features until much later. This was to agree with Auguste Comte that the empire of the dead increases over the living, but with far more positive implications. Cooley was suggesting the kind of weight that tradition can have in modern life—not the oppressive weight of an inert mass, but the pervasive weight of an atmosphere, necessary for one to draw a social breath.[88]

Cooley's sense of tradition as part of the environment suggested the modification of a further dichotomy, that of tradition and convention, which had become influential largely through Tarde's *Les lois de l'imitation*. "Tradition," Cooley acknowledged, "comes down from the past, while convention arrives, sidewise as it were, from our contemporaries; the fireside tales and maxims of our grandparents illustrate the one, the fashions of the day the other." In the standard comparison, medieval society was traditional and modern society conventional. But Cooley found the description inadequate, for in reality tradition and convention were not opposites or even separate from each other. Traditional usages were conventional for the groups which observed them, he pointed out, and enforced by the same informal sanctions. Conversely, conventions might also be traditions: "The new fashions are adaptations of old ones, and there are no really new ideas of any sort, only a gradual transformation of those that have come down from the past." Tradition and convention, in sum, were simply different phases of the same continuous "transmission of thought."[89]

Having reduced such artificial antinomies, Cooley pointed to the role of tradition in specific departments of modern society. The real life of the Constitution, for obvious example, derived from the accumulated ideas of generations of jurisprudence; the written document itself was simply "an Ark of the Covenant, ensuring the integrity of the tradition." Religion had necessarily the same character, he thought, for even the most exalted sentiment needed forms of expression which only tradition and usage could provide. The arts no less required traditions to nurture individual genius, and when traditions became attenuated, as he believed they had in his own time, art suffered accordingly. Even science had to pursue its empirical investigations within a framework of traditional method and precept.[90]

Education and scholarship, to which Dewey and others imparted an anti-traditionalist bias during the first part of the twentieth century, remained for Cooley properly tradition-based activities. On the lower levels, at least, tradition supplied an essential morality: "The great thing in the education of children," he declared, "is to have, in the school, a strong current of good tradition running, in which a child may be placed and so floated into integrity, honor, purity, industry, and the like." On an advanced level, he emphasized, universities furnished the matrices of cumulative scholarly endeavor needed for creative work. They might also, he suggested, draw upon the best traditions of the community at large to serve as model communities governed by ideals of service.[91]

Recognizing the pervasive presence of tradition in environment, convention, and institutions, Cooley liberated it from narrow definitions which suggested that it was irrelevant or obstructive to modern life. This gave him a somewhat distinctive place among Progressives and pragmatists; at least it would be difficult to ascribe to Cooley the view that John Patrick Diggins ascribed to John Dewey, that "culture was useless to the extent to which it concerned the past." Cooley saw more clearly, perhaps—or drew more positive implications from the perception—that the past and present necessarily involve each other. And understanding tradition as properly a source of individuality and possibility rather than as a limitation upon them, he found for it a human space between the determining hand of the biological or historical past and a disembodied presentist rationalism—between William Graham Sumner's rigorous application of natural selection to society and the rather airless planning which Lester Frank Ward's "Sociocracy" now suggests.[92]

For Cooley this would not have been a human space had it not been also in some aspect a sacred space, a meeting ground of the striving social self with its highest possibilities—with God, as Cooley said. Enduring, progressively unfolding traditions, transcending particularities of time and place, could indicate these possibilities. Cooley's religious temperament conditioned his receptivity to tradition, placing him in a familiar generational context while withholding something of his essence from any facile pigeonholing. Broadly, he fell into a pattern

characteristic of the educated and progressive-minded of his generation, retaining a strong religious impulse from the wreckage of late
Victorian doubt, but seeking a replacement for creeds no longer credible. The God who answered to this summons was one immanent in
society, most fully in democratic society, as Jean B. Quandt suggests,
and He signified a social salvation.[93]

This quasi-theology offered at least a provisional solution to the
core problem of Cooley's thought. He viewed Christianity, with which
he continued closely to identify, as an ineluctably social phenomenon;
Jesus, it seemed clear, had commanded his followers "to live in the *we*
rather than in the *I*." To follow this precept made of religion, he
believed, "a powerful instrument of social unification," signifying the
loyalty of the individual to the group and its culture. This was a loyalty,
he believed, which could in a fashion surmount the limitations of mortality. He speculated that "an intense sense of the general social life will
perhaps replace that definite belief in an individual future after death
that now seems no longer possible."[94]

Religion so conceived seemed merely the echo of faith in a secular
world, never more so than when Cooley defined his own as "only conscience determined by ideals." Yet "ideals" covered a lot of ground; they
were shaped, he added, by institutions, traditions, and creeds. And
however we might see his significance as a thinker today, his own
impulse seemed as much to sacralize the secular as to secularize the
sacred. The "We," conceived as mere society, did not quite absorb an
"I" capable of its own transcendent insights and visions. Despite his
more abstract formulations of divinity, Cooley's religious sensibility
insisted on something very like a personal deity. God remained for him
an intimate and active although by his own acknowledgment necessarily "vague" presence. "It helps me sometimes to think of myself as a
delicate instrument for the divine will to play upon," he wrote to his
fiancée in his mid-twenties. The important thing was "absolute self-
abandonment and willingness for something better than self to fill you
and raise you up." Suggestive of the conversion experience, the comment represented as well an abiding sense of spiritual service. "If I do a
good work," he noted later, "it is after all done *through* me; it is God
working by means of me."[95]

This formulation was, of course, well in keeping with Christian tradition, and other basic Christian precepts helped Cooley to find the religious terms to express the relationship between the individual and the social body. He restated the old prescription to be in the world but not of the world. "To be strong and significant a man must be at once quite separate from other men and perfectly united to them," was how he put it. Cooley appeared also to draw on the biblical proposition that there is one spirit but many gifts. God's love was offered to all, he remarked; yet with this outreaching 'we' there comes also a distinctive 'I,' an 'I' that seeks its own modes of service." But even in making use of the peculiar talents of His servants, this was a God of continuity and development. If Cooley's contemporary, the philosopher Josiah Royce, conceived of God as a great community of wills, Cooley's preferred and reiterated term was "Process"—"the process of God in human life," he noted briefly in his journal. "That, I take it, is my subject."⁹⁶

Idealist and pragmatic elements in Cooley's thought met in this idea of the "process of God," and in so doing they helped to define the uses of tradition. This was not an outcome which all Americans of the time would have expected. Tradition seemed allied with ideals increasingly at odds with social realities and simply in the way of pragmatic solutions to social problems. That tradition itself could have a pragmatic character was not a possibility that announced itself with any confidence to the Progressive mind-set, certainly. Yet for Cooley tradition played a doubly pragmatic role: having arisen as he assumed to meet practical needs, it continued to provide resources for solving practical problems and constructing a better society; and when so employed it pointed beyond itself to enduring and even transcendent verities which made the universe "work."

Cooley came to his pragmatism by that double Victorian path which offered on one side faith in progress and on the other faith in the possibilities of the individual in his ultimate freedom and integrity. When progress came to be encased in an iron determinism, as it seemed to with Herbert Spencer's law of evolution, the contradiction inherent in this double path became apparent, and Cooley was part of the journey of thought which during his lifetime struggled to reconcile authentic personal choice with the promise of social betterment. Instructed by

Emerson and Thoreau in the primacy of the individual, schooled in the continuities of evolution, he felt keenly the need to find room within the social process for the quotidian, indeterminate mutability of life.

Progressive evolution in the Spencerian mode, as Cooley perceived it, offered only a false movement, a progression past never-changing scenery. "Is not a new logic necessary?" he asked at the beginning of the new century, "a logic of life, motion or process?" Contrary to the established practice of conceiving of phenomena as at least provisionally fixed, and motion as "a series of stations," he thought, "the *movement* of organic life is of the essence of it; our science must teach us to see it as systematic flux." This has a strong Bergsonian ring ("the flux of time is the reality itself, and the things which we study are the things which flow," Henri Bergson wrote in *Creative Evolution*), and although rather slighting of the Frenchman as lacking personal weight, Cooley recognized in his work a confirmation of his own conception of the "onward impulse" of humanity.[97]

Flux, of course, was not incompatible with direction—either historical or moral. It permitted a moral universe in which good and evil, right and wrong, remained sharply distinct qualities in themselves, but were not to be sorted out by absolute rules of conduct. Contrary to the older moralists, "not only each age and each man, but every mood, each moment, has its own right and wrong," Cooley observed. On a social plane the right might then be located in "an equilibrium of personal claims" rather than in the realization of a single, "literal" truth.[98]

About the most obvious source of the pragmatic side of his thought, William James, Cooley was disparaging to a surprising degree. Oddly, he perceived in James "too much of the atmosphere of a library," without "the feeling of ordinary, homely life." From an almost opposite angle he later described James as clear, honest, naïve, and popular, without subtlety or much originality, with little interest in, or sense of, "organization." Except for the "substantial contribution" of *Varieties of Religious Experience*, James seemed to Cooley most significant as a "slashing critic" of technical philosophy—certainly not as a thinker "to cherish and brood over."[99]

Such comments, confided to Cooley's journal, certainly understated his debt to the thinker who in Talcott Parsons's estimation provided the sociologist's "major theoretical reference point." Cooley's key notion of the looking-glass self, in particular, was rooted in Jamesian psychology. In some ways James may chiefly have reinforced compatible elements in Cooley's thought without changing its direction. The younger man's sense of life as experimental, clearly expressed as early as 1890, suggests a pragmatic disposition well before James's own articulation of pragmatism. Cooley maintained his own version of the experimental life, never underpinned by James's pluralism, but approaching a Modernist consciousness of disjunction and risk. "Is not the recognition of experiment, uncertainty, partial failure, the cost of growth, the most distinctive thing in modern thought?" he asked in 1913. "You might call it the tentative character of life."[100]

Other pronouncements had even a more decided Jamesian cast. In a 1904 observation—"as to what is beyond knowledge, do not hesitate to believe what you desire to be true"—there was certainly a whiff of "The Will to Believe," not diminished by the added comment that one could help make the belief in question true, or at least find in it a "vehicle for the spirit." James's proposition that the meaning of life was to be found in the application of a man's or woman's pains to the pursuit of some "unhabitual ideal" has parallel (and almost simultaneous) expression in Cooley: "I say the fight makes the man; but it must be the good fight, for the inmost peculiar truth which you alone can grasp."[101]

Cooley's ungrudging praise for *Varieties of Religious Experience* is not surprising; like James and others born in the middle generations of the nineteenth century he carried a sense of religious urgency into an age of theological doubt. Paradoxically—considering the admitted vagueness of his own idea of divinity—it was often religion which provided Cooley with the terms in which he most clearly and strikingly articulated his views. His religious vision shared ground with both the "Soldier's Faith" of Oliver Wendell Holmes, Jr., and with James's hypothesizing of an embattled finite deity. "I am of God's army," he proclaimed. "Like a soldier I may not know just what I am fighting for, and may be wounded to death in a lonesome place; but I believe in my commander and my cause." Like James, Cooley rejected the orthodox idea of an omnipotent, all-controlling God. It seemed to him rather that the deity, "like us, . . . does his best. He is a growth, a process, an onward striving force: and we are members of him, real agents in the work." Like James too, he wished to absolve the deity of responsibility for evil. "No intelligence planned the slaughter and filth of the Great War," he observed late in life. "We win our battles as we can, and so, perhaps, must God." (No mere expression of postwar disillusionment, this echoed a 1909 comment on an Italian earthquake.)[102]

For James this indeterminism was the corollary of pluralism and individualism. It was equally essential to Cooley's organicism—a view which, he explained, was always partial and tentative—"never more than relatively true." God, representing for Cooley an ideal expression of the organic and dynamic whole, was no serene and omniscient deity: "He strives and experiments like us; . . . he is strenuous, advancing, adventurous." Such a deity, feeling His way into incarnation with no more than faith in the unknown, was more like a child than an old man, and Cooley did not hesitate to reverse the conventional paternal imagery. "He has enormous vitality and potentiality," the sociologist confided like a hopeful parent himself, "but no maturity."[103]

This infantile deity contrasted sharply with James's image of God as a chieftain leading His troops into dubious battle, and although Cooley also employed the military metaphor, his use of it suggests the difference between the two thinkers. A youthful God, like an embattled warrior, could stand for incompletion and uncertainty, but He could also stand for the continuity of development in which boy became man or a deity realized Himself. James's venturesome hero was, for Cooley, also a process.

The distinction was crucial. James and Cooley had much in common, personally as well as intellectually. Both had struggled against physical and neurasthenic infirmities; both learned to engage life strenuously; in both agonistic religious temperaments contended with agnostic intellectual reservations. The real sticking point for Cooley, in his estimation of James, was the philosopher's "militant individuality." James did not share Cooley's concern with the "We" nearly so much as shared that with the "I." Cooley granted James "insight into the social nature of the self," but lamented that he failed to "develop this into a really organic conception of the relation of the individual to the social whole." (A truly social pragmatism remained to be worked out, it seemed to him in 1921.)[104]

Certainly Cooley's conception of the role of tradition in the "social whole" was a part of what he found missing in James. If for Philip Bruce tradition provided an alternative route to the creedal American goods of liberty and individualism, and if Ralph Adams Cram conducted a medieval detour to arrive at the country's accustomed democratic ideal, Cooley's traditionist strain led to a different expression of the American venturesomeness so forcefully articulated by William James. To James's life "on the perilous edge" Cooley counterposed the less dramatic prescription of adaptive growth. He found a master-image in the grapevine, which "feels its way and has a system of behavior which insures its growth along the line of successful experiment." Similarly in human life he discovered a vital impulse, never breaking continuity with the past but capable of advancing in any number of different directions. Taking the form of traditions, institutions, associations, and ideas, these lines of development were stimulated or repressed by the situations they encountered.[105]

As a way of understanding human—and specifically American— experience, Cooley's thought on the whole complemented rather than contradicted the more original thought of William James. The traditions which the sociologist valued were of a sort to nurture the pluralism at least of everyday life, and to elicit experimentation and innovation in its living. They were as well suited to an immature and practical-minded country as was his baby God; they made not for the propagation of static forms but for adaptive growth. After all, Cooley pointed out, customs and traditions had originally developed to "meet the exigencies to which the tribe is liable," and still properly performed this practical function.[106]

There is a strain of conservatism in these themes, although of a European and Burkean rather than an American and individualist variety. (Not that the two entirely excluded each other: the sociologist's own father, Thomas McIntyre Cooley, adhered firmly to an American brand of laissez-faire individualism, yet at the same time much admired Burke's political philosophy.) Charles Cooley recognized a degree of affinity with the English Whig; although critical of his rhetorical excesses, he acknowledged that "a conservatism like that of Burke is always worth considering." More enthusiastically, he commended Burke's perception of the unconscious aspect of social growth, agreeing that "the traditional organisms of society—language, folkways, common law and the like—exhibit on the whole an adaptability to conditions, a workableness, that could not be equaled by reflective consciousness alone." Ratiocenation could invent an artificial language like Volapuk, as he illustrated his point, but never the language of Shakespeare. Burke's pronouncement that society is a partnership of generations could have inspired Cooley's own comment that "man is formed to be a member of a social whole embracing not only the men of his lifetime but those past and to come. To live in the present only is as unnatural as to live in solitude."[107]

In such comments Cooley articulated a Burkean sense of society more clearly than did someone like Philip Alexander Bruce, although in lifestyle and practical politics the Virginian was far closer to the British statesman. "Progressivism" of the age of Theodore Roosevelt and Woodrow Wilson was characteristically founded upon a conservatism of values and interests, so it is not incongruous that in the conventional terms of American political and social-scientific discourse Cooley remained decidedly a Progressive. He usually eschewed the anti-traditionalist rhetoric of Ward and Ross because he believed more strongly than they that tradition knit together the social organism and furnished the means to a better society.

There remained a more fundamental tension than that between Progressive and conservative. Tradition conceived as a mundane continuity of life, however adaptive and experimental, could hardly speak to the Cooley who responded to Thomas à Kempis and Ralph Waldo Emerson, and emulated their aspiration to communion with ultimate reality. But there was also, the sociologist discovered, a kind of tradition capable of rising above itself, and it was this to which he finally looked to reconcile an illimitable "I" with an earthbound but aspiring "We." Toward the end of his life he provided in his journal his clearest articulation of such a reconciliation, making of tradition the very stuff of transcendence: "It is not unnatural that one should live *sub specie aeternitatis*. Our minds move in the general flow of life coming down from the past, and this is made up predominantly of that which has been preserved as of more lasting human interest and value, as worthy to endure beyond the individual term. Thus when we live understandingly we are formed by a select and enduring social heritage and derive our aims and motives from that. It requires no special effort, no peculiar virtue, to live for eternal things; we are by nature of them." Whereas for Ralph Adams Cram tradition transcends itself by a heroic aesthetic and spiritual effort, for Cooley living in tradition, in ordinary good faith, is to live in a milieu of the transcendent. The individual need only recognize the fact.[108]

It was then entirely natural for the Jews to have brought to the East Side the Old World traditions which harbored eternal truths. That the East Side was part of modern America made a difference, however, one which Cooley's figure of the grapevine recognized. Flexible and opportunistic, the grapevine provided a more fitting organic emblem for whatever continuities the twentieth century sustained than did Burke's sturdy English oaks. In Cooley's rendering, tradition had less the solid mystique of authority which endeared it to European conservatives and frightened American individualists, and more of an instrumental character. It was, first of all, a set of resources. Cooley observed of his own life that in his family background and institutional affiliations he "float[ed] on the current of tradition," and yet was an innovator in sociology, itself a relatively new discipline. Generalizing, he pointed out that it was the challenge of education to foster experiments which took the relevant social heritage as a starting point. Thus, once again, apparent antinomies proved congruent: "All innovation is based on conformity, all heterodoxy on orthodoxy, all individuality on solidarity."[109]

Tradition so conceived, clearly, was a boon for all seasons, as necessary to the modern world as to "traditional society." Cooley recognized, indeed, that the special conditions of modernity doomed tradition in certain of its forms. Aware from his own late-life forays on the highway that the automobile was working to diminish provincialism, he looked for no lasting bastions of tradition in agrarianism or rural isolation. Nor did he pin his hopes on a medieval revival, for all his admiration of the Gothic cathedral. Any kind of traditionalism based on the separation of communities or the effort to recapture the past was foreign to Cooley's sense of a progressive, integrative social process.[110]

And yet, he was convinced, tradition remained central to that process. The need was existential as well as practical. That the United States was so far lacking in "traditionary character" he perceived—without using the term—as alienating. Extracted from a traditional context, the individual lacked place and weight; society became in a strange way remote. "So rather unimportant details about England or Italy impose upon us because they connect with history and literature," Cooley suggested. "They are nearer to us, in a sense, than our own country." But even in America the primary groups nourished a sense of rootedness in space and time, and thus prepared one for larger venues: "We all need to belong to an intimate group of persons, which leads out into the society and to God," Cooley observed. And despite the dizzying mobility of American society, he clung to the belief that it still had room for "simple ideals of the family and neighborhood group." Offered a position at Columbia University by Franklin Henry Giddings in 1910, Cooley agonized for several weeks before deciding against the move from Ann Arbor. "I can be a distincter man here than transplanted," he mused in his journal. "I see myself clothed in a tradition, a reputation, in local associations, that I could not carry away with me. I should half-die in moving. Here I have incarnated myself."[111]

In post-frontier America, the home needed not to be carried outward in the old literal sense of physical relocation to the geographical margins, and the mobility which continued to mark American society might be accepted. But domesticity was more than neighborhood sentiment, and Cooley argued that the very complexity and diversity of modern life gave the traditionary qualities of "home" an extended utility. "Both consciously and unconsciously the larger mind is continually building itself up into wholes—fashions, traditions, institutions, tendencies, and the like—which spread and diversify like the branches of a tree, and so generate an even higher and more various structure of differentiated thought and symbols." Tradition conceived as part of such a proliferation did not limit choice; rather it enriched and multiplied it.[112]

This was no luxury, in Cooley's view; advanced society required many different types of persons, formed by "many traditions and environments." An authentic democracy, especially, was based on the kind of individuality which could arise only from diverse social settings. The country needed, in consequence, "many kinds of family, of school, of church, of community, of occupational and culture associations, each with a tradition and spirit of its own." America might lack the diversities of class and region which nourished such traditions in Europe, but it could develop a comparable culture deriving from distinctions of function, he suggested. His ultimate vision was of society as "a continuous and unified organism, with rich and varied traditions, intricate cooperation, and a wide interplay of thought and sentiment." Such resources were the more valuable in that they could liberate a generation from the particular shibboleths of its age. "Culture must always mean, in part, that we rise above the special atmosphere of our time and place to breathe the large air of great traditions that move tranquilly on the upper levels," Cooley explained. The micro-traditions of the neighborhood prepared one for the macro-traditions of humanity.[113]

Tradition in this view was never really lost; it was conserved in the great web of connections which linked past with present. And human beings were really "not less dependent upon the past than before," Cooley thought; "it is only that tradition is so intricate and so spread out over the face of things that its character as tradition is hardly to be discovered." He preferred a society which was able creatively to revise rather than simply discard old traditions, but in the end tradition in some form was inescapable. Even the youth of the twenties, rebelling against the institutions of their elders, worked out their own traditions and mores, Cooley noted—based though they might be on iconoclastic ideas taken from H. L. Mencken or Havelock Ellis.[114]

Mencken, at least, might have suggested some of the problems inherent in so sanguine a view of the role of tradition in the modern world. The Sage of Baltimore indeed was more of a traditionalist than his liberal devotees of the twenties—and probably Cooley himself—realized. He was an admirer of genuine aristocracy with every man in his place, a lover of the time-hallowed "Beer and Bach" gemütlichkeit which Cooley had found so attractive in Munich. But Mencken's public value derived from his "irreverence"—his scorn for particular traditions and conventions honored by the "Booboisie." Continuities were no doubt as inescapable as Cooley contended, but he never fully conjured with the discontinuities which, even if largely psychological, gave Modernist sensibilities their force and modern life much of its character, and which made tradition in itself seem merely exotic or nostalgic.

Cooley did his best to adapt tradition to the conditions of modernity, but in those conditions it tended always to dissolve, as Cooley's God tended always to dissolve into a mere apotheosis of society. For tradition to be "spread out over the face of things" could mean extinction by absorption. One counterstrategy proposed the eclectic observance of tradition. In modern society, the sociologist pointed out, "all the known past becomes accessible anywhere, and instead of the cult of immediate ancestors we have a long-armed, selective appropriation of whatever traditional ideas suit our tastes." Yet to remove from tradition its aura of authority and make it a matter of personal or collective selection from the options of a multifarious heritage was to offer a cultural smorgasbord far removed from the prescribed continuities of "traditional life." The individual was likely to end not so much by living in tradition as by consuming it.[115]

Cooley perceived something of these problems. As early as 1894 he had invested in the proposition that modern transportation and communications simply extended the scope and reach of tradition. They were capable, he thought, of combining "the widest unity with very great complexity of detail." The railroad and the telegraph were simply the most efficient means of "carrying the home outward." Experience taught him that the physical and intellectual mobility which such media generated worked against the particularities of tradition which fed the whole, however. If a true social pluralism was "no longer possible to our shifting life," he remarked with a trace of desperation, "perhaps we can make America itself a neighborhood and absorb that."[116]

Cooley did not pursue this thought, although he has been charged with the larger project of trying to make a village of the world. Such aggrandizing tendencies, although well rooted in the Anglo-American propensity to conflate home and empire, threatened his own first principles. A continental neighborhood or a global village confounded incommensurable kinds of "We." It identified the primary group, which was supposed to school the individual for the larger world, with the larger world itself. Despite modern colloquial usage, the grapevine of communication which increasingly linked instantaneously the far reaches of the world could not easily stand in for Cooley's grapevine of steadily accreting, adaptive growth.[117]

Cooley's organicism was most vulnerable when most diffuse: in expanding the scale of social relationships, in indistinct linkage of general and particular, in its overgenerous reliance on pluralism and multiple options. C. Wright Mills criticized Cooley for the "many sided fluidity" of his ideal society, a society in which nothing was fixed and everything was plastic. Such a "structureless flux" resisted or absorbed political action—a fatal objection for Mills—and the propagation of the instruments of mass society only compounded the problem. In particular the mass communications media, in which his predecessor had placed such confidence, had deadened rather than enlightened public opinion, Mills believed.[118]

If from this leftist point of view Cooley vitiated politics, he has also been taxed with opening the way to an all-too-effective exercise of public power. Pointing out that in Cooley's system authority has "no content and meaning superior to or anterior to society," John Patrick Diggins suggested that in delivering the self to such an omnipotent society Cooley may have produced a "formula for tyranny." Cooley's emphasis on the role of tradition would appear to mitigate the opposite dangers to which Mills and Diggins called attention, however. Tradition can provide direction and sense of purpose in the otherwise "structureless flux"; it can also restrain or obstruct the power of society as constituted at any particular moment—as sociologists like Ward and Ross feared.[119]

Cooley expressed himself most simply, but also perhaps most truly, when he remarked that his amateur work at his carpenter's table connected him to the incomparably greater work of the master-builders of the Gothic cathedrals. There was nothing diffuse or "fluid" in this apposition; it linked the homely to the exalted, medieval to modern, the particular and transient to the enduring and universal, within a broad but definable tradition of craft. Cooley's comment can lead us through such connections to the heart of his philosophy. Paul Creelan points to the "self-transcending tradition of Christian mysticism" which the sociologist found in Thomas à Kempis, and which represented for him an "open and expansive I" in contrast to the "self-centered Me" associated with Adam Smith. The juxtaposition of carpenter's table and cathedral, reaching across not only degrees of craftsmanship but the generations extending back to the time of Thomas and beyond, demonstrates tradition as a medium of self-transcendence. It seems also to vindicate Cooley's essential paradigm: family and neighborhood—and the workshop or corner where his table may have been—leading out into the larger world. In transcending itself the "I" touched a "We" great in space and time.[120]

The web of relationships which such a world contained seemed to Cooley so powerful a reality as to overcome even mortal limitations. In the spring of 1929, suffering from cancer and convalescing from an operation which he had learned would not prolong his life, Cooley wrote a final entry in his journal. "This is our world," he mused, "the world of the social heritage and the cumulative achievements of men, of great traditions, of history, literature and arts, of great men, great hopes and great endeavors; the world which has been growing from immemorial time, and will continue to grow for unmeasured time to come." It was also, he consoled himself, "my world. . . . In this world I shall go on living; for the immediate future in my known works, and in the memories of men, for all time as an influence absorbed into the whole." The impending dissolution of his own organism and consciousness seemed, in consequence, "a notable change" but not "calamitous . . . for what I care most about shall not die but live hopefully on."[121]

In this denouement lay both the defeat and the vindication of tradition, seen as an integral part of the venturous, experimental continuity of life in which Cooley so fervently believed. Particularities of place and time, the very stuff of tradition, were finally dissolved, yet the man or woman struggling productively in tradition was shown to have lived, in the term Cooley adopted, *sub specie aeternitatis*.

Although he was in some ways a typical Victorian, and although Ralph Adams Cram and Edward Alsworth Ross long survived him, Cooley was in the essentials of his thought the most modern of the figures considered here. He looked to tradition not to underwrite what might seem almost atavistic goals of quasi-racial expansion, the vindication of the vanquished, or medieval restoration, but rather a very modern search for community in the face of social disintegration and anomie. Despite his private parochial attachments, he carried no special banner for the Teutonic idea, Old Virginia (or his native Michigan), or the Gothic quest. His home was a generic one and he proclaimed the cosmopolitan efficacy of the "great traditions." (Tribal uses of tradition would reemerge later in the century.)

But community, with its stores of tradition, was also a truth-seeking enterprise, and in his recognition of this paramount function Cooley faced both backward and forward. Inspired by ancient Israel and by the Brethren of the Common Life of Thomas à Kempis, he also anticipated late-twentieth-century philosophers who recognized in traditions the necessary vehicles of intellectual and moral inquiry. In the relationship of the prophet to his people, of the mystic to his monastery, of the scholar to his school, there was for Cooley if not the ultimate resolution of the problem of the "I" and the "We"—this he recognized in dying—then at least the most promising prescription for the life of the venturing spirit in the world.

Conclusion:
Sub Specie Aeternitatis

Unable to take traditionary matters for granted, Americans have been prone to a sharp ambivalence about them. The Atlantic has served equally as Thoreau's "Lethean stream" freeing American minds from unwanted memories and as the royal road to "heritage," conveying Van Wyck Brooks's "sightseers" to their Old World castles and cathedrals. Americans have perceived tradition as impoverishment, narrowing and constricting human possibilities, but also as abundance, providing the treasures of the past for the uses of the present. There was warrant in the national experience for both interpretations. The country had religious roots in the Protestant search for scriptural purity. This entailed a distrust of traditional accretions to faith which it was not difficult for Yves Congar to contrast to the Catholic preference for the plenitude of tradition. Yet materially the United States was a nation of plenty, and in time tradition itself became an article of enjoyment and consumption. However the problem is stated, the Tennysonian riddle remained: were the ages to which Americans were heirs presumptive the source of "honeyed sweets," as Augustine Jones half-believed, or only of dregs and corruptions better left behind? In wanting to have it both ways the amateur historian was no more than representative of his countrymen.[1]

In the late nineteenth century, a time both of rapid change and of retrospection, of a sense of breaking with the past and of fascination with history, this conflictedness about tradition was at its most intense. Yet the faith of the century in continuous and progressive development offered a way to contain apparent disjunctions and reconcile tradition with innovation. In such a representative thinker as John Fiske, tradition could become part and parcel of "progressive evolution," bearing humanity forward on one great tide. Tradition retained its old associations with home and town, but the home was to be "carried outward," the lares and penates of the hearthside to become the totems of nation and empire.

Although satisfying to Fiske and many others of his time, this solution worked less well for those born later. Advancing gradually from one historical station to the next, tradition seemed at last exhausted of anything fresh or vital to offer an impatient modernity. It seemed at worst a perverse defense of one troublesome "inner circle" or another— of knots of unreconstructed rebels or "clots" of immigrant benighted-ness—at best a futile last stand against the big and soulless aggrega-tions which Ralph Adams Cram described as "imperial modernism." For progressive reformers like Lester Frank Ward and Edward Alsworth Ross it was difficult to comprehend as other than dead weight, justifi-able if at all in service to social control as a corollary of social progress.

There was, however, another, more complex modernism, which helps to illuminate the adaptive utility of tradition during the last century. Relying on Daniel Joseph Singal, Norman F. Cantor, and other recent cultural historians, I am using the term (as capitalized) in reference to the cultural and intellectual movement which arose in revolt against Victorian precepts at the end of the nineteenth century and beginning of the twentieth. Modernists of this sort typically rejected Victorian hierar-chies such as those of race, sex, and class and sharp dichotomies like that between "civilized" and "savage." They found experience more compelling than morality and conflict more significant than harmony. They accepted a universe without certainty or absolute answers. Most to the point here, these Modernists rejected the linear historical conscious-ness beloved of the Victorians. "The modern mind grew indifferent to history, for history, conceived as a continuous nourishing tradition, became useless to its projects," according to Carl Schorske.[2]

Yet there was another side to Modernism, and while changes in the meaning and significance of tradition have been part of the making of the "modern mind," these changes have not been all of negative value. As a guide to everyday life, perhaps, tradition has continued to recede; as a guide to thought it arguably enjoys a higher standing now than it did a century ago. Inundated in the precincts of the quotidian, it might be said, tradition has retreated to more rarified levels.

The more considered verdict of Modernism was not so much a rejection of tradition as a redefinition of it. Modernists effected a reconsideration of tradition by calling into question both the terms of its accessibility and the import of its message, as these had been understood by Victorians like John Fiske. Tradition had been assumed to be available through the continuous sequence of generations, which from the perspective of the present receded into a remote, often mistily Germanic, past. It had come widely to be regarded also as the bearer of transcending truths and goods progressively realized and universally applicable. Modernists rejected both the premise of continuous transmission and that of universal applicability.

This was not, however, to deny the enduring significance of the past. On the contrary, leading Modernists insisted upon the complete immanence of past experience. They were "all atavists in some way," Herbert N. Schneidau observes of figures like Ezra Pound and T. S. Eliot, but atavists who sought to recover "not the pastness of the past but its presentness, its presence *in* the present." The inheritance of tradition through a succession of generations both obscured the bequest itself and bore it down with the oppressive weight of accumulated time and authority to the Modernist mind. In a sense, access to the past required the elimination of the temporal dimension altogether. Eliot's *Waste Land*, Louis Menand points out, "seems to regard the present moment—as it is experienced by the individual subject—as a reinscription of the whole of the cultural past." Stephen Spender attributed this flatness of perspective to the American "Newness" exploiting "the truism that the past can only attain consciousness in the minds of the living," in contrast to the clearer European sense of the depth of the past. Thus for Eliot, Spender believed, "the past is the dead pressing down on the consciousness of the living; and every past, in being realized through that consciousness, is contemporaneous with every other past." (Whether or not it represents a peculiarly American disposition, the collapse of time continues in the Postmodern age. A recent critic suggests that "'old' and 'new' are exhausted categories. The past is present now.")[3]

This omnipresent past made possible a new conception of tradition as the source of a "comprehensive mind" or "unity of experience." It was not experienced as oppressive because Modernists tendered the initiative to the present consciousness. This meant too that it was intelligently accessible only with the collaboration of the living individual. Tradition "cannot be inherited, and if you want it you must attain it by great labour," Eliot advised. Requisite to such endeavor was a "historical sense, which is a sense of the timeless as well as of the temporal and of the timeless and of the temporal together," and which permitted the artist to be at once traditional and conscious of his own "contemporaneity." But Eliot emphasized that as a new work of art changed the whole body of art, the past was altered by the present as much as the present is directed by the past. Far from merely constraining the individual, tradition empowered him—even to change the tradition itself.[4]

We are thus "heir of all the ages" in a new sense, and one which claimed for the sovereign present consciousness the prerogative of recognizing within a tradition the quality of transcendence. In contrast to the romantic desire to perceive the divine in everything, Ricardo Quinones remarks, Modernists were disposed to allow an object to be just what it was. But Quinones points also to "the mythic needs of Modernism, the need to have, as in Greek tragedy, 'the immediate present appear sub specie aeternitatis, and in a certain sense timeless,' and to give to everyday experience 'the stamp of the eternal.'"[5]

This was not a timelessness gauged in relation to a fixed hierarchy of values or truths, however, but one which was deemed to arise from the very integrity and significance of the thing in its particularity. It is most clearly applicable to aesthetic judgments, such as those we make in speaking of the "timeless beauty" of the Parthenon or Chartres Cathedral, without claiming an exclusive validity or absolute superiority for Greek or Gothic architecture. But the association of value with particularity, and even with the limitations which particularity necessarily entails, suggests other uses of tradition as well.

This is not a trivial point, for tradition in recent thought has proved able in some degree to compensate for the collapse of the universals which were fundamental both to Enlightenment and Victorian thought—gaining in consequence a renewed significance as a necessary context for the pursuit of truth. This was in keeping with the familiar pattern of tradition, which cleaved to the particular and local even while, like Jaroslav Pelikan's icon, pointing to things beyond itself. The chastening in the twentieth century of claims to universal understanding have brought such functions of tradition back into view. Thus Christopher Shannon calls attention to the final abandonment of the "driving principle" of Enlightenment rationalism: "the opposition of reason to tradition" and the rediscovery of the principle that reason and matters of belief "make sense only in the context of some received tradition of inquiry."[6]

Richard Rorty notes similarly that "contemporary intellectuals have given up the Enlightenment assumption that religion, myth, and tradition can be opposed to something ahistorical, something common to all human beings qua human." Confronting the "dilemma formed by ethnocentrism on the one hand and relativism on the other," Rorty proposes that we grasp the ethnocentric horn, recognizing that we must in practice "privilege our own group." We must, that is to say, "work by our own lights. . . . What we cannot do is to rise above all human communities, actual and possible." Rorty's call to work from within a tradition is particularly striking in a pragmatic philosopher; no previous pragmatist, John Patrick Diggins remarks, had been so inclined to seek guidance from the past. (I would argue that Charles Cooley, in his pragmatic character, was an exception.)[7]

The insight cut across philosophical boundaries, however. From a very different, Aristotelian-Augustinian, perspective, Alasdair MacIntyre arrived at some similar conclusions. Not even Americans, MacIntyre commented, could escape the formative influences of the past. There was accordingly "no way to possess the virtues except as part of a tradition in which we inherit them and our understanding of them from a series of predecessors." In seeming paradox he offered the proposition that "reason can only move towards being genuinely universal and impersonal insofar as it is neither neutral nor disinterested."[8]

In a time of fundamental shifts of thought and sensibility, the figures of this study moved between a confidence in possessing universally applicable truths and the realization articulated later by Rorty and MacIntyre that the search for such truths can be carried on only from the particular and limited vantage which time and space, society and tradition, provide. John Fiske and the Virginia historians were confident enough of their hold on universal truth to identify it with their own special traditions, assuming alternatives to Anglo-American or Anglo-Virginian modes to fall more or less short of complete validity. Cram and Cooley most significantly qualified their faith in universals. Cram, while looking to the ultimate catholicity claimed by his Christian faith, had an architect's sense that different traditions might legitimately seek to represent transcending beauty and truth. He had as well of course a healthy reactionary's resentment of the universalizing pretensions of "imperial modernism." Cooley, although grounded in a monistic idealism, cherished diversity within the organic whole. He emphasized the importance of particular traditions, such as that which he had observed in the Jewish community of the Lower East Side, both in nourishing the individual's quest for truth and in enriching society.

In other ways too these figures occupied a middle ground. In broadest perspective, they fell between the largely unreflective adherence to tradition of truly "traditional" society and the deliberate and unfettered uses of it which became common in the late twentieth century. Tradition in the years between the Civil War and World War II retained an aura of authority, most solidly when as in Virginia it rested on deep social foundations, but even in the aesthetic and academic worlds of Ralph Adams Cram and Charles Horton Cooley. But it was coming to be a matter of considered and voluntary adherence; it was increasingly eclectic and selective rather than a legacy accepted all in all.

These concessions to modern introspection and multiplicity did not necessarily diminish the force of tradition. Tradition has always at least a passive role, conveying its store of culture and custom with quiet inertia. What is most striking in the late nineteenth and early twentieth centuries is the strong active role it also sustained. It was the harbinger of national expansion and empire, it was the means of sectional vindication and intersectional reconciliation, it was the ground of transcendent spiritual values, it was the ligament of the "I" and the "We" in the organic community. Like the "invention of tradition," the employment of it in these positive and often self-conscious ways could indicate both an uncertain sense of relationship to the past and an uncertain sense of social coherence in the present.

It is against the backdrop of Modernism that the transitional character of the traditionism of this time stands in clearest perspective. Except for Fiske, all of the figures considered here lived well into the period of Modernist maturation. None could be called a Modernist in any full sense, although in varying degrees and ways they resembled the "reluctant modernists" whom George Cotkin describes as "attempting to synthesize the traditions and ideals of Victorianism with the challenges and possibilities of modernist streams of thought."[9]

Even in such cultural conservatives as Philip Bruce and Lyon G. Tyler, traditionism had certain affinities with Modernism, somewhat in the way that premodern painting, lacking perspective, has an affinity with the two-dimensional modern canvas. The immanence of all pasts, as invoked by T. S. Eliot, was a psychological possibility not merely for Modernists—or else we have to call Bruce and Tyler, in this respect, Modernists in spite of themselves. As historians, the Virginians grappled skillfully enough with change; as defenders of tradition their instinct was to deny it. So closely did they identify with Lee, with Washington and Jefferson, with the early settlers whom with varying qualifications they designated as cavaliers, and so closely did they identify these with each other, that it was as if, in the Modernist mode, every significant part of their past was "contemporaneous with every other past."

More deliberately, although without explicit reference to Modernism, Charles H. Cooley contended that the conditions of modernity made all traditions immediately accessible; they became part of the atmosphere of cultural life, to be appropriated as willed. Along with the Modernists, Cooley aspired to live, as he said, *sub specie aeternitatis*, realizing a timelessness in the mundane. Cooley's earnest Progressivism and faith in an organic social process would discourage a Modernist label, but he illustrates the common ground that traditionism, Modernism, and Progressivism could occupy.

Historians, and even those who dabbled in history for polemical purposes like Ralph Adams Cram, could not rely entirely on the immanence of all pasts, however. To speak in the historical voice, after all, required them to connect past to present in ways that accounted for the passage of time, for the development of the village-community into the imperious, industrialized nation-state, if that was the relevant thesis, or of the seventeenth-century cavalier into Woodrow Wilson. Even historically minded traditionists shared ground with Modernists, however, in seeking linkages to the past which escaped the straight-line, evolutionary, progressive model that both groups, after the generation of John Fiske, found unsatisfactory.

The Victorian penchant for linear progression, as if on a temporal railroad track, could leave past and present so remote from each other as to drain tradition of all but antiquarian interest. But tradition did not have to be captive to the linear mode. It was premodern in essence: subjective and therefore rough in temporal texture, gnarly, unbonded to strict chronology, associated with place and locality, it could survive— and compensate for—the failure of progressive evolution as well as of universal values in modern consciousness.

Even in Fiske, the preeminent champion of progressive evolution, a tendency to couch tradition in such terms is discernible. Federalism, the lynchpin of Fiske's "Teutonic Idea" (and failed bulwark of the Virginians' "inner circle"), provided temporal as well as spatial bonding. Middletown, Connecticut, and Washington, D.C., might stand for political cultures which respectively looked back to colonial times and ahead to global dominion, but Fiske's broad version of federalism fixed backwater and capital as integral parts of the same system.

Similarly, typological patterns of thought enabled the Virginians to perceive in Washington and Lee the lineaments of the seventeenth-century cavalier, and Ralph Adams Cram to find in feudal society a model of the "true democracy" which America might yet restore. Cram's five-hundred-year cycles of history made even the remote past accessible on the crest of successive creative waves, with the Middle Ages particularly immanent in the wreckage of modern civilization. Even Cooley's figure for "adaptive growth," the grapevine, suggested twistings and turnings and doublings-back not confined to a straight-line connection to the past.

The danger in such devices was, again, a false familiarity with the past. The Virginians' inclination to believe that they were at one with the Jamestown settlers and cavaliers, Cram's confidence that the Gothic spirit could be resurrected in twentieth-century America, even Cooley's slightly too easy identification with medieval artisans and the progressive Fiske's eager acclaim of the Aryans as the "Yankees of Antiquity," bespoke an insufficiently critical approach to tradition. Theodor Adorno, although dismissive of the very possibility of tradition in "a radically bourgeois country like the US," proposed a "critical approach to tradition" which would avoid alike the "bad traditionalism" which "reduces distance and reaches for the irretrievable," and a self-congratulatory acceptance of the fruits of historical development. Such a critical approach would seek out in tradition "that which was left along the way, passed over or overpowered," that especially which "throws light on the present" not because of an easy affinity with it but because of its distance from it.[10]

Political implications aside, this critical approach might sometimes have served the American defenders of tradition better than their usual lines of argument. But they were at once too enamored of tradition, and too American and optimistic, to deal with the problem in this critical fashion. (Cram came closest in his effort to reveal the lost "democracy" of the Middle Ages, but as he failed to make important distinctions and lacked sufficient empirical evidence to support his thesis, it came across as another essay in false affinity.)

At bottom perhaps it was a lingering devotion to the domestic trope which kept these figures from embracing a Modernist sense of the past, let alone the kind of "critical" relationship proposed by Adorno. A spiritual comfort in the universe, never quite relinquished, preserved them from a more profound sense of dispossession than any that mundane history could impart. Clare Cavanagh, in *Osip Mandelstam and the Modernist Creation of Tradition* (1995), points out that the Modernist version of tradition is "based not on continuity or succession, on direct transmission from father, or mother, to son: it derives instead from dislocation and interruption." Further, it will not stay put even after being dislocated, but is subject to endless remaking. Modernist tradition "relies as much on homelessness as home," Cavanagh concludes. "It thus makes orphans of us all."[11]

This prospect could only have appalled those who cleaved to village or farm, walled town, cathedral, or primary group as "home," and especially to those who wanted to "carry the home outward" or upward. Edward Alsworth Ross, alone of those considered here, seems to have glimpsed the specter of cosmic homelessness. His brief vision of moderns as "social derelicts," unable to "lay our course in the light of the experience of our ancestors," did not signify the death of tradition, but it did suggest that tradition could no longer be accepted with traditional assurance or followed entirely in traditional ways.

Notes

Introduction

1. Henry David Thoreau, "Walking," in *The Writings of Henry David Thoreau* (Boston: Houghton Mifflin, 1906; repr. New York: AMS Press, 1968), 5: 218; Anthony Kemp, *The Estrangement of the Past: A Study in the Origins of Modern Historical Consciousness* (New York: Oxford University Press, 1991), 105, called attention to this passage.

2. Daniel J. Boorstin, *The Lost World of Thomas Jefferson* (Boston: Beacon Press, 1960), 204.

3. Ralph Waldo Emerson, *The Works of Ralph Waldo Emerson* (Boston: Houghton Mifflin, 1883), 2: 297 ("Circles"); 3: 173 ("Nature"); 3: 69 ("Experience"); R. W. B. Lewis, *The American Adam: Innocence, Tragedy and Tradition the Nineteenth Century* (Chicago: University of Chicago Press, 1955); Henry James, *The Sense of the Past* (New York: Scribner's, 1917; repr. Fairfield, N. J.: Augustus M. Kelley, 1976), 34.

4. James Russell Lowell, "A Great Public Character," in *Literary Essays: Among My Books, My Study Windows, Fireside Travels*, vol. 2, *The Works of James Russell Lowell* (Boston: Houghton Mifflin, 1899), 273–74.

5. David Gross, *The Past in Ruins: Tradition and the Critique of Modernity* (Amherst: University of Massachusetts Press, 1992), 8; H. B. Acton, "Tradition and Some Other Forms of Order," *Proceedings of the Aristotelian Society*, n.s., 53 (1952–1953), 2; Edward Shils, "Tradition and Liberty: Antinomy and Interdependence," *Ethics* 68 (April 1958): 154; S. N. Eisenstadt, "Intellectuals and Tradition," *Daedalus* 101 (Spring 1972): 3; Edward Shils, *Tradition* (Chicago: University of Chicago Press, 1981), 168; Kenneth Zaretzke, "The Idea of Tradition," *Intercollegiate Review* 17 (Spring/Summer 1982): 91.

6. Eric Hobsbawm and Terence Ranger, eds., *The Invention of Tradition* (Cambridge: Cambridge University Press, 1983), 2; Edward Shils, "Intellectuals, Tradition, and the Traditions of Intellectuals: Some Preliminary Considerations," *Daedalus* 101 (Spring 1972): 23.

7. Acton, "Tradition," 5; Garrett Barden, *After Principles* (Notre Dame, Ind.: University of Notre Dame Press, 1990), 110–11; Shils, "Tradition and Liberty," 154.

8. Edward Alsworth Ross, *Social Psychology: An Outline and Source Book* (New York: Macmillan, 1909), 196; Edward Sapir, "Custom," *Encyclopaedia of the Social Sciences*, ed. Edwin R. A. Seligman (New York: Macmillan, 1957), 3: 658; Max Radin, "Tradition," ibid., 15: 62; Josef Rupert Geiselmann, *The Meaning of Tradition*, trans. W. J. O'Hara (New York: Herder and Herder, 1966), 46.

9. Peter Richard Rohden, "Traditionalism," *Encyclopaedia of the Social Sciences*, 15: 69–70; Samuel Coleman, "Is There Reason in Tradition?" in *Politics and Experience:*

Essays Presented to Professor Michael Oakeshott on the Occasion of His Retirement, ed. Preston King and B. C. Parekh (Cambridge: Cambridge University Press, 1968), 252; Bert F. Hoselitz, "Tradition and Economic Growth," in *Tradition, Values, and Socio-Economic Development*, ed. Ralph Braibanti and Joseph J. Spengler (Durham, N.C.: Duke University Press, 1961), 100; Jaroslav Pelikan, *The Vindication of Tradition* (New Haven: Yale University Press, 1984), 72; Shils, "Tradition and Liberty," 161.

10. David Lowenthal, *Possessed by the Past: The Heritage Crusade and the Spoils of History* (New York: Free Press, 1996), 119–22.

11. T. J. Jackson Lears, *No Place of Grace: Antimodernism and the Transformation of American Culture, 1880–1920* (New York: Pantheon, 1981), xv–xvi, 13.

12. Gross, *Past in Ruins*, 80; J. H. Plumb, *The Death of the Past* (Boston: Houghton Mifflin, 1970), 14–17, 108, 136. This was not in Plumb's view a bad thing, the past having always been "the handmaid of authority" (p. 40). See also J. G. A. Pocock, "Time, Institutions and Action: An Essay on Traditions and Their Understanding," in *Politics and Experience*, ed. King and Parekh, 209–37.

13. The effect of Weber's analysis, Talcott Parsons noted, was radically to devalue tradition. Max Weber, *The Theory of Social and Economic Organization*, trans. A. M. Henderson and Talcott Parsons (New York: Oxford University Press, 1947), 80, 328; Michael Oakeshott, *Rationalism in Politics and Other Essays* (New York: Basic Books, 1962), 1–4; Shils, *Tradition*, 323.

14. George Allan, *The Importances of the Past: A Meditation on the Authority of Tradition* (Albany: State University of New York Press, 1986), 240; Gross, *Past in Ruins*, 12, 84.

15. Daniel Lerner, *The Passing of Traditional Society: Modernizing the Middle East*, with the collaboration of Lucille W. Pevsner and an introduction by David Riesman (Glencoe, Ill.: Free Press, 1958), 50, 133–35, 146, and passim.

16. H. T. Wilson, *Tradition and Innovation: The Idea of Civilization as Culture and Its Significance* (London: Routledge and Kegan Paul, 1984), vii; Joseph R. Gusfield, "Tradition and Modernity: Misplaced Polarities in the Study of Social Change," *American Journal of Sociology* 72 (January 1967): 356–57. Michael Kammen points out that there has been a "relentlessly dialogical relationship between the values of tradition and progress." *Mystic Chords of Memory: The Transformation of Tradition in American Culture* (New York: Knopf, 1991), 14.

17. Brian Stock, *Listening for the Text: On the Uses of the Past* (Baltimore: Johns Hopkins University Press, 1990), 1; Stephen Spender, *The Struggle of the Modern* (Berkeley: University of California Press, 1963), 60.

18. William M. Sloane, "History and Democracy," *American Historical Review* 1 (October 1895): 1, 4, 6–7, 9–11, 15–16.

19. Van Wyck Brooks, *The Wine of the Puritans: A Study of Present-Day America* (Folcroft, Pa.: Folcroft Press, 1969), 132–36.

20. Donald B. Meyer, "Myth, Memory, and Tradition in American Culture," *Canadian Review of American Studies* 23 (Fall 1992): 151.

21. Emerson, "History," *Works*, 2: 9, 14–15.

22. John Olin Eidson, *Tennyson in America: His Reputation and Influence from 1827 to 1858* (Athens: University of Georgia Press, 1943), xii, 96–97; Alfred Lord Tennyson, "Locksley Hall," lines 177–78, *The Poetic and Dramatic Works of Alfred Lord Tennyson* (Boston: Houghton Mifflin, 1898), 94.

23. Henry Kozicki, *Tennyson and Clio: History in the Major Poems* (Baltimore: Johns Hopkins University Press, 1979), 71–72, 75.

24. George Bancroft, *Address at Hartford, Before the Delegates to the Young Men of Connecticut, on the Evening of February 18, 1840* (pamphlet, n.d.), 10.

25. Wyndham Lewis, *Time and Western Man* (Boston: Beacon Press, 1957), 36, 212; Kammen, *Mystic Chords,* 7 (original italics omitted).

26. Robert A. Nisbet, *The Sociological Tradition* (New York: Basic Books, 1966), 70–76.

27. Extensive literature on these developments includes Michael Kammen, *Mystic Chords of Memory: The Transformation of Tradition in American Culture* (New York: Knopf, 1991); T. J. Jackson Lears, *No Place of Grace*; John C. Fraser, *America and the Patterns of Chivalry* (Cambridge: Cambridge University Press, 1982); Wallace Evan Davies, *Patriotism on Parade: The Story of Veterans' and Hereditary Organizations in America, 1783–1900* (Cambridge: Harvard University Press, 1955); Calder Loth and Julius Trousdale Sadler, Jr., *The Only Proper Style: Gothic Architecture in America* (Boston: Little, Brown, 1975); Eileen Boris, *Art and Labor: Ruskin, Morris, and the Craftsman Ideal in America* (Philadelphia: Temple University Press, 1986); David Glassberg, *American Historical Pageantry: The Uses of Tradition in the Early Twentieth Century* (Chapel Hill: University of North Carolina Press, 1990); Maxwell Geismar, *Rebels and Ancestors: The American Novel, 1890–1915* (Boston: Houghton Mifflin, 1953); Karal Ann Marling, *George Washington Slept Here: Colonial Revivals and American Culture, 1876–1986* (Cambridge: Harvard University Press, 1988); James M. Lindgren, *Preserving the Old Dominion: Historic Preservation and Virginia Traditionalism* (Charlottesville: University Press of Virginia, 1993) and *Preserving Historic New England: Preservation, Progressivism, and the Remaking of Memory* (New York: Oxford University Press, 1995).

28. Lindgren contends that historical preservation fundamentally "concerned what Michel Foucault called the 'relations of power.'" *Preserving Historic New England,* 5. For Lears's interpretation, see *No Place of Grace,* 7–32.

29. Stephen H. Watson, *Tradition(s): Refiguring Community and Virtue in Classical German Thought* (Bloomington: Indiana University Press, 1997), 18, 32; Theodor W. Adorno, "On Tradition," *Telos* 94 (Winter 1992): 75. The latter two characterizations are from Edward A. Ross, *Social Control: A Survey of the Foundations of Order* (New York: Macmillan, 1922), 169; Edmund Burke, *Reflections on the Revolution in France, and on the Proceedings in Certain Societies in London Relative to that Event,* ed. Conor Cruise O'Brien (Harmondsworth, England: Penguin Books, 1969), 315; K. R. Minogue, "Revolution, Tradition and Political Continuity," in *Politics and Experience,* ed. King and Parekh, 286; Spender, *Struggle of the Modern,* 232.

30. Allan, *Importances of the Past,* 93, 117; Shils, "Tradition and Liberty," 154, 156.

Josef Geiselmann noted that the language of tradition suggests initiation rites, revealing "to each new generation a world which opens out on things transcending the human world." *Meaning of Tradition*, 95–96.

31. Gerhart Niemeyer, "In Praise of Tradition," *Modern Age* 36 (Spring 1994): 233; James S. Cutsinger, "An Open Letter," *Modern Age* 36 (Spring 1994): 295. S. N. Eisenstadt comments that "the upholding of criteria of sacredness . . . contains the most important elements of what has usually been called 'traditionality'"—an aspect of tradition especially likely to be weakened by the processes of modernization. Samuel Noah Eisenstadt, *Tradition, Change, and Modernity* (New York: John Wiley & Sons, 1973), 139, 209; Pelikan, *Vindication of Tradition*, 54–56. Tradition becomes an idol, Pelikan adds, "when it makes the preservation and repetition of the past an end in itself." Ibid., 55.

32. Pocock, "Time, Institutions and Action," 216–17; Eisenstadt, *Tradition, Change, and Modernity*, 122.

33. J. G. A. Pocock, *Politics, Language, and Time: Essays on Political Thought and History* (New York: Atheneum, 1971), 143.

34. Johann Gottfried v. Herder, *Outlines of a Philosophy of the History of Mankind*, trans. T. Churchill (London: 1800; repr. New York: Bergman Publishers, n.d.), 227.

35. Norman F. Cantor, *Twentieth-Century Culture: Modernism to Deconstruction* (New York: Peter Lang, 1988), 380. See also Richard Wolin, "Modernism vs. Postmodernism," *Telos* 62 (Winter 1984–85): 20.

CHAPTER I. *Carrying the Home Outward*

Portions of this chapter were previously published in "The Empire of the Dead and the Empire of the Living: John Fiske and the Spatialization of Tradition," *American Studies* 38 (Fall 1997): 91–107. Reprinted by permission.

1. *National Cyclopaedia of American Biography* (Ann Arbor: University Microfilms, 1967), 6: 203.

2. Augustine Jones, *The Life and Work of Thomas Dudley, the Second Governor of Massachusetts* (Boston: Houghton Mifflin, 1899), 9, 15–17, 51, 103.

3. Ibid., 52.

4. Ibid., 8–9, 69, 289, 344, 369–70.

5. Ibid., 76–77.

6. Ibid., 57.

7. Ibid., 261–62.

8. Ursula Brumm, *American Thought and Religious Typology* (New Brunswick, N.J.: Rutgers University Press, 1970); Jonathan Edwards, *Images or Shadows of Divine Things*, ed. Perry Miller (New Haven: Yale University Press, 1948; repr. Westport, Conn.: Greenwood Press, 1977); Heather Henderson, *The Victorian Self: Autobiography and Biblical Narrative* (Ithaca, N.Y.: Cornell University Press, 1989); George P. Landow, *Victorian Types, Victorian Shadows: Biblical Typology in Victorian Literature, Art, and Thought*

(Boston: Routledge and Kegan Paul, 1980); Earl Miner, ed., *Literary Uses of Typology: From the Late Middle Ages to the Present* (Princeton: Princeton University Press, 1977).

9. Charles Francis Adams, *Massachusetts: Its Historians and Its History: An Object Lesson* (Boston: Houghton Mifflin, 1893), 8, 41, 99; Henry Adams, *The Education of Henry Adams* (Boston: Houghton Mifflin, 1961), 382, 408–10.

10. Herbert Baxter Adams to Daniel Coit Gilman, July 3, 1882, in *Historical Scholarship in the United States, 1876–1901: As Revealed in the Correspondence of Herbert Baxter Adams*, ed. W. Stull Holt (Westport, Conn.: Greenwood Press, 1970), 55; Herbert Baxter Adams, *The Germanic Origin of New England Towns. Read Before the Harvard Historical Society, May 9, 1881* (Baltimore: Johns Hopkins University Press, 1882; repr. New York: Johnson Reprint Corporation, 1973), 7–11, 18.

11. Frederick Jackson Turner, *The Frontier in American History* (New York: Henry Holt, 1920), 37–38.

12. Donald Davidson, *The Attack on Leviathan: Regionalism and Nationalism in the United States* (Chapel Hill: University of North Carolina Press, 1938; repr. Gloucester, Mass.: Peter Smith, 1962), 16, 37–38.

13. John Higham, "Herbert Baxter Adams and the Study of Local History," *American Historical Review* 89 (December 1984): 1225–39, is a negative assessment. David Hackett Fischer, *Albion's Seed: Four British Folkways in America* (New York: Oxford University Press, 1989), stirred controversy but shows the possibilities of an approach emphasizing Anglo-American continuity. See also Dorothy Ross, "Historical Consciousness in Nineteenth-Century America," *American Historical Review* 89 (October 1984): 923–24.

14. Bronson Alcott, *The Journals of Bronson Alcott*, ed. Odell Shepard (Boston: Little, Brown, 1938), 41 (April 24, 1834). Sacvan Berkovitch called attention to this passage in *The Rites of Assent: Transformations in the Symbolic Construction of America* (New York: Routledge, 1993), 181.

15. "Recent Books on American History," *Atlantic Monthly* 65 (February 1890): 274.

16. Henri Bergson, *Time and Free Will: An Essay on the Immediate Data of Consciousness*, trans. F. L. Pogson (London: George Allen, 1913), 237; Ricardo J. Quinones, *Mapping Literary Modernism: Time and Development* (Princeton: Princeton University Press, 1985), 38, 68, 71–72. In 1927 Wyndham Lewis decried Modernist development of a "cult of Time" at the expense of the "greater reality" of space in *Time and Western Man* (Boston: Beacon Press, 1957), 211–12, 429. Stephen Kern, *The Culture of Time and Space, 1880–1918* (Cambridge: Harvard University Press, 1983), is essential for understanding the meanings of the two terms in the period.

17. Stephen Spender, *Love-Hate Relations: English and American Sensibilities* (New York: Random House, 1974), 15, 77–78.

18. Walter Scott, ed., *Sir Tristrem; A Metrical Romance of the Thirteenth Century; by Thomas of Erceldoune Called the Rhymer*, 3d ed. (Edinburgh: Archibald Constable, 1811), xxvii–xxviii. Michael Kammen calls attention to this passage in *Mystic Chords of Memory: The Transformation of Tradition in American Culture* (New York: Knopf, 1991),

272; George P. Marsh, *The Goths in New-England: A Discourse Delivered at the Anniversary of the Philomathesian Society of Middlebury College, August 15, 1843* (Middlebury [Vt.]: Printed by J. Cobb, Jr., 1843), 33. T. S. Eliot made a prerequisite of tradition the persistence of "the same people living in the same place." *After Strange Gods: A Primer of Modern Heresy* (New York: Harcourt, Brace, 1934), 18.

19. Charles Hirschfeld, "Edward Eggleston, Pioneer in Social History," in *Historiography and Urbanization: Essays in American History in Honor of W. Stull Holt*, ed. Eric F. Goldman (Baltimore: Johns Hopkins University Press, 1941; repr. Port Washington, N.Y.: Kennikat Press, 1968), 201; Edward Eggleston, *The Transit of Civilization from England to America in the Seventeenth Century* (New York: D. Appleton, 1901), 1; Edward Eggleston, *The Beginners of a Nation: A History of the Source and Rise of the Earliest English Settlements in America with Special Reference to the Life and Character of the People* (New York: D. Appleton, 1896; repr. New York: Johnson Reprint Corporation, 1970).

20. Eggleston, *Transit of Civilization*, 1, 48, 127, 207, 279.

21. Ibid., 277–79.

22. R. Jackson White, *In Quest of Community: Social Philosophy in the United States, 1860–1920* (New York: John Wiley, 1968), 27; David D. Hall and Alan Taylor, "Reassessing the Local History of New England," in *New England: A Bibliography of Its History*, ed. Roger Parks (Hanover, N.H.: University Press of New England, 1989), xix–xxvi.

23. William B. Weeden, *Economic and Social History of New England, 1620–1789* (Williamstown, Mass.: Corner House Publishers, 1978), 1: 19, 49.

24. Ibid., 1: 19–20, 67.

25. Ibid., 1: 87, 99, 281.

26. Ibid., 1: 403; 2: 786.

27. William B. Weeden, *Early Rhode Island: A Social History of the People* (New York: Grafton Press, 1910; repr. Bowie, Md.: Heritage Books, 1991), 11; William B. Weeden, "The Development of the American People," *Proceedings of the American Antiquarian Society* 13 (April 1899): 27–29.

28. Lois Kimball Mathews, *The Expansion of New England: The Spread of New England Settlement and Institutions to the Mississippi River, 1620–1865* (New York: Russell and Russell, 1962), 1–5, 10, 250, 261.

29. William Stubbs, *Lectures on Early English History* (London: Longmans, Green, 1906), 185.

30. Milton Berman, *John Fiske: The Evolution of a Popularizer* (Cambridge: Harvard University Press, 1961), is the most thorough treatment. Other studies include George Parsons Winston, *John Fiske* (New York: Twayne, 1972); Henry Steele Commager, "John Fiske: An Interpretation," *Proceedings of the Massachusetts Historical Society* 66 (1942): 332–45; Russel B. Nye, "John Fiske and His Cosmic Philosophy," *Papers of the Michigan Academy of Science, Arts and Letters* 28 (1942): 685–98; Jennings B. Sanders, "John Fiske," in *The Marcus W. Jernigan Essays in American Historiography: By*

His Former Students at the University of Chicago, ed. William T. Hutchinson (New York: Russell and Russell, 1937), 144–70; Philip P. Wiener, *Evolution and the Founders of Pragmatism* (Cambridge: Harvard University Press, 1949), 129–51; and Bruce Kuklick, *The Rise of American Philosophy: Cambridge, Massachusetts, 1860–1930* (New Haven: Yale University Press, 1977), 80–91. I discussed other aspects of Fiske's thought in "The Meaning of Freedom for George Bancroft and John Fiske," *Midcontinent American Studies Journal* 10 (Spring 1969), 60–75, and *Worldly Theologians: The Persistence of Religion in Nineteenth-Century American Thought* (Washington, D.C.: University Press of America, 1981), 69–126.

31. Berman, *John Fiske*, 77–79, 84–85, 125; John Fiske to Abby Brooks, March 30, 1862 (FK 30). This item is reproduced by permission of The Huntington Library, San Marino, California. Fiske wrote later that he would willingly "devote my life to the study [of history] if I could get this chance to teach here at Harvard. I should at last get the opportunity for which I have been waiting all my life, of doing the sort of work I love best, instead of merely makeshift work." John Fiske to Edward Everett Hale, April 8, 16, 1879 (FK 117–18). These items are reproduced by permission of The Huntington Library, San Marino, California.

32. William Dean Howells, "John Fiske," *Harper's Weekly* 45 (July 20, 1901): 732; John Fiske to Abby Fiske, August 24, 1873 (FK 170). This item is reproduced by permission of The Huntington Library, San Marino, California. Patrick D. Hazard remarked upon Fiske's personal excesses in "John Fiske as American Scholar: A Study in the Testing of a Native American Tradition" (Ph.D. diss., Western Reserve University, 1957), 203.

33. Phyllis Ann O'Callaghan, "The Philosophy of History of John Fiske" (Ph.D. diss., Saint Louis University, 1957), 108; John Fiske, *Myths and Myth-Makers: Old Tales and Superstitions Interpreted by Comparative Mythology* (Boston: Houghton Mifflin, 1872), 21, 36.

34. Berman, *John Fiske*, 259.

35. Hazard, "John Fiske," 516, 543; Berman, *John Fiske*, 246. Charles M. Andrews faulted Fiske's lack of original research and ideas and noted the early fading of his influence in "John Fiske, Philosopher and Historian," *Yale Review*, n.s., 7 (July 1918): 865–69.

36. Berman, *John Fiske*, 77–79, 84–85, 125; John Fiske to Abby Brooks, March 30, 1862 (FK 30), John Fiske to Herbert Spencer, September 29, 1871 (FK 1144). These items are reproduced by permission of The Huntington Library, San Marino, California; John Fiske, *Outlines of Cosmic Philosophy: Based on the Doctrine of Evolution, with Criticisms on the Positive Philosophy*, 4 vols. (Boston: Houghton Mifflin, 1874), 4: 231–61.

37. Vernon Louis Parrington, *Main Currents in American Thought: The Beginnings of Critical Realism in America, 1860–1920* (New York: Harcourt, Brace, 1930), 13.

38. John Fiske to Rev. J. E. Barnes, May 1860 (FK 1103). This item is reproduced by permission of The Huntington Library, San Marino, California.

39. John Fiske, *Excursions of an Evolutionist*, 16th ed. (Boston: Houghton Mifflin, 1894), 259; John Fiske, *The Beginnings of New England: or the Puritan Theocracy in Its Relations to Civil and Religious Liberty* (Boston: Houghton Mifflin, 1896), 58, 246.

40. John Fiske, *A Century of Science and Other Essays* (Boston: Houghton Mifflin, 1899), 142–45, 149; John Fiske, *New France and New England* (Boston: Houghton Mifflin, 1902), 222–25.

41. H. Burnell Pannill, *The Religious Faith of John Fiske* (Durham, N.C.: Duke University Press, 1957), 92–93, 206–7.

42. John Fiske to Rev. J. E. Barnes, May 1860 (FK 1103). This item is reproduced by permission of The Huntington Library, San Marino, California; John Fiske, *The Idea of God as Affected by Modern Knowledge* (Boston: Houghton Mifflin, 1885), 82–84, 111–12, 150–54.

43. Jon H. Roberts, *Darwinism and the Divine in America: Protestant Intellectuals and Organic Evolution, 1859–1900* (Madison: University of Wisconsin Press, 1988), 137–39, 157–58; Alexander V. G. Allen, *The Continuity of Christian Thought: A Study of Modern Theology in the Light of Its History* (Boston: Houghton Mifflin, 1884), 8, 176, 373–82, 438.

44. John Fiske, *The Destiny of Man: Viewed in the Light of His Origin* (Boston: Houghton Mifflin, 1884), 103, 107–18. An early assertion of the "complete harmony" between science and Christianity appears in a letter from Fiske to his mother, Mary Stoughton, March 31, 1872 (FK 850). This item is reproduced by permission of The Huntington Library, San Marino, California.

45. Pannill, *Religious Faith of John Fiske*, 175.

46. Herbert Spencer, *The Principles of Sociology* (London: Williams and Norgate, 1897–1906), 1: 13, 299, 423; 3: 106; Herbert Spencer, *First Principles* (New York: De Witt Revolving Fund, 1958), 130.

47. Spencer, *Principles of Sociology*, 1: 701; 2: 321–22; 3: 102.

48. Fiske, *Cosmic Philosophy*, 3: 289, 297, 313 (original italics omitted); 4: 20, 24, 157–58.

49. Ibid., 3: 344.

50. Ibid., 4: 161–62; John Fiske, *Through Nature to God* (Boston: Houghton Mifflin, 1899), 88, 97; John Fiske to Mary Stoughton, September 7, 1884 (FK 1039). This item is reproduced by permission of The Huntington Library, San Marino, California.

51. Fiske, *Century of Science*, 209, 213.

52. Fiske, *Cosmic Philosophy*, 3: 327–28, 285–88; 4: 19–24; Fiske, *Through Nature*, 66; John Fiske, *Darwinism and Other Essays*, rev. ed. (Boston: Houghton Mifflin, 1886), 164. Phyllis O'Callaghan usefully delineated the distinction in Fiske's thought between evolution and social progress. "Philosophy of History of John Fiske," 66–79.

53. Fiske, *Cosmic Philosophy*, 3: 287; 4: 27.

54. Ibid., 3: 292, 344.

55. Edward Shils, "Tradition and Liberty: Antinomy and Interdependence," *Ethics* 68 (April 1958): 154.

56. Fiske, *Idea of God*, 138; John Fiske, *Life Everlasting* (Boston: Houghton Mifflin, 1901), 57; O'Callaghan, "Philosophy of History of John Fiske," 145, 155, 163. Tony Judt notes that the English language does not lend itself as readily as German, French, and the Slavic languages to "the easy and chilling conflation of hearth, home, homeland, homogeneity, and Heimat." *New Republic* 219 (September 7, 1998): 34. Even with a degree of linguistic prophylaxis, however, nineteenth-century Anglo-Americans found it natural to trace the virtues of home over time and space to larger institutional embodiments.

57. Fiske, *Idea of God*, 45. Cf. Fiske, *Through Nature*, 115.

58. J. W. Burrow, *A Liberal Descent: Victorian Historians and the English Past* (Cambridge: Cambridge University Press, 1981), 107, 22.

59. Fiske, *Century of Science*, 271; Edward Augustus Freeman, *Lectures to American Audiences* (Philadelphia: Porter and Coates, 1882), 10–12; Edward Augustus Freeman, *The Growth of the English Constitution from the Earliest Times* (New York: Frederick A. Stokes, 1890), 41.

60. Henry Sumner Maine, *Village-Communities in the East and West* (New York: Henry Holt, 1889; repr. New York: Arno Press, 1974), 107–8, 146, 166; Henry Sumner Maine, *Lectures on the Early History of Institutions* (New York: Henry Holt, 1875), 388. J. W. Burrow discusses the influence of these ideas in "'The Village Community' and the Uses of History in Late Nineteenth-Century England," in *Historical Perspectives: Studies in English Thought and Society in Honour of J. H. Plumb*, ed. Neil McKendrick (London: Europa Publications, 1974), 255–84.

61. Maine, *Village-Communities*, 201; J. W. Burrow, *Whigs and Liberals: Continuity and Change in English Political Thought* (Oxford: Clarendon Press, 1988), 131–35; Freeman, *English Constitution*, 17–18; Edward Augustus Freeman, *History of Federal Government in Greece and Italy*, 2d ed. (London: Macmillan, 1893), 38–39, 82–84.

62. John Fiske, *Old Virginia and Her Neighbours* (Boston: Houghton Mifflin, 1897), 1: 228, 2: 147–48; Fiske, *Beginnings of New England*, 24–25.

63. John Fiske, *American Political Ideas: Viewed from the Standpoint of Universal History* (New York: Harper, 1885), 18, 36–37, 41; Fiske, *Old Virginia*, 2: 252, 309; Fiske, *Century of Science*, 280.

64. Fiske, *American Political Ideas*, 36–37.

65. John Fiske, "Cambridge as Village and City," *A Century of Science*, 284.

66. John Fiske, "The Story of a New England Town," *Atlantic Monthly* 86 (December 1900): 722, 726, 734–35. Hazard notes Fiske's early opinion of Middlebury. "John Fiske," 42.

67. Fiske, *American Political Ideas*, 35; Fiske, *Old Virginia*, 2: 42–44, 147–49, 323–24; John Fiske, *The Dutch and Quaker Colonies in America* (Boston: Houghton Mifflin, 1899), 1: 225.

68. Fiske, *Beginnings of New England*, 49–52.

69. Ibid., 7–12, 20–25 (original italics omitted).

70. Fiske, *Cosmic Philosophy*, 4: 33; John Fiske, *The Unseen World and Other Essays*

(Boston: Houghton Mifflin, 1876), 333–34; Fiske, *American Political Ideas*, 87, 120–24, 129; Fiske, *Beginnings of New England*, 25, 52.

71. Fiske, *Beginnings of New England*, 26, 52, 58, 246–47; Fiske, *American Political Ideas*, 120–23, 129; John Fiske, *The Critical Period of American History, 1783–1789* (Boston: Houghton Mifflin, 1888), 64.

72. Philip P. Wiener, *Evolution and the Founders of Pragmatism* (Cambridge: Harvard University Press, 1949), 143; Burrow, *Liberal Descent*, 175.

73. Fiske, *Cosmic Philosophy*, 4: 147–48; Fiske, *American Political Ideas*, 6, 87–88; Fiske, "New England Town," 723.

74. Fiske, *American Political Ideas*, 6, 35, 87–88, 91–93; Fiske, "New England Town," 723–27.

75. Fiske, *American Political Ideas*, 85; Fiske, *Critical Period*, 237–38.

76. Fiske, *Century of Science*, 38.

77. Fiske, *American Political Ideas*, 123, 128, 146–47, 151–52.

78. Ibid., 92–93, 143.

79. See Reginald Horsman, *Race and Manifest Destiny: The Origins of American Racial Anglo-Saxonism* (Cambridge: Harvard University Press, 1981).

80. John Fiske, *The American Revolution* (Boston: Houghton Mifflin, 1899), 2: 18–20. Cf. Fiske, *American Political Ideas*, 115.

81. John Fiske, *The Discovery of America: With Some Account of Ancient America and the Spanish Conquest* (Boston: Houghton Mifflin, 1894), 1: 23; Fiske, *Excursions*, 103; Fiske, *Darwinism*, 242; Berman, *John Fiske*, 251–52. On Fiske's attitudes toward immigration, see also Hazard, "John Fiske," 426–28. In a letter never sent, Fiske noted that he had been prepared to join the protest against annexation of the Philippines until he became aware of pro-annexation arguments which he was unable to refute. John Fiske to "Mr. Bradford," June 14, 1898 (FK 1107). This item is reproduced by permission of The Huntington Library, San Marino, California.

82. Fiske, *Century of Science*, 211–12.

83. John Fiske, *Colonization of the New World*, vol. 21 of *A History of All Nations* (Philadelphia: Lea Brothers, 1905), 43; Edward W. Said, *Culture and Imperialism* (New York: Knopf, 1993), 222.

84. Fiske, *Discovery of America*, 1: vi, 130–31; 2: 290–91, 319–38, 405.

85. Ibid., 1: 33, 49n–50n; 2: 261, 292.

86. Dorothy Ross, "Historical Consciousness in Nineteenth-Century America," *American Historical Review* 89 (October 1984): 909–10. Ross provides a more extended treatment of the subject in *The Origins of American Social Science* (Cambridge: Cambridge University Press, 1991).

87. Quinones, *Mapping Literary Modernism*, 257.

88. Alasdair MacIntyre, *Three Rival Versions of Moral Enquiry: Encyclopaedia, Genealogy, and Tradition* (Notre Dame, Ind.: University of Notre Dame Press, 1990), 59–60, 65, 125.

89. Ibid., 182.

Portions of this chapter were previously published in "More English than the English: Cavalier and Democrat in Virginia Historical Writing, 1870–1930," *Journal of American Studies* 27 (1993): 2, 187–206. Reprinted with the permission of Cambridge University Press.

1. See, e.g., Lyon G. Tyler to J. Franklin Jameson, May 26, 1914, Tyler Family Papers, Group B, Manuscripts and Rare Books Department, Earl Gregg Swem Library, College of William and Mary; John Fiske, *Old Virginia and Her Neighbours*, 2 vols. (Boston: Houghton Mifflin, 1897), 1: 102–111; 2: 12–13, 26–29; Lyon Gardiner Tyler, review of *Old Virginia and Her Neighbours*, by John Fiske, in *American Historical Review* 3 (July 1898): 735; John Fiske to Abby Fiske, October 26, 1895 (FK 443). This item is reproduced by permission of The Huntington Library, San Marino, California. On the Culpepper protest see Patrick D. Hazard, "John Fiske as American Scholar: A Study in the Testing of a Native American Tradition" (Ph.D. diss., Western Reserve University, 1957), 347–48.

2. James M. Lindgren, *Preserving the Old Dominion: Historic Preservation and Virginia Traditionalism* (Charlottesville: University Press of Virginia, 1993), 165; Lyon G. Tyler to W. B. Cridlin, March 30, 1922, Tyler Family Papers.

3. Thomas Nelson Page, *The Old Dominion: Her Making and Her Manners* (New York: Scribner's, 1908), 335.

4. Edward Ingle, *Local Institutions of Virginia*, Johns Hopkins Studies in Historical and Political Science, ed. Herbert Baxter Adams, 3d ser., 2–3 (Baltimore: Johns Hopkins University Press, 1885), 9–10, 47, 71.

5. Philip Alexander Bruce, *Social Life of Virginia in the Seventeenth Century: An Inquiry into the Origin of the Higher Planting Class, Together with an Account of the Habits, Customs, and Diversions of the People* (Richmond: Whittet and Shepperson, 1907), 104; Philip A. Bruce, Lecture before Christ Church, ca. 1909, Philip Alexander Bruce Papers, Special Collections, Alderman Library, University of Virginia, Charlottesville, Va.

6. Philip Alexander Bruce, *Institutional History of Virginia in the Seventeenth Century: An Inquiry into the Religious, Moral, Educational, Legal, Military, and Political Condition of the People, Based Upon Original and Contemporaneous Records*, 2 vols. (New York: Putnam's, 1910; repr. Gloucester, Mass.: Peter Smith, 1964), 2: 605, 635.

7. Philip Alexander Bruce, "The Birds of My English Water Meadow," *South Atlantic Quarterly* 15 (April 1916): 113–28; Lyon G. Tyler to Philip A. Bruce, May 18, 1915, Tyler Family Papers; Philip A. Bruce to Joseph Edmunds Gaines, May 9, 1915, July 21, 1917, Philip Alexander Bruce Papers, Virginia Historical Society, Richmond.

8. Alexander Brown, *The First Republic in America: An Account of the Origin of this Nation, Written from the Records then (1624) Concealed by the Council, Rather than from the Histories then Licensed by the Crown* (Boston: Houghton Mifflin, 1898), 329, 651; Thomas Nelson Page, *Address at the Three Hundredth Anniversary of the Settlement of Jamestown* (Richmond: Whittet and Shepperson, 1919), 18; Thomas Nelson Page, *Robert E. Lee:*

Man and Soldier (New York: Scribner's, 1911), 48. J. W. Burrow similarly notes that for such a Victorian historian as Edward A. Freeman, English history was "a drama of rebirths and resurrections" which approached typology. *A Liberal Descent: Victorian Historians and the English Past* (Cambridge: Cambridge University Press, 1981), 221.

9. Philip A. Bruce, Lecture before Christ Church, ca. 1909, Bruce Papers, University of Virginia; Philip Alexander Bruce, *The Rise of the New South*, vol. 17 of *The History of North America* (Philadelphia: George Barrie and Sons, 1905), 4, 407.

10. Philip Alexander Bruce, *The Plantation Negro as a Freeman: Observations on His Character, Condition, and Prospects in Virginia* (1910; repr. Williamstown, Mass.: Corner House Publishers, 1970), 129, 256, 259; Thomas Nelson Page, *The Negro: The Southerner's Problem* (New York: Scribner's, 1904; repr. New York: Johnson Reprint Company, 1970), 282–83; Lyman Moody Simms, Jr., "Philip Alexander Bruce and the Negro Problem, 1884–1930," *Virginia Magazine of History and Biography* 75 (July 1967): 361–62. See also Lyman Moody Simms, "Philip Alexander Bruce: His Life and Works" (Ph.D. diss., University of Virginia, 1966), 28–30, 85–106; and William S. Powell, "Philip Alexander Bruce, Historian," *Tyler's Quarterly Historical and Genealogical Magazine* 30 (January 1949): 165–71.

11. Lyon G. Tyler to J. Skottowe Wanamaker, June 6, 1919; Lyon G. Tyler to Philip A. Bruce, May 18, 1915, Tyler Family Papers.

12. Philip A. Bruce to Lyon G. Tyler, July 15, 1925, Tyler Family Papers; Philip Alexander Bruce, *Robert E. Lee* (Philadelphia: George W. Jacobs, 1907), 72; Bruce, *Institutional History*, 2: 633.

13. Wilbur J. Cash, *The Mind of the South* (New York: Knopf, 1941), 59–70; Dewey W. Grantham, *Southern Progressivism: The Reconciliation of Progress and Tradition* (Knoxville: University of Tennessee Press, 1983), 65; Raymond H. Pulley, *Old Virginia Restored: An Interpretation of the Progressive Impulse, 1870–1930* (Charlottesville: University Press of Virginia, 1968), 32–40, 59.

14. Pulley, *Old Virginia Restored*, ix, 5, 58–59, 112; Grantham, *Southern Progressivism*, xvi, 65, 72–74, 418–19.

15. A[rthur] G[ranville] Bradley, *Sketches from Old Virginia* (London: Macmillan, 1897), 242. Examples of the description of the plantation as a kingdom or principality are found in Philip Alexander Bruce, *Economic History of Virginia in the Seventeenth Century: An Inquiry into the Material Condition of the People, Based Upon Original and Contemporaneous Records* (New York: Macmillan, 1896), 2: 522–23; and Thomas Jefferson Wertenbaker, *Patrician and Plebeian in Virginia: or The Origin and Development of the Social Classes of the Old Dominion* (1910; repr. New York: Russell and Russell, 1958), 58.

16. Philip Alexander Bruce, *Brave Deeds of Confederate Soldiers* (Philadelphia: George W. Jacobs, 1916), 15. "The more we cherish the noble social and political traditions of the South, the more we adhere to the customs and feelings that have come down to us from our fathers, the more we venerate our heroes, . . . the greater we will be as a people," Bruce had written in similar spirit twenty-seven years earlier. Philip A.

Bruce, editorial in the *Richmond Times-Dispatch*, December 1889, Bruce Papers, University of Virginia.

17. Philip A. Bruce, editorial in the *Richmond Times-Dispatch*, December 1889, Bruce Papers, University of Virginia .

18. Henry Watterson, "A Plea for Provincialism" [address at Georgetown, Ky., 1874], in *The Compromises of Life and Other Lectures and Addresses, Including Some Observations on Certain Downward Tendencies of Modern Society* (New York: Duffield and Company, 1906), 272; Thomas Nelson Page, "The American Home: The Source of Our Liberties," 1–2, 6–7, 9–10, Special Collections, Alderman Library, University of Virginia, Charlottesville, Va.

19. Moncure Daniel Conway, *Barons of the Potomack and the Rappahannock* (New York: Grolier Club, 1892), 135.

20. Philip A. Bruce, editorial in the *Richmond Times-Dispatch*, December 1889, Bruce Papers, University of Virginia. Basil L. Gildersleeve held local feeling to be part of the "creed of the Old South." *The Creed of the Old South* (Baltimore: Johns Hopkins University Press, 1915), 32–35; John Fiske, *American Political Ideas: Viewed from the Standpoint of Universal History. Three Lectures Delivered at the Royal Institution of Great Britain in May 1880* (New York: Harper and Brothers, 1885), 7; Page, *Robert E. Lee*, 46.

21. John E. Hobeika, *The Sage of Lion's Den: An Appreciation of the Character and Career of Lyon Gardiner Tyler and of His Writings on Abraham Lincoln and the War Between the States* (New York: Exposition Press, 1948), 16; Lindgren, *Preserving the Old Dominion*, 72; Lila Meade Valentine to Lyon G. Tyler, December 13, 1909, January 11, 1910; Philip A. Bruce to Lyon G. Tyler, November 10, 1911; Lyon G. Tyler to Alice O. Tyler, April 16, 1914, Tyler Family Papers.

22. Lindgren, *Preserving the Old Dominion*, 26; Simms, "Philip Alexander Bruce," 86; Philip Alexander Bruce, "Some American Impressions of Europe," *The Nineteenth Century and After* 49 (March 1901): 472, 476–77.

23. Philip A. Bruce to Lyon G. Tyler, November 5, 1922, Tyler Family Papers.

24. Archibald Henderson to Philip A. Bruce, June 7, 1920; John T. Latané to Philip A. Bruce, July 21, 1917, Bruce Papers, University of Virginia; Albert B. Hart to Lyon G. Tyler, September 24, 1929; Worthington Chauncey Ford to Lyon G. Tyler, May 19, 1922, Tyler Family Papers.

25. Lyon Gardiner Tyler, *A Criticism by Lyon Gardiner Tyler of History of the American People By David S. Muzzey of Massachusetts*, 2d ed. (Richmond: Richmond Press, 1932), 54; Lyon G. Tyler to William E. Dodd, November 4, 1920, Tyler Family Papers; *Time*, April 9, 1928, pp. 11–12; Philip A. Bruce to Lyon G. Tyler, April 28, 1927; Lyon G. Tyler to Robert M. Hughes, June 20, 1928; Lyon G. Tyler to the treasurer of the New York Southern Society, November 10, 1933, Tyler Family Papers.

26. Philip A. Bruce to Lyon G. Tyler, July 10, 1926, Tyler Family Papers. Bruce's fears were perhaps not unfounded. "In the late 1920s schoolboys in three Alabama cities cited Lincoln more often than Lee as a historical or public character after whom they wished to model themselves," Gaines Foster notes, though, he adds,

"both Lincoln and Lee ranked well below Washington and Lindbergh." *Ghosts of the Confederacy: Defeat, the Lost Cause, and the Emergence of the New South, 1865 to 1913* (New York: Oxford University Press, 1987), 197.

27. Tyler, *Criticism of Muzzey*, 11, 18, 79, 85; Philip A. Bruce to Lyon G. Tyler, May 16, 1928, Tyler Family Papers.

28. Bruce, "Some American Impressions," 481; Philip A. Bruce to Lyon G. Tyler, September 29, 1916, Tyler Family Papers; Philip A. Bruce, letter to *Richmond Times-Dispatch*, April 30, 1926, Bruce Papers, University of Virginia.

29. Philip Alexander Bruce, *The Virginia Plutarch*, 2 vols. (Chapel Hill: University of North Carolina Press, 1929), 1: 68; Lyon Gardiner Tyler, *The Cradle of the Republic: Jamestown and James River* (Richmond: Heritage Press, 1906), 182; Tyler, *Criticism of Muzzey*, 5.

30. Philip A. Bruce, letter to *Richmond Times-Dispatch*, April 30, 1926; Philip A. Bruce, letter to Springfield [Mass.] Daily Republican, August 20, 1923, Bruce Papers, University of Virginia.

31. Watterson, *Compromises of Life*, 322–23. Lincoln was "a Southern man," Watterson insisted. He "sprang from a Virginia pedigree and was born in Kentucky." Ibid., 163, 364.

32. Mary Newton Stanard, *The Story of Virginia's First Century* (Philadelphia: J.B. Lippincott, 1928), 11.

33. Philip A. Bruce to Lyon G. Tyler, August 25, 1925, Tyler Family Papers.

34. Brown, *First Republic in America*, 184–85, 249, 252, 258.

35. Ibid., xx, 332, 615, 650; Alexander Brown, *English Politics in Early Virginia History* (Boston: Houghton Mifflin, 1901; repr. New York: Russell and Russell, 1968), 53, 143–44, 262.

36. Brown, *English Politics*, 13, 235; Brown, *First Republic*, 434, 651.

37. Wesley Frank Craven, *Dissolution of the Virginia Company: The Failure of a Colonial Experiment* (New York: Oxford University Press, 1932), 1–23, traces the historiography of the problem. See also Wesley Frank Craven, "'. . . And So the Form of Government Became Perfect,'" *Virginia Magazine of History and Biography* 77 (April 1969): 133–34. Alden T. Vaughan, "The Evolution of Virginia History: Early Historians of the First Colony," in *Perspectives on Early American History: Essays in Honor of Richard B. Morris*, ed. Alden T. Vaughan and George Athan Billias (New York: Harper and Row, 1973), 9–39, deals especially with the histories of Smith, Robert Beverley, and William Stith.

38. Wertenbaker, *Patrician and Plebeian*, i, 11, 20, 23.

39. Tunstall Smith to Betty Bruce, May 8, 1919; Fairfax Harrison to Philip A. Bruce, September 23, 1926, Bruce Papers, University of Virginia.

40. Tunstall Smith to Betty Bruce, May 8, 1919; Thomas Jefferson Wertenbaker to Philip A. Bruce, August 22, 1917, Bruce Papers, University of Virginia; Thomas Jefferson Wertenbaker to Lyon G. Tyler, March 24, 1914; Philip A. Bruce to Lyon G. Tyler, June 12, 1920, Tyler Family Papers. See also Philip A. Bruce, review of *Virginia*

under the Stuarts, by Thomas J. Wertenbaker, in *American Historical Review* 20 (October 1914): 163–64.

41. Lyon G. Tyler to Philip A. Bruce, July 8, 1926, Bruce Papers, University of Virginia ; Philip A. Bruce to Lyon G. Tyler, July 10, 1926, Tyler Family Papers.

42. Wertenbaker, *Patrician and Plebeian*, 32n–33n, 58, 102.

43. Philip A. Bruce to Lyon G. Tyler, July 10, 1926, Tyler Family Papers.

44. Thomas Nelson Page, *The Old South: Essays Social and Political* (New York: Scribner's, 1896), 40.

45. Lyon G. Tyler to Philip A. Bruce, February 27, 1923, August 5, 1925, Bruce Papers, University of Virginia; Lyon Gardiner Tyler, *The Cavalier in America* (Richmond: Whittet and Shepperson, 1913), n.p.

46. Edward L. Ayers, *Southern Crossing: A History of the American South, 1877–1906* (Oxford: Oxford University Press, 1995), 251. Dewey Grantham points out a "dialectical process" between the South and the nation as a whole in *The Democratic South* (Athens: University of Georgia Press, 1963), 98; Page, *Old Dominion*, 60–61.

47. Lindgren, *Preserving the Old Dominion*, 123.

48. "The Ter-Centenary of Jamestown," *Virginia Magazine of History and Biography* 8 (April 1901): 416; Julian A. C. Chandler and Travis B. Thames, *Colonial Virginia* (Richmond: Times Dispatch Co., 1907), 247.

49. Page, *Three Hundredth Anniversary*, 11–12, 18, 27.

50. Ibid., 28; Foster, *Ghosts of the Confederacy*, 135; Julia Wyatt Bullard, *Jamestown Tributes and Toasts* (Lynchburg, Va.: J. P. Bell, 1907), passim.

51. Lyon G. Tyler to W. B. Cridlen, Secretary, Virginia Historical Pageant Association, March 30, 1922, Tyler Family Papers.

52. Francis Pendleton Gaines, *The Southern Plantation: A Study in the Development and Accuracy of a Tradition* (New York: Columbia University Press, 1925), 157; David Hackett Fischer, *Albion's Seed: Four British Folkways in America* (New York: Oxford University Press, 1989), 897; Conway, *Barons*, 135. Kenneth S. Greenberg emphasizes how important to the antebellum southern culture of honor was the presumption of an essential equality among men of the upper class. *Honor and Slavery* (Princeton: Princeton University Press, 1996).

53. John Esten Cooke, *Virginia: A History of the People* (Boston: Houghton Mifflin, 1883), iv–vi, 155–56, 365, 370.

54. Page, *Old South*, 106–7; Page, *Old Dominion*, 366; Page, *Three Hundredth Anniversary*, 16, 22. Michael Flusche, in "Thomas Nelson Page: The Quandary of a Literary Gentleman," *Virginia Magazine of History and Biography* 84 (October 1976): 478–79, comments that Page depicted colonial Virginia "alternately as aristocratic or democratic." I would emphasize Page's efforts to combine the two views.

55. Page, *Old Dominion*, 137–41; Page, *Old South*, 9.

56. Philip A. Bruce to Lyon G. Tyler, May 9, 1925, Tyler Family Papers; Tyler, *Cradle of the Republic*, 191, 199–200; Lyon Gardiner Tyler, *England in America, 1580–1652* (New York: Harper and Brothers, 1904; repr. New York: Greenwood Press, 1969), 116;

Lyon Gardiner Tyler, review of *Old Virginia and Her Neighbours*, by John Fiske, *American Historical Review* 3 (July 1898): 736–37.

57. Rosewell Page, *Thomas Nelson Page: A Memoir of a Virginia Gentleman* (New York: Scribner's, 1923), 84–85; Bradley, *Sketches*, 94, 97; Philip Alexander Bruce, "The Social Life of the Upper South," in *The South in the Building of the Nation*, ed. Samuel Chiles Mitchell (Richmond: Southern Historical Publication Society, 1909), 10: 9. Timothy Curtis Jacobson points out the importance of small-farming agrarianism as a tradition linking the Old South with the New. "Tradition and Change in the New South, 1865–1910" (Ph.D. diss., Vanderbilt University, 1974), 112, 128–29, 180.

58. *New York Times*, February 13, 1935, p. 19.

59. Lyon Gardiner Tyler, *The Letters and Times of the Tylers* (Richmond: Whittet and Shepperson, 1884–85), 1: 26–27, 37–42, 45, 192.

60. Ibid., 1: 122, 406, 471; 2: 197, 299–300, 468.

61. Ibid., 1: 6, 26, 33–34; 2: 537.

62. Lyon G. Tyler to J. B. C. Spencer, November 25, 1907, Tyler Family Papers.

63. Tyler, *Criticism of Muzzey*, 13–14; Lyon G. Tyler to L. Lamprey, July 19, 1928, Bruce Papers, University of Virginia.

64. Philip A. Bruce to Lyon G. Tyler, May 9, 1925, Tyler Family Papers; Lyon G. Tyler to Philip A. Bruce, May 25, 1925, April 30, 1927, Bruce Papers, University of Virginia.

65. William Alexander Caruthers, *The Cavaliers of Virginia, or The Recluse of Jamestown: An Historical Romance of the Old Dominion* (1835; repr. Ridgewood, N.J.: Gregg Press, 1968), 1: 4; John Esten Cooke, *The Virginia Comedians: or, Old Days in the Old Dominion* (New York: D. Appleton, 1883), 2: 107. Ritchie Devon Watson provides an extended treatment of the literary uses of the "cavalier myth" in *The Cavalier in Virginia Fiction* (Baton Rouge: Louisiana State University Press, 1985).

66. William H. Whitmore, *The Cavalier Dismounted: An Essay on the Origin of the Founders of the Thirteen Colonies* (Salem, Mass.: G. M. Whipple and A. A. Smith, 1864), iv, 1, and passim.

67. William R. Taylor, *Cavalier and Yankee: The Old South and American National Character* (New York: George Braziller, 1961); Paul H. Buck, *The Road to Reunion, 1865–1900* (Boston: Little, Brown, 1937); Robert Darden Little, "The Ideology of the New South: A Study in the Development of Ideas, 1865–1910" (Ph.D. diss., University of Chicago, 1950); Paul M. Gaston, *The New South Creed: A Study in Southern Mythmaking* (New York: Knopf, 1970) are fundamental for understanding the Old and New South uses of the cavalier.

68. Wertenbaker, *Patrician and Plebeian*, 222; Watson, *Cavalier*, 37, 133.

69. William Edward Walker, "John Esten Cooke: A Critical Biography" (Ph.D. diss., Vanderbilt University, 1957), ii, 231–32, 242, 728; Cooke, *Virginia*, 159–61, 200, 229.

70. John Esten Cooke, *Stonewall Jackson: A Military Biography* (New York: D. Appleton, 1876), 170–72, 175. Cooke also likened J. E. B. Stuart to Prince Rupert.

The royalist cavalry leader was a favorite type of the cavalier, and according to Cooke kin to Stuart—himself a "model cavalier." See Steve Davis, "John Esten Cooke and Confederate Defeat," *Civil War History* 24 (March 1978): 74–75.

71. Cooke, *Stonewall Jackson*, 9, 12, 22–23, 44, 136, 165, 172, 464.

72. Philip A. Bruce, Lecture before Christ Church, ca. 1909, Bruce Papers, University of Virginia.

73. Page, *Old South*, 8–9, 16–17.

74. Maud Wilder Goodwin, *The Colonial Cavalier* (1895; repr. New York: Arno Press, 1975), 7.

75. Tyler, *Cavalier in America*, n. p.

76. Ibid.

77. William Peterfield Trent, *William Gilmore Simms* (1892; repr. New York: Greenwood Press, 1969), 31; Cooke, *Virginia*, 229–30. In an early novel Cooke described eighteenth-century "cavaliers," including George Washington, as meriting the title by nature as much as by family status—"by God's patent, as by the King's." *Fairfax: or The Master of Greenway Court. A Chronicle of the Valley of the Shenandoah* (New York: G. W. Carleton and Co., 1868), 301. Matthew C. O'Brien comments on these efforts to fuse aristocratic and democratic values in "John Esten Cooke, George Washington, and the Virginia Cavaliers," *Virginia Magazine of History and Biography* 84 (July 1976): 259–65.

78. Lindgren, *Preserving the Old Dominion*, 135.

79. Page, *Three Hundredth Anniversary*, 24; Lyon Gardiner Tyler, "Bacon's Rebellion: From Dr. Tyler's Unpublished History," *Tyler's Quarterly Historical and Genealogical Magazine* 23 (July 1941): 23. See also Page, *Old South*, 17–19. J. V. Ridgely notes William Alexander Caruthers's portrayal of Bacon as a cavalier leader of the people in *Nineteenth-Century Southern Literature* (Lexington: University Press of Kentucky, 1980), 45. For parallels between Bacon and Patrick Henry, see Tyler, "Bacon's Rebellion," 23, and Mary Newton Stanard, *The Story of Bacon's Rebellion* (New York: Neale Publishing, 1907), 47, 57; Thomas Jefferson Wertenbaker, *Virginia under the Stuarts: 1607–1688* (Princeton: Princeton University Press, 1914; repr. New York: Russell and Russell, 1957), v–vi.

80. Philip Alexander Bruce, "The National Spirit of General Lee," *South Atlantic Quarterly* 10 (January 1911): 29–30.

81. Page, *Lee*, 6; John Esten Cooke, *A Life of General Robert E. Lee* (New York: D. Appleton, 1871), 5–6.

82. Bruce, *Lee*, 106. Bruce suggested that "it was the stern spirit of his Covenanter forefathers that disclosed itself" in General Grant's "apparently reckless sacrifice of human lives" (ibid., 259).

83. Page, *Lee*, 10, 12, 687–88; Davis, "Cooke and Confederate Defeat," 69.

84. Philip Alexander Bruce, "Recollections of My Plantation Teachers," *South Atlantic Quarterly* 16 (January 1917): 3–5; Philip Alexander Bruce, "Autobiographical Sketch of Philip A. Bruce," 1–2, Bruce Papers, University of Virginia.

85. Bruce, "Autobiographical Sketch," 2–4; Simms, "Bruce: Life and Works," 7–8, 19–23, 30–35. William Cabell Bruce noted a "tone of reservation" in Lyon G. Tyler's comments on his life of Randolph. He wrote to Philip Bruce about his brother's friend: "It is hardly possible to lose sight of the fact that he is a bigoted partisan where his father or State rights are concerned, and it may be that his views about my book have been colored by my failure to say anything laudatory about his father in connection with the Tyler-Randolph competition for a seat in the U.S. Senate, and my freedom from sectional partisanship." W. C. Bruce to Philip A. Bruce, May 5, 1923, Bruce Papers, University of Virginia.

86. Simms, "Bruce: Life and Works," 47, 169, 240–41. James M. Lindgren contends that Bruce "represented a group of historians, novelists, and artists who glorified the plantation culture of the Old South and vindicated its ideals." *Preserving the Old Dominion*, 20–21. Hobeika, *Sage of Lion's Den*, 40, quotes Bruce's acknowledgment of his historiographical debt to Tyler.

87. Simms, "Bruce: Life and Works," 192–94; Philip A. Bruce, Lecture before Christ Church, ca. 1909, pp. 5–10, Bruce Papers, University of Virginia. Recently David Hackett Fischer has given support to Bruce's interpretation in its more pro-Cavalier aspects. See *Albion's Seed*, 225n.

88. Simms, "Bruce: Life and Works," 60; Henry Steele Commager, review of *The Virginia Plutarch*, by Philip Alexander Bruce, in *New York Herald Tribune Book Review*, March 2, 1930.

89. Philip A. Bruce to Lyon G. Tyler, July 15, 1925, Tyler Family Papers; Philip A. Bruce to Thomas N. Page, December 11, 1897, Thomas Nelson Page Papers, Special Collections, Alderman Library, University of Virginia, Charlottesville, Va.

90. Philip A. Bruce to Joseph Edmunds Gaines, July 21, 1917, August 27, 1919, Bruce Papers, Virginia Historical Society.

91. Philip A. Bruce to Joseph Edmunds Gaines, March 5, 1915, Bruce Papers, Virginia Historical Society.

92. Philip A. Bruce to Joseph Edmunds Gaines, April 16, May 9, July 10, August 20, October 4, 29, November 20, December 18, 1915; September 1, 1918; April 17, May 31, 1920; August 5, 1921, Bruce Papers, Virginia Historical Society.

93. Philip A. Bruce to Joseph Edmunds Gaines, October 9, n.y.; August 13, June 27, 1919, Bruce Papers, Virginia Historical Society.

94. Philip A. Bruce to Lyon G. Tyler, May 16, 1928, Tyler Family Papers.

95. Ibid.

96. Richard M. Weaver, *The Southern Tradition at Bay: A History of Postbellum Thought*, ed. George Core and M. E. Bradford (New Rochelle, N.Y.: Arlington House, 1968), 39. Cf. Eugene D. Genovese, who remarks that Burke "has long been a hero to southern conservatives." This may be, but I think that it has mainly been post–World War II conservatives who have applied the Burkean understanding of society to the South. See Genovese, *The Southern Tradition: The Achievement and Limitations of an American Conservatism* (Cambridge: Harvard University Press, 1994), 27; Philip

Alexander Bruce, review of *Robin Aroon*, by Armistead C. Gordon, *Richmond Times-Dispatch*, October, 1908, Bruce Papers, University of Virginia.

97. Bruce, *Social Life*, 25–27; Philip Alexander Bruce, "Cape Henry, 1607," *William and Mary Quarterly*, 2d ser., 6 (April 1926): 110–11.

98. Bruce, *Institutional History*, 1: 106; Bruce, *Social Life*, 253.

99. Bruce, *Economic History*, 2: 522–23; Philip Alexander Bruce, *History of the University of Virginia, 1819–1919: The Lengthened Shadow of One Man* (New York: Macmillan, 1921), 3: 273; Bruce, *New South*, 423.

100. Bruce, *Economic History*, 2: 568–69; Philip Alexander Bruce, "Some Aspects of Southern Development," typescript, n.d., Bruce Papers, University of Virginia, 6–7; Barry Alan Shain, *The Myth of American Individualism: The Protestant Origins of American Political Thought* (Princeton: Princeton University Press, 1994), 84–87, 95, 179. In a broader formulation, less applicable here, Richard M. Weaver contrasted the "social bond individualism" represented by John Randolph of Roanoke with the "anarchic individualism" of Henry David Thoreau. See *The Southern Essays of Richard M. Weaver*, ed. George M. Curtis III and James J. Thompson, Jr. (Indianapolis: Liberty Press, 1987), 82, 100, 102.

101. Bruce, "Some Aspects of Southern Development," 7; Bruce, "Social Life of the Upper South," 4; Philip Alexander Bruce, "The Co-operative Spirit," editorial in *Richmond Times-Dispatch*, July 6, 1890, Bruce Papers, University of Virginia.

102. Bruce, *Social Life*, 254–55; Bruce, *Institutional History*, 2: 613–14. See also Bruce, *Economic History*, 2: 568–69.

103. Gerald Smythe to Philip A. Bruce, July 6, 1916, Bruce Papers, University of Virginia.

104. Philip Alexander Bruce, review of *Robin Aroon*, by Armistead C. Gordon, *Richmond Times-Dispatch*, October, 1908, Bruce Papers, University of Virginia.

CHAPTER 3. *Tradition and Transcendence*

Portions of this chapter were previously published in "Ralph Adams Cram and the Americanization of the Middle Ages," *Journal of American Studies* 23 (1989): 2, 195–213. Reprinted with the permission of Cambridge University Press.

1. "Order of the White Rose. To the Companies and Associates of the White Rose in North America. Boston. St. George's Day, 1899," n.p., Louise Imogen Guiney Papers, College of the Holy Cross Archives and Special Collections.

2. Ibid.; Douglass Shand-Tucci, *Boston Bohemia, 1881–1900*, vol. 1 of *Ralph Adams Cram: Life and Architecture* (Amherst: University of Massachusetts Press, 1995), 317; Robert Muccigrosso, *American Gothic: The Mind and Art of Ralph Adams Cram* (Washington, D.C.: University Press of America, 1980), 9.

3. Louise Imogen Guiney to Rev. W. H. van Allen, May 8, 1899; to Herbert E. Clarke, June 23, 1899, in *Letters of Louise Imogen Guiney*, ed. Grace Guiney (New York: Harper and Brothers, 1926), 1: 257; 2: 4; Ralph Adams Cram to Louise Imogen

Guiney, 1899, Guiney Papers; E. M. Tenison, *Louise Imogen Guiney: Her Life and Works, 1861–1920* (London: Macmillan, 1923), 215, 132.

4. Ralph Adams Cram to Louise Imogen Guiney, n.d.; May 12, 1916, Guiney Papers.

5. "Skyward," *Time,* December 13, 1926, p. 20; Ann Miner Daniel, "The Early Architecture of Ralph Adams Cram, 1889–1902" (Ph.D. diss., University of North Carolina, 1978), 15; Shand-Tucci, *Boston Bohemia,* 193.

6. Muccigrosso, *American Gothic,* 8–9, 11; Shand-Tucci, *Boston Bohemia,* 6, 12, 366.

7. Ralph Adams Cram, *My Life in Architecture* (Boston: Little, Brown, 1936), 40; Shand-Tucci, *Boston Bohemia,* 6, 79, 116, 120, 123, 128, 132, 274.

8. Cram, *My Life,* 6–9, 46. The depiction of "dirt, meanness, ugliness" is from [Ralph Adams Cram], *The Decadent: Being the Gospel of Inaction: Wherein are Set Forth in Romance Form Certain Reflections Touching the Curious Characteristics of These Ultimate Years and the Divers Causes Thereof* (Boston: Privately Printed for the Author [Issued by Copeland and Day, of Cornhill, Boston. Printed by John Wilson and Son, Cambridge, at the University Press], 1893), 2.

9. Shand-Tucci, *Boston Bohemia,* 274, 291, and passim; Robert Muccigrosso, review of *Boston Bohemia,* by Douglass Shand-Tucci, in *Journal of American History* 83 (June 1996): 233; Mary W. Blanchard, review of *Boston Bohemia,* by Douglass Shand-Tucci, in *New England Quarterly* 69 (June 1996): 331. John Shelton Reed similarly concludes that English Anglo-Catholics were accused of effeminacy, but that the lack of evidence, and of any clear concept of homosexuality, preclude definite conclusions about their sexual composition. *Glorious Battle: The Cultural Politics of Victorian Anglo-Catholicism* (Nashville: Vanderbilt University Press, 1996), 221–23.

10. Cram, *My Life,* 52, 61–66.

11. Ibid., 57, 59; Arthur F. Beringause, *Brooks Adams: A Biography* (New York: Knopf, 1955), 145.

12. Cram, *My Life,* 19–20, 59–60, 97; Ralph Adams Cram to Louise Imogen Guiney, March 3, 1919, Guiney Papers.

13. Yves M.-J. Congar, *Tradition and Traditions: An Historical and a Theological Essay,* trans. Michael Naseby and Thomas Rainborough (New York: Macmillan, 1967), 465; Reed, *Glorious Battle,* xxiii–xxiv, 174, 183.

14. Shand-Tucci, *Boston Bohemia,* 391. See also Muccigrosso, *American Gothic,* 90.

15. Ralph Adams Cram, "Concerning the Restoration of Idealism and the Raising to Honour Once More of the Imagination," *The Knight Errant* 1 (April 1892): 11–13.

16. Cram, *My Life,* 33, 50; James F. O'Gorman, *Three American Architects: Richardson, Sullivan, and Wright, 1865–1915* (Chicago: University of Chicago Press, 1991), 32.

17. Cram, *My Life,* 33.

18. William R. Lethaby, *Mediaeval Art: From the Peace of the Church to the Eve of the Renaissance, 312–1350,* rev. ed. (London: Duckworth and Co., 1912), 2, 80, 136, 141, 188. On Lethaby's influence on Cram see Shand-Tucci, *Boston Bohemia,* 40.

19. Ralph Adams Cram, *The Catholic Church and Art* (New York: Macmillan, 1930),

23, 26, 108; Ralph Adams Cram, *Convictions and Controversies* (Boston: Marshall Jones, 1935), 38–40.

20. Ralph Adams Cram, "Reflections upon Art," *Commonweal* 10 (June 5, 1929): 121; Cram, *My Life*, 7, 26, 152, 195.

21. For Lears's own treatment of Cram as an antimodernist see *No Place of Grace: Antimodernism and the Transformation of American Culture, 1880–1920* (New York: Pantheon Books, 1981), 203–9.

22. Shand-Tucci, *Boston Bohemia*, 252–54, 432–33; Carl E. Schorske, *Thinking with History: Explorations in the Passage to Modernism* (Princeton: Princeton University Press, 1998), 146.

23. Arthur Tappan North, *Ralph Adams Cram: Cram and Ferguson* (New York: McGraw-Hill, 1931), 8. "Cram did not see himself as a traditionalist nor did those who commissioned his designs," Ann Miner Daniel observes. "Early Architecture of Cram," 267. This is true if "traditionalism" be taken to mean a servile devotion to forms established in the past. Ralph Adams Cram, *The Ministry of Art* (1914; repr. Freeport, N.Y.: Books for Libraries Press, 1967), 122; Ralph Adams Cram, "The Limits of Modernism in Art: When the New Art Means Progress and When It Means Degeneracy," *Arts and Decoration* 20 (January 1924): 11, 13.

24. Cram, "Limits of Modernism," 12.

25. Ibid., 12–13.

26. Cram, *Ministry of Art*, 123.

27. Robert M. Torrance, *The Spiritual Quest: Transcendence in Myth, Religion, and Science* (Berkeley: University of California Press, 1994), 66, 70, 98. Torrance gives credit to John S. Mbiti as a source of these insights.

28. Yves Congar, *The Meaning of Tradition*. trans. A. N. Woodrow (New York: Hawthorn Books, 1964), 17, 51, 113, 152.

29. Ralph Adams Cram, *Impressions of Japanese Architecture and the Allied Arts* (Boston: Marshall Jones, 1930; repr. New York: Dover, 1966), 174; Ralph Adams Cram, ms. of article on the founding of the Mediaeval Academy of America, p. 21, Ralph Adams Cram to Sarah Blake Cram, December 18, 1906, Ralph Adams Cram Papers, Print Department, Boston Public Library, Boston, Mass.

30. Ralph Adams Cram, "Reims Cathedral," *Yale Review*, n.s., 8 (October 1918): 34–35.

31. Ralph Adams Cram, "On the Religious Aspect of Architecture," *Architectural Record* 2 (January–March 1893): 352; Ralph Adams Cram, *Architecture in Its Relation to Civilization. Occasional Pamphlets Bearing on the World After the War as This Appears through Study of the Past or Conditions of the Present*. Number II (Boston: Marshall Jones, 1918), 3.

32. Ralph Adams Cram, "The Approach to Religion," *Atlantic Monthly* 160 (October 1937): 469–70.

33. Ibid., 470.

34. Ralph Adams Cram, *The Ruined Abbeys of Great Britain* (New York: James Pott and

Company, 1905), 162; Kenneth Clark, *The Gothic Revival: An Essay in the History of Taste* (New York: Scribner's, 1929), 150–52; Schorske, *Thinking with History*, 71; Robert Muccigrosso, "Ralph Adams Cram and the Modernity of Medievalism," *Studies in Medievalism* I (Spring 1982): 28–29, 34.

35. See, e.g., John C. Fraser, *America and the Patterns of Chivalry* (New York: Cambridge University Press, 1982); Mark Girouard, *The Return to Camelot: Chivalry and the English Gentleman* (New Haven: Yale University Press, 1981); Eric Hobsbawm and Terrence Ranger, eds., *The Invention of Tradition* (Cambridge: Cambridge University Press, 1983); Bernard Rosenthal and Paul E. Szarmach, eds., *Medievalism and American Culture: Papers of the Eighteenth Annual Conference of the Center for Medieval and Early Renaissance Studies* (Binghamton, N.Y.: Medieval and Renaissance Texts and Studies, 1989).

36. On the Gothic influence in America, see Henry Seidel Canby, *Alma Mater: The Gothic Age of the American College* (New York: Farrar and Rinehart, 1936); Kristine Ottesen Garrigan, *Ruskin on Architecture: His Thought and Influence* (Madison: University of Wisconsin Press, 1973); Roger B. Stein, *John Ruskin and Aesthetic Thought in America, 1840–1900* (Cambridge: Harvard University Press, 1967).

37. Robin Fleming, "Picturesque History and the Medieval in Nineteenth-Century America," *American Historical Review* 100 (October 1995): 1077.

38. Kim Moreland, *The Medievalist Impulse in American Literature: Twain, Adams, Fitzgerald, and Hemingway* (Charlottesville: University Press of Virginia, 1996), 15, 26. See Fraser, *Patterns of Chivalry*, passim, for latter-day American "knights." Carl Schorske points out that Pugin emphasized the antithesis of the Middle Ages and the modern world; Coleridge and Disraeli attempted to adapt medieval values to modern uses. *Thinking with History*, 76–88.

39. Henry Adams, *Mont-Saint-Michel and Chartres* (Garden City, N.Y.: Doubleday, 1959), 37.

40. Ibid., 153, 307.

41. Kathleen Verduin, "Medievalism and the Mind of Emerson," in *Medievalism in American Culture*, ed. Rosenthal and Szarmach, 143.

42. Charles Eliot Norton, *Notes of Travel and Study in Italy* (Boston: Houghton Mifflin, 1887), 3, 13n, 163, 237.

43. Ibid., 103–6.

44. Ibid., 110, 126–27, 312, 315–16.

45. James Jackson Jarves, *The Art-Idea*, ed. Benjamin Rowland, Jr. (Cambridge: Cambridge University Press, 1960), 112, 236. Charles Eliot Norton similarly described the popular and communal spirit of the medieval cathedral in "The Building of the Church of St.-Denis," *Harper's New Monthly Magazine* 79 (October 1889): 766–76, and "The Building of the Cathedral at Chartres," *Harper's New Monthly Magazine* 79 (November 1889), 944–55; Mrs. Schuyler [Mariana] Van Rensselaer, *English Cathedrals: Canterbury, Peterborough, Durham, Salisbury, Litchfield, Lincoln, Ely, Wells, Winchester, Gloucester, York, London* (New York: Century, 1892), 282;

Charles Herbert Moore, *Development and Character of Gothic Architecture*, 2d ed. (New York: Macmillan, 1906), 25–26.

46. Moore, *Development and Character*, 29, 189–90; Russell Sturgis and A. L. Frothingham, *A History of Architecture* (Garden City, N.Y.: Doubleday, Page, 1915), 3: 22; 4: 89.

47. "An American Definition of Gothic Architecture," *Atlantic Monthly* 66 (July 1890): 126–27, 130.

48. Robert S. Peabody, "Architecture and Democracy," *Harper's New Monthly Magazine* 81 (July 1890): 219, 221–22.

49. Ralph Adams Cram to Louise Imogen Guiney, February 23, n.y., Guiney Papers; Adams, *Mont-Saint-Michel*, vii; Cram, *My Life*, 226.

50. Cram, *Architecture in Its Relation to Civilization*, 19; Ralph Adams Cram, *The Gothic Quest*, rev. ed. (Garden City, N.Y.: Doubleday, Page, 1915), 54–57; Ralph Adams Cram, *The Significance of Gothic Art. Occasional Pamphlets Bearing on the World After the War as This Appears through Study of the Past or Conditions of the Present* (Boston: Marshall Jones, 1918), 13.

51. Cram, *Gothic Quest*, 56–57; Cram, "Reims Cathedral," 36–37; Cram, *Japanese Architecture*, 31.

52. Ralph Adams Cram, *The Great Thousand Years* (Boston: Marshall Jones, 1918), 31; Cram, *Gothic Quest*, 20; Ralph Adams Cram, *Heart of Europe* (New York: Scribner's, 1915), 157, 192–94; Cram, *Convictions and Controversies*, 271; Ralph Adams Cram, *Walled Towns* (Boston: Marshall Jones, 1919), 81–82.

53. Ralph Adams Cram, *The Substance of Gothic: Six Lectures on the Development of Architecture from Charlemagne to Henry VIII* (Boston: Marshall Jones, 1917), 103; Ralph Adams Cram, *The End of Democracy* (Boston: Marshall Jones, 1937), 29, 55; Ralph Adams Cram, *The Nemesis of Mediocrity* (Boston: Marshall Jones, 1917), 42.

54. Ralph Adams Cram, "Scrapping the Slums" [Address at the Seventh National Conference of Housing in America, Boston, November 26, 1918], *The American Architect* 114 (December 18, 1918): 761–62. Shand-Tucci, *Boston Bohemia*, 87, notes Cram's interest in workers' housing in the 1890s; Ralph Adams Cram, "The Pre-eminence of Our Own Domestic Architecture: The Best of Its Sort Seen in Any Country for More Than a Hundred Years," *Arts and Decoration* 22 (April 1925): 22, 73.

55. Cram, "The Pre-eminence of Our Own Domestic Architecture," 22; Cram, *Heart of Europe*, 147; Cram, *Convictions and Controversies*, 122.

56. Cram, *Substance of Gothic*, 57; Ralph Adams Cram, *The Sins of the Fathers* (Boston: Marshall Jones, 1919), 17; Cram, *Significance of Gothic Art*, 12–13.

57. Ralph Adams Cram, "What Is Civilization? III—The Answer of the Middle Ages," *The Forum* 73 (March 1925): 354–55; Ralph Adams Cram, *Introduction to The Story of My Misfortunes*, by Peter Abelard, trans. Henry Adams Bellows (Glencoe, Ill.: Free Press, 1958), iii.

58. Cram, *Substance of Gothic*, 108.

59. Ibid., 38; Ralph Adams Cram, *Towards the Great Peace* (Boston: Marshall Jones, 1922), 5–7.

60. Mary Cram Nichols to Douglass Shand-Tucci, June 1977, Ralph Adams Cram Papers; Cram, *Convictions and Controversies*, 80–81, 91.

61. Cram, *Nemesis of Mediocrity*, 28; Cram, *End of Democracy*, 44–45; Cram, *Towards the Great Peace*, 14.

62. Cram, *End of Democracy*, 20–21, 40; Cram, *Nemesis of Mediocrity*, 35; Ralph Adams Cram, "Notes Abroad" [1886], Journal, Ralph Adams Cram Papers.

63. Cram, *Convictions and Controversies*, 54–55, 60, 142–46; Cram, *Towards the Great Peace*, 253–59.

64. Ralph Adams Cram to Louise Imogen Guiney, October 22, 1915, Guiney Papers; Cram, *Significance of Gothic Art*, 3; Cram, *Substance of Gothic*, 3.

65. Cram, *Gothic Quest*, 160–61.

66. Ibid., 73, 75, 161, 202.

67. Ralph Adams Cram, "The Unity of the Arts," *Landscape Architecture* 23 (April 1933): 196; Cram, "Limits of Modernism," 12; Ralph Adams Cram, *The Cathedral of Palma de Mallorca: An Architectural Study* (Cambridge, Mass.: Mediaeval Academy of America, 1932; repr. New York: Kraus Reprint Co., 1971), 5; Cram, *Gothic Quest*, 43.

68. Ralph Adams Cram, ms. of article on the founding of the Mediaeval Academy of America, p. 1, Ralph Adams Cram Papers; Cram, *Significance of Gothic Art*, 25; Cram, *Convictions and Controversies*, 13; Cram, *Walled Towns*, 13; Muccigrosso, "Cram and the Modernity of Medievalism," 31.

69. Muccigrosso, "Cram and the Modernity of Medievalism," 33; Robert Muccigrosso, "American Gothic: Ralph Adams Cram," *Thought* 47 (Spring 1972): 115.

70. Ralph Adams Cram to Edith Guerrier, May 3, 1935, Boston Public Library/Rare Books Department. Courtesy of the Trustees. Cram also listed works by Dean Gauss, Oswald Spengler, Henry Adams, James Henry Breasted, Lewis Mumford, and Christopher Dawson, and a volume by the American Institute of Architects, *Appreciation of the Fine Arts*. Cram recommended Madariaga in a letter to his daughter, Mrs. Wallace M. Scudder, Jr., February 25, 1937, Ralph Adams Cram Papers.

71. William Aylott Orton, *America in Search of Culture* (Boston: Little, Brown, 1933), 23–24, 76, 87–91, 103, 106, 298.

72. José Ortega y Gasset, *The Revolt of the Masses* (New York: Norton, 1957), 36, 91, 96.

73. Ibid., 17, 72, 82, 116, 139.

74. Salvador de Madariaga, *Anarchy or Hierarchy* (London: George Allen and Unwin, 1937), 33–35, 81, 122, 151–58, 164–65, 187, 205.

75. Nicholas Berdyaev, *The End of Our Time: Together with an Essay on the General Line of Soviet Philosophy*, trans. Donald Attwater (London: Sheed and Ward, 1933), 57, 179–80, 201–2.

76. Ibid., 13, 60, 69ff., 75, 85, 112.

77. Ralph Adams Cram, "The Mass-Man Takes Over," *American Mercury* 45 (October 1938), 166–67, 174–75.

78. Cram, *Convictions and Controversies*, 150–52; Cram, *End of Democracy*, 35.

79. Cram, *End of Democracy*, 100–101; Cram, *Great Thousand Years*, 63–66; Cram, *Towards the Great Peace*, 56–60.

80. Cram, *Towards the Great Peace*, 6–7; Cram, *End of Democracy*, 93–94.

81. Cram, *End of Democracy*, 94, 103–8.

82. Ralph Adams Cram, "The Return to Feudalism," *American Review* 8 (January 1937): 338–40; Ralph Adams Cram, "Invitation to Monarchy," *American Mercury* 37 (April 1936): 482–86.

83. Cram, *Significance of Gothic Art*, 10; Cram, "Return to Feudalism," 340; Ralph Adams Cram, *A Plan for the Settlement of Middle Europe: On the Principle of Partition without Annexation. Occasional Pamphlets Bearing on the World After the War as this Appears through Study of the Past or Conditions of the Present. Number III* (Boston: Marshall Jones, 1918), 16.

84. Cram, *Convictions and Controversies*, 13.

85. Cram, *The Decadent*, 9–12, 25, 33, 40–41.

86. Ralph Adams Cram, "An American Congregation of the Canons Regular of St. Norbert," n.d., , 1, 9, 31, 42–43, Ralph Adams Cram Papers.

87. Ralph Adams Cram, "Princeton Architecture," *American Architect* 96 (July 21, 1909): 24–25.

88. Ralph Adams Cram to Louise Imogen Guiney, April 1, 1907, Guiney Papers.

89. Cram, *Walled Towns*, 35–37, 41, 65, 78, 80, 91. See also Cram, *Great Thousand Years*, 34–35.

90. Ralph Adams Cram, "Cities of Refuge," *Commonweal* 22 (August 16, 1935), 380. See also Cram, *Great Thousand Years*, 63; Cram, *Convictions and Controversies*, 208, 267–68; Cram, *Ministry of Art*, 52; Cram, *My Life*, 292–93; Cram, *End of Democracy*, 66.

91. Cram, *Substance of Gothic*, 4.

92. Cram, *Japanese Architecture*, 32–33.

93. Margaret Ellen O'Shaughnessey, "The Middle Ages in the New World: American Views and Transformations of Medieval Art and Literature" (Ph.D. diss., Duke University, 1989), 53–73; Cram, *My Life*, 98–100.

94. Cram, *Japanese Architecture*, 38; Ralph Adams Cram, "Japanese Domestic Interiors," *Architectural Review* 7 (January 1900): 10.

95. Cram, "Pre-eminence of Our Own Domestic Architecture," 21, 73.

96. Cram, *Japanese Architecture*, 30–31, 37, 89.

97. Ibid., 39, 171–72.

98. Ibid., 107, 210, 221, 227.

CHAPTER 4. *The I and the We*

Portions of this chapter were previously published in "Charles H. Cooley and the Modern Necessity of Tradition," *Modern Age* 36 (Spring 1994): 277–85. Reprinted by permission.

1. Thomas L. Haskell, *The Emergence of Professional Social Science: The American Social Science Association and the Nineteenth-Century Crisis of Authority* (Urbana: University of Illinois Press, 1977), 66, 87, 251. The term "community of the competent" was that of Francis E. Abbot.

2. Philip Abrams, "The Sense of the Past and the Origins of Sociology," *Past and Present* 55 (May 1972): 18–22.

3. Franz Boas, *The Mind of Primitive Man* (New York: Macmillan, 1927), 242; W. Warren Wagar, *Good Tydings: The Belief in Progress from Darwin to Marcuse* (Bloomington: Indiana University Press, 1972), 38; George W. Stocking, Jr., *Victorian Anthropology* (New York: Free Press, 1987), 53–54; Robert A. Nisbet, *The Sociological Tradition* (New York: Basic Books, 1966), 293–94.

4. Nisbet, *Sociological Tradition*, 47, 116; Jean B. Quandt, *From the Small Town to the Great Community: The Social Thought of the Progressive Intellectuals* (New Brunswick: Rutgers University Press, 1970), 1, 18–19.

5. Franklin Henry Giddings, *The Principles of Sociology: An Analysis of the Phenomena of Association and of Social Organization* (New York: Macmillan, 1908), 17–18, 141–45.

6. Franklin Henry Giddings, *Civilization and Society: An Account of the Development and Behavior of Human Society*, abridged and edited by Howard W. Odum (New York: Henry Holt, 1932), 107–8, 314–15; Franklin Henry Giddings, *Studies in the Theory of Human Society* (New York: Macmillan, 1922), 18, 285, 393–94; Giddings, *Principles of Sociology*, 220; Franklin Henry Giddings, *The Elements of Sociology: A Text-Book for Colleges and Schools* (New York: Macmillan, 1916), 87, 98, 124–25.

7. Giddings, *Theory of Human Society*, 263–93; William Graham Sumner, *Essays of William Graham Sumner*, ed. Albert Galloway Keller and Maurice R. Davie (New Haven: Yale University Press, 1911; repr. New York: Archon Books, 1969), 1: 73–74; William Graham Sumner, *Folkways: A Study of the Sociological Importance of Usages, Manners, Customs, Mores, and Morals* (Boston: Ginn and Company, 1906), 4.

8. Robert C. Bannister, *Sociology and Scientism: The American Quest for Objectivity, 1880–1940* (Chapel Hill: University of North Carolina Press, 1987), 89; Sumner, *Folkways*, 28–29.

9. Sumner, *Essays*, 1: 68–69, 314.

10. Ibid., 1: 470; William Graham Sumner, *War and Other Essays*, ed. Albert Galloway Keller (New Haven: Yale University Press, 1919), 170.

11. Sumner, *War*, 332.

12. Lester Frank Ward, *Glimpses of the Cosmos: Comprising His Minor Contributions, Together with Biographical and Historical Sketches of All His Writings* (New York: Putnam's, 1973), 1: 46.

13. Ibid., 1: 46, 48, 92–94 (from *The Iconoclast*, 1870).

14. Ibid., 1: lxvi; Lester Frank Ward, *Dynamic Sociology: or Applied Social Science as Based upon Statical Sociology and the Less Complex Sciences*, 2d ed. (New York: D. Appleton, 1897), 1: 647; 2: 435, 499.

15. Clifford H. Scott, *Lester Frank Ward* (Boston: Twayne, 1976), 48, 71–76, 142;

Alvin F. Nelson, *The Development of Lester Ward's World View* (Fort Worth: Branch-Smith, 1968), 53ff., 60; Samuel Chugerman, *Lester F. Ward: The American Aristotle* (Durham, N.C.: Duke University Press, 1939), 245; Lester Frank Ward, *Pure Sociology: A Treatise on the Origin and Spontaneous Development of Society*, 2d ed. (New York: Macmillan, 1907; repr. New York: Augustus M. Kelley, 1970), 573–74.

16. Ward, *Pure Sociology*, 16, 31–33; Ward, *Glimpses*, 6: 28; Lester Frank Ward, *Applied Sociology: A Treatise on the Conscious Improvement of Society by Society* (Boston: Ginn and Company, 1906; repr. New York: Arno Press, 1974), 122.

17. Ward, *Pure Sociology*, 230.

18. Ward, *Dynamic Sociology*, 1: 662; Ward, *Applied Sociology*, 281.

19. Julius Weinberg, *Edward Alsworth Ross and the Sociology of Progressivism* (Madison: State Historical Society of Wisconsin, 1972), 3–5, 10, 21–33.

20. Ibid., 43–55, 102–4, 142–43, 188–89; Fay Berger Karpf, *American Social Psychology: Its Origins, Development, and European Background* (New York: McGraw-Hill, 1932), 177, 308. For the Emma Goldman episode, see Sean Howard McMahon, "Sentinel of Social Control: An Intellectual Biography of Edward Alsworth Ross" (Ph.D. diss., Florida State University, 1996), 193–200. No anarchist himself but a staunch advocate of free speech, Ross served as chairman of the National Committee of the American Civil Liberties Union from 1940 to 1950 (ibid., 300).

21. Edward Alsworth Ross, "Turning Towards Nirvana," *The Arena* 24 (November 1891): 736–38.

22. Ibid., 739–43.

23. Ibid., 739, 741; J. Bernhard Stern, ed., "The Ward-Ross Correspondence," *American Sociological Review* 3 (June 1938): 365 (Ross to Ward, December 13, 1891); Edward Alsworth Ross, *Social Control: A Survey of the Foundations of Order* (New York: Macmillan, 1922), 264.

24. Ross, *Social Control*, 184, 192; Edward Alsworth Ross, *Foundations of Sociology* (New York: Macmillan, 1905), 94.

25. Edward Alsworth Ross, *Social Psychology: An Outline and Source Book* (New York: Macmillan, 1909), 4, 210–11, 227; Ross, *Social Control*, 169; Edward Alsworth Ross, *Standing Room Only?* (New York: Century, 1927; repr. New York: Arno Press, 1977), 348; Edward Alsworth Ross, "The Balance in Government," *La Follette's Magazine* (June 1917): 10, reel 39, Edward A. Ross Papers (microfilm edition, 1982), Wisconsin Historical Society Archives. See also Edward Alsworth Ross, "Ossification," *American Journal of Sociology* 25 (March 1920): 530.

26. Ross, *Social Control*, 181 (original emphasis omitted); Ross, *Social Psychology*, 198.

27. Ross, *Social Psychology*, 200–204.

28. Edward Alsworth Ross, *South of Panama* (New York: Century, 1917), 60, 137, 191, 199; *New York Times*, October 29, 1911, reel 39, Ross Papers; Edward Alsworth Ross, *The Changing Chinese: The Conflict of Oriental and Western Cultures in China* (New York: Century, 1911), 174–82.

29. Edward Alsworth Ross, *Russia in Upheaval* (New York: Century, 1919), 129–30, 243, 247, 330; McMahon, "Sentinel of Social Control," 289.

30. *New York Times*, October 29, 1911, reel 39, Ross Papers; Weinberg, *Edward Alsworth Ross*, 176.

31. Edward Alsworth Ross, *The Old World in the New: The Significance of Past and Present Immigration to the American People* (New York: Century, 1914), 133, 136; Fred L. Holmes, "Preserving Democracy—America's Task," *Dearborn Independent*, November 12, 1921, reel 39, Ross Papers. The *Independent* was a xenophobic paper sponsored by Henry Ford.

32. Edward Alsworth Ross to Robert U. Johnson, April 1, 1911, reel 5, Ross Papers; Edward Alsworth Ross, "The Mob-Mind," *Popular Science Monthly* 51 (July 1897): 390–98, reel 39, Ross Papers; Edward Alsworth Ross, "The American Race Suffers from 'Will Cramp,'" *Fremont [Neb.] Tribune*, September 30, 1905, reel 39, Ross Papers; Edward Alsworth Ross, "Individuation," *American Journal of Sociology* 25 (January 1920): 469.

33. Edward Alsworth Ross, *Principles of Sociology* (New York: Century, 1920), 16; Edward Alsworth Ross, *Changing America: Studies in Contemporary Society* (New York: Century, 1912), 39, 142–43, 146. Ross was reported as warning that immigrants were making the American population ugly: *Shelby [N.C.] Highlander*, December 14, 1922; cf. *New York Evening World*, March 5, 1917, reel 39, Ross Papers.

34. "An Unprofessorial Professor," *American Hebrew*, November 13, 1914; "Some Notes on Professor Ross, the Anti-Semite," *The Jewish Voice*, ca. 1914; *American Hebrew*, September 18, 1914, quoting Professor Gotthard Deutsch in *The American Israelite*, reel 39, Ross Papers; Ross, *Old World in the New*, 165–66.

35. Ross, *Social Psychology*, 315, 326; Ross, *Social Control*, 415.

36. Ross, *Old World in the New*, 166; Ross, *Social Psychology*, 241–42; Ross, *Principles of Sociology*, 224; Edward Alsworth Ross, *Roads to Social Peace: The Weil Lectures, 1924, on American Citizenship* (Chapel Hill: University of North Carolina Press, 1924), 53–54.

37. Ross, *Changing America*, 39–40; Ross, *Foundations of Sociology*, 196–97; Ross, *Social Psychology*, 243. See also Ross, *Roads to Social Peace*, 56.

38. Ellsworth R. Fuhrman, *The Sociology of Knowledge in America, 1883–1915* (Charlottesville: University Press of Virginia, 1980), 185; Ross, *Social Control*, 84–85.

39. Georges Gurvitch, "Social Control," in *Twentieth Century Sociology*, ed. Georges Gurvitch and Wilbert E. Moore (Freeport, N.Y.: Books for Libraries Press, 1945), 267, 269; McMahon, "Sentinel of Social Control," 118; Ross, *Foundations of Sociology*, 112–13; Ross, *Principles of Sociology*, 506. Weinberg, *Edward Alsworth Ross*, 97, provides background.

40. Ross, *Social Control*, 3, 20–21.

41. Ibid., 293; Ross, *Social Psychology*, 270 (original italics omitted), 273.

42. Ross, *Social Control*, 74, 221–22; Ross, "Balance in Government," 10. See also Edward Alsworth Ross, "Capsules of Social Wisdom," *Social Forces* 27 (December 1948): 209; Ross, *Social Psychology*, 286, 292.

43. Ross, *Social Control*, 17; Ross, *Social Psychology*, 228.

44. Stern, ed., "Ward-Ross Correspondence," 11: 747 (Ross to Ward, July 7, 1901); Ross, *Social Psychology*, viii, 276–77; Gabriel de Tarde, *The Laws of Imitation*, trans. Elsie Clews Parsons (New York: Henry Holt, 1903; repr. Gloucester, Mass.: Peter Smith, 1962), 50. See Karpf, *American Social Psychology*, 89–108, on Tarde's influence on American social psychology.

45. Tarde, *Laws of Imitation*, xxii, 295; Ferdinand Tönnies, *Custom: An Essay on Social Codes*, trans. A. Farrell Borenstein (New York: Free Press of Glencoe, 1961), 75–76, 98, 101, 104, 117.

46. Ross, *Social Psychology*, 276–77; Ross, *Foundations of Sociology*, 113; Ross, *Social Control*, 150.

47. Ross, *Principles of Sociology*, 414, 520; Edward Alsworth Ross, *The Social Trend* (New York: Century, 1922), Introduction, n.p.; Ross, *Foundations of Sociology*, 114. Cf. Ross, *Social Psychology*, 26.

48. Ross, *Social Control*, 183; Ross, *Principles of Sociology*, 4.

49. Charles H. Cooley to Elsie Jones, June 9, 1889, Charles Horton Cooley Papers, Bentley Historical Library, University of Michigan.

50. Charles H. Cooley, Journal, n.d. [1889–91], Cooley Papers; Charles Horton Cooley, *Social Organization: A Study of the Larger Mind* (New York: Schocken Books, 1962), 94, 168–70; Charles Horton Cooley, *Life and the Student: Roadside Notes on Human Nature, Society, and Letters* (New York: Knopf, 1927), 25.

51. Charles H. Cooley to Elsie Cooley, September 9, 16, 1904, Cooley Papers.

52. Charles H. Cooley to Elsie Cooley, September 12, 15, 1904, Cooley Papers.

53. Charles H. Cooley, Journal, September 18, 1904, Cooley Papers,.

54. Edward A. Ross to Charles H. Cooley, November 2, 1894; Charles H. Cooley, Journal, June 16, 1908, April 10, 1910, Cooley Papers.

55. Thomas Bender, *Community and Social Change in America* (New Brunswick: Rutgers University Press, 1978), 32–37.

56. Fuhrman, *Sociology of Knowledge*, 214; Charles H. Cooley, Journal, September 3, 1906, Cooley Papers.

57. Charles H. Cooley, Journal, January 29, 1898, September 3, 1906, Cooley Papers.

58. Charles H. Cooley, student notes at the University of Munich, 1884; Journal, January 18, 1903, Cooley Papers.

59. Charles H. Cooley, Journal, July 21, 1895, June 30, 1899, July 3, 1902; Charles H. Cooley to Elsie Jones, January 5, 1890, Cooley Papers.

60. Alan Jones, "Law and Economics v. A Democratic Society: The Case of Thomas M. Cooley, Charles H. Cooley, and Henry C. Adams," *American Journal of Legal History* 36 (April 1992): 120, 125, 135.

61. Marshall J. Cohen, *Charles Horton Cooley and the Social Self in American Thought* (New York: Garland, 1982), 2–5, 11–14, provides biographical information.

62. Ibid.; Karpf, *American Social Psychology*, 303; Edward Shils, *The Calling of*

Sociology and Other Essays on the Pursuit of Learning (Chicago: University of Chicago Press, 1980), 97.

63. Charles H. Cooley, Journal, May 12, 1890, November 23, 1902, December 5, 1903, January 22, 1904, Cooley Papers.

64. Charles H. Cooley to John Phelan, March 4, 1926; Charles H. Cooley, Journal, February 19, 1882, March 15, 1882, July 21, 1895, September 3, 1919, September 11, 1928, Cooley Papers.

65. Charles H. Cooley, Journal, July 21, 1895, May 22, 1890, March 17, 1898, September 4, 1919, Cooley Papers.

66. Charles Horton Cooley, "The Roots of Social Knowledge," *American Journal of Sociology* 32 (July 1926): 68–73.

67. Charles H. Cooley, Journal, March 2, 1915, Cooley Papers.

68. Charles H. Cooley, Journal, January 5, 1913, February 14, 1915, February 2, 1898, March 1, 1896; Charles H. Cooley to Elsie Jones, December 19, 1888, July 27, 1889, March 21, 1890, Cooley Papers. "He has been the tree on which I have climbed up to whatever spiritual heights I may have attained," Cooley added later. Charles H. Cooley to Elsie Jones, July 27, 1889; Charles H. Cooley to Otto H. Boesser, March 1, 1929 (extracts from a paper prepared in 1928 for Professor Bernard's projected History of Sociology in the United States); Charles H. Cooley, "The Teachings of Emerson," 1887, Cooley Papers. On Emerson's influence see Quandt, *From the Small Town*, 12–13.

69. Charles Horton Cooley, *Sociological Theory and Social Research* (New York: Henry Holt, 1930), 184–86.

70. Charles H. Cooley, Journal, September 20, 1897, Cooley Papers.

71. Charles H. Cooley, Journal, February 2, 1898, February 18, 1912, Cooley Papers.

72. Charles H. Cooley, Journal, November 21, 1915, February 17, 1901, September 1, 1928, August 22, 1927; Charles H. Cooley to Mary Horton Cooley, March 16, 1884, Cooley Papers.

73. Charles H. Cooley, Journal, January 21, 1911, April 30, 1905, Cooley Papers. For Cooley, as Caroline Winterer puts it, "it was not democracy and easy communication that blighted culture and genius; it was the newness of American society." Maturity, he hoped, would provide traditions to support individual work. "A Happy Medium: The Sociology of Charles Horton Cooley," *Journal of the History of the Behavioral Sciences* 30 (January 1994): 26.

74. Charles H. Cooley, Journal, July 11, 1909, April 7, 1924, Cooley Papers; Charles Horton Cooley, *Social Process* (Carbondale: Southern Illinois University Press, 1966), 363–65; Cooley, *Life and the Student*, 24, 39.

75. Charles H. Cooley, Journal, November 24, 1918, February 17, 1901, September 1, 1928, August 22, 1927, Cooley Papers; Cooley, *Social Process*, 348.

76. Charles H. Cooley, "Account of Development of Sociology Program at the University of Michigan," 2–3; Charles H. Cooley to Elsie Jones, December 28, 1888, November 11, 1889, Cooley Papers; Cooley, *Sociological Theory*, 263. Marshall Cohen

contends that Cooley "determined in large measure" the "fate of Spencerian thought" in the United States. Cohen, *Cooley and the Social Self*, 2, 15–34.

77. Charles H. Cooley, Journal, May 2, 1909, July 21, 1895, Cooley Papers; Cooley, *Social Process*, 116.

78. Cooley, *Sociological Theory*, 269–73.

79. Cooley, *Social Organization*, 315; Charles Horton Cooley, *Human Nature and the Social Order*, rev. ed. (New York: Schocken Books, 1964), 4–5. One type of transmission, Cooley added, "flows through the germ-plasm; the other comes by way of language, intercourse, and education. The road is more recent than the stream: it is an improvement that did not exist at all in the earliest flow of animal life, but appears later as a vague trail alongside the stream," developing still later into a busy highway.

80. J. David Lewis and Richard L. Smith, *American Sociology and Pragmatism: Mead, Chicago Sociology, and Symbolic Interaction* (Chicago: University of Chicago Press, 1980), 157–58. See also Cohen, *Cooley and the Social Self*, 71–73, 174–75; and Quandt, *From the Small Town*, 54–55. Other sources useful in placing Cooley in the context of his discipline include Hamilton Cravens, *The Triumph of Evolution: American Scientists and the Heredity-Environment Controversy, 1900–1941* (Philadelphia: University of Pennsylvania Press, 1978); Roscoe C. Hinkle, *Founding Theory of American Sociology, 1881–1915* (Boston: Routledge and Kegan Paul, 1980); Arthur J. Vidich and Stanford M. Lyman, *American Sociology: Worldly Rejections of Religion and Their Directions* (New Haven: Yale University Press, 1985); Bruce Mazlish, *A New Science: The Breakdown of Connections and the Birth of Sociology* (New York: Oxford University Press, 1989); Don Martindale, *The Nature and Types of Sociological Theory* (Boston: Houghton Mifflin, 1960); Edward Shils, *The Calling of Sociology and Other Essays on the Pursuit of Learning* (Chicago: University of Chicago Press, 1980); Margaret Wilson Vine, *An Introduction to Sociological Theory*, 2d ed. (New York: David McKay, 1969); and Werner J. Cahnman and Alvin Boskoff, eds., *Sociology and History: Theory and Research* (London: Free Press of Glencoe, 1964). Studies devoted wholly or in large part to Cooley include Sister Mary Edward Healy, *Society and Social Change in the Writings of St. Thomas, Ward, Sumner, and Cooley* (Westport, Conn.: Greenwood Press, 1972); Edward C. Jandy, *Charles Horton Cooley: His Life and His Social Theory* (New York: Dryden Press, 1942); Richard Dewey, "Charles Horton Cooley: Pioneer in Psychosociology," in *An Introduction to the History of Sociology*, ed. Harry Elmer Barnes (Chicago: University of Chicago Press, 1948), 833–52; Albert J. Reiss, Jr., ed., *Cooley and Sociological Analysis* (Ann Arbor: University of Michigan Press, 1968); and George Herbert Mead, "Cooley's Contribution to American Social Thought," *American Journal of Sociology* 35 (March 1930): 693–706.

81. Charles H. Cooley, Journal, January 4, 1914, Cooley Papers; Mead, "Cooley's Contribution," 695; Roscoe C. Hinkle, Jr., and Gisela J. Hinkle, *The Development of Modern Sociology: Its Nature and Growth in the United States* (New York: Random House, 1954), 30–31; John Patrick Diggins, "The Socialization of Authority and the Dilemmas of American Liberalism," *Social Research* 46 (Autumn 1979): 464.

82. Charles H. Cooley, Journal, July 21, 1895, July 30, 1903, September 5, 1908, Cooley Papers. See also Quandt, *From the Small Town*, 58. Cooley perceived that the primary group could provide refuge as well as nurture. "Barrett Wendell is a signal example of how sensitive, imaginative people seek to live in the sense of an intimate and continuing life by cherishing the memories and heirlooms of their ancestors, the whole body and atmosphere in fact of the family and community which they inherit and expect to transmit," he observed wryly of the Harvard literary critic and historian. "It keeps them feeling warm and safe, shuts them in out of the cold and desolation of alien life." Charles H. Cooley, Journal, June 28, 1925, Cooley Papers.

83. Charles H. Cooley, "Living Together Well: A Preliminary Impression," n.d. [post–World War I], 2–3, Cooley Papers.

84. Cooley, *Social Organization*, 313; Charles H. Cooley, Journal, March 16, 1927, Cooley Papers.

85. Cooley, *Human Nature*, 35, 50; Cooley, *Social Process*, 200; Cooley, *Life and the Student*, 9; Charles H. Cooley, Journal, March 12, 1905, July 16, 1916, July 21, 1895, Cooley Papers.

86. Cooley, *Social Process*, 3; Charles H. Cooley, Journal, January 1, 1910, June 22, 1921, July 30, 1922, Cooley Papers; Charles Horton Cooley, "Moderate Behaviorism," review of *An Introduction to Social Psychology*, by L. L. Bernard, in *The New Republic* 49 (December 8, 1926): 85–86. Cooley remarked in 1926, "I am a behaviorist as far as I think I can be without being a fanatic," but he balked when behaviorists failed to acknowledge that the meanings of symbols or actions could only be known through consciousness. Consciousness and behavior, he contended, "mutually complement and explain each other." "Roots of Social Knowledge," 68–70.

87. Charles Horton Cooley, "Heredity or Environment," *Journal of Applied Sociology* 10 (March–April 1926): 303, 305, 307.

88. Cooley, *Human Nature*, 48, 74–76.

89. Cooley, *Social Organization*, 335–38.

90. Ibid., 314, 373; Charles H. Cooley, Journal, April 30, 1922, Cooley Papers.

91. Charles H. Cooley, Journal, September 19, 1902, May 9, 1913, May 2, 1915, Cooley Papers.

92. John Patrick Diggins, *The Promise of Pragmatism: Modernism and the Crisis of Knowledge and Authority* (Chicago: University of Chicago Press, 1994), 318.

93. Quandt, *From the Small Town*, 11–13, 74–75.

94. Charles H. Cooley, Journal, September 12, 1902, November 23, 1895, July 18, 1896, Cooley Papers.

95. Charles H. Cooley, Journal, July 3, 1902, January 2, 1903, October 2, 1902; Charles H. Cooley to Elsie Jones, June 3, 1889, Cooley Papers.

96. Charles H. Cooley, Journal, June 7, 1898, September 12, 1902, December 3, 1909, Cooley Papers.

97. Charles H. Cooley, Journal, May 13, 1901, July 6, 1913, August 31, 1913, Cooley

Papers; Henri Bergson, *Creative Evolution*, trans. Arthur Mitchell (New York: Henry Holt, 1913), 344.

98. Charles H. Cooley, Journal, December 9, 1900, March 25, 1903, April 12, 1903, Cooley Papers.

99. Charles H. Cooley, Journal, October 6, 1903, March 20, 1921, Cooley Papers.

100. Talcott Parsons, "Cooley and the Problem of Internalization," in *Cooley and Sociological Analysis*, ed. Reiss, 59; Martindale, *Nature and Types of Sociological Theory*, 344; Lewis and Smith, *American Sociology and Pragmatism*, 163–66; Diggins, "Socialization of Authority," 464; Charles H. Cooley, Journal, May 14, 1890, March 14, 1913, Cooley Papers.

101. Charles H. Cooley, Journal, March 21, 1904, February 7, 1908, Cooley Papers; William James, *Talks to Teachers on Psychology and to Students on Some of Life's Ideals* (London: Longmans Green, 1908), 299. Whether James inspired Cooley on this point is not known.

102. Charles H. Cooley, Journal, January 3, 1909, December 20, 1903, Cooley Papers; Cooley, *Life and the Student*, 250.

103. Charles H. Cooley, Journal, July 8, 1916, July 22, 1909, May 2, 1920, March 9, 1919, Cooley Papers.

104. Charles H. Cooley, Journal, March 25, 1921, Cooley Papers.

105. Cooley, *Social Process*, 3, 8–9.

106. Ibid., 244.

107. Charles H. Cooley, Journal, February 14, 1915, Cooley Papers; Cooley, *Social Process*, 383, 418; Cooley, *Life and the Student*, 246. Alan Jones notes Burkean overtones in Thomas Cooley's later views. "Law and Economics," 127.

108. Charles H. Cooley, Journal, December 6, 1926, Cooley Papers.

109. Charles H. Cooley, Journal, October 15, 1900, "Living Together Well: A Preliminary Impression," n.d. [post–World War I], 4, Cooley Papers; Cooley, *Social Organization*, 321.

110. Charles H. Cooley, Journal, July 6, 1924, Cooley Papers.

111. Charles H. Cooley, Journal, January 21, 1911, March 2, 1907, March 14, 1913, August 1, 1907, Cooley Papers. Cooley later generalized upon his own experience in *Life and the Student* (p. 199): "One is a distincter man if he can root himself somewhere and grow with the neighborhood," he pointed out; "he gains in depth, significance, flavor, absorbs a local tradition and spirit, sees himself as a part of a continuing whole."

112. Cooley, *Social Organization*, 21.

113. Cooley, *Social Process*, 67–68, 363–65, 369; Charles H. Cooley, Journal, April 7, 1924, Cooley Papers. Cf. Cooley, *Life and the Student*, 39.

114. Cooley, *Social Organization*, 338–39; Charles H. Cooley to J. H. Hanford, April 19, 1928, Cooley Papers.

115. Cooley, *Social Organization*, 339.

116. Charles Horton Cooley, *The Theory of Transportation* (Baltimore: American

Economic Association, 1894), 42, 139; Cooley, *Social Organization*, 339; Cooley, *Life and the Student*, 199.

117. "Cooley took the idealists' absolute and gave it the characteristics of an organic village; all the world should be an enlarged, Christian democratic version of a rural village. He practically assimilated 'society' to the primary group community, and he blessed it emotionally and conceptually." C. Wright Mills, *Power, Politics and People: The Collected Essays of C. Wright Mills*, ed. Irving Louis Horowitz (New York: Oxford University Press, 1963), 543.

118. Ibid., 362–63, 536. More recently Peter Simonson has cited Cooley, along with John Dewey and others, as an example of "communication hope," an over-reliance on communications as the means to building a democratic community, which emerged among Progressive Age intellectuals. With Cooley, especially, it was the process of communication which was important, Simonson argues, more than what was actually communicated. "Dreams of Democratic Togetherness: Communication Hope from Cooley to Katz," *Critical Studies in Mass Communication* 13 (December 1996): 324, 330–33.

119. Diggins, "Socialization of Authority," 466–67, 470.

120. Paul Creelan, "The Degradation of the Sacred: Approaches of Cooley and Goffman," *Symbolic Interaction* 10 (Spring 1987): 33, 44.

121. Charles H. Cooley, Journal, April 7, 1929, Cooley Papers.

Conclusion

1. Yves M.-J. Congar, *Tradition and Traditions: An Historical and a Theological Essay* (New York: Macmillan, 1967), 152–53.

2. Carl Schorske, *Thinking with History: Explorations in the Passage to Modernism* (Princeton: Princeton University Press, 1998), 4. Daniel Joseph Singal provides a useful summary in "Towards a Definition of American Modernism," *American Quarterly* 39 (Spring 1987): 7–26. Norman F. Cantor distinguishes between "classical" and "expressionist" modernism, noting that both "reject sequential temporality." *The American Century: Varieties of Culture in Modern Times* (New York: Harper Collins, 1997), 99.

3. Herbert N. Schneidau, *Waking Giants: The Presence of the Past in Modernism* (New York: Oxford University Press, 1991), vii, 16; Louis Menand, *Discovering Modernism: T. S. Eliot and His Context* (New York: Oxford University Press, 1987), 81; Stephen Spender, *Love-Hate Relations: English and American Sensibilities* (New York: Random House, 1974), 29–30, 45–49; Peter Schjeldahl, "The Elegant Scavenger: John Currin's Low Comedy of High Style," *New Yorker* (February 22 & March 1, 1999), 175.

4. P. G. Ellis, "The Development of T. S. Eliot's Historical Sense," *Review of English Studies*, n.s., 23 (August 1972): 301; T. S. Eliot, "Tradition and the Individual Talent," in *Selected Essays*, new ed. (New York: Harcourt, Brace, 1950), 4–5.

5. Ricardo J. Quinones, *Mapping Literary Modernism: Time and Development* (Princeton: Princeton University Press, 1985), 29 (quoting Nietzsche), 131.

6. Christopher Shannon, *Conspicuous Criticism: Tradition, the Individual, and Culture in American Social Thought, from Veblen to Mills* (Baltimore: Johns Hopkins University Press, 1996), xi, xv.

7. Richard Rorty, *Objectivity, Relativism, and Truth* (Cambridge: Cambridge University Press, 1991), 29, 38, 176; John Patrick Diggins, *The Promise of Pragmatism: Modernism and the Crisis of Knowledge and Authority* (Chicago: University of Chicago Press, 1994), 478.

8. Alasdair MacIntyre, *After Virtue: A Study in Moral Theory* (Notre Dame, Ind.: University of Notre Dame Press, 1981), 119, 122; Alasdair MacIntyre, *Three Rival Versions of Moral Inquiry: Encyclopaedia, Genealogy, and Tradition* (Notre Dame, Ind.: University of Notre Dame Press, 1990), 59–60, 65–66.

9. George Cotkin, *Reluctant Modernism: American Thought and Culture, 1880–1900* (New York: Twayne, 1992), xi.

10. Theodor W. Adorno, "On Tradition," *Telos* 94 (Winter 1992): 75, 79–80.

11. Clare Cavanagh, *Osip Mandelstam and the Modernist Creation of Tradition* (Princeton: Princeton University Press, 1995), 102, 143.

Index

Acton, H. B., 3
Adamic myth, 2, 9, 12, 15, 124
Adams, Brooks, 122, 145
Adams, Charles Francis, Jr., 30, 107
Adams, Henry, 6, 30, 134–35, 138–40, 145, 250n70
Adams, Herbert B., 30–32, 34–35, 140
Adams, John, 120
Adorno, Theodor, 18, 224
Alcott, Bronson, 32
Alfred the Great, King, 28, 53, 57
Allen, Alexander V. G., 45–46
Ambler, Charles Henry, 84
American Revolution, 56, 67–69, 83, 94, 103–4, 114
antimodernism, 5–6, 12, 126, 145
Arnold, Matthew, 120
Ashby, Turner, 98
Astor, Nancy, 78
Augustine of Canterbury, 28–29

Bacon, Nathaniel, 81, 93–94, 102, 243n79
Bagby, George W., 92
Bagehot, Walter, 49, 165, 172
Bancroft, George, 13–14, 30, 44
Beard, Charles A., 31–32
Berdyaev, Nicholas, 149, 151
Bergson, Henri, 33, 49–50, 204
Berkeley, William, 93, 102
Billikopf, Jacob, 184
Blake, Ira, 119, 144
Blavatsky, Helena, 120
Boas, Franz, 63, 163
Bradley, Arthur Granville, 92
Breasted, James Henry, 250n70
Brooks, Van Wyck, 11–12, 132, 216

Brown, Alexander, 82–83, 86
Brownson, Orestes, 122
Bruce, Philip Alexander: introduced, 21–22; on aristocracy and democracy, 80, 86, 91–92, 95–96, 103; and cavaliers, 84, 99, 106; defense of southern history, 77, 79–80; early life of, 105–9; and English tradition, 67–68, 74–75, 111, 113–14; as historian, 76, 105–7; home and family of, 74, 76, 104–5, 107, 109, 112–13, 238n16; politics of, 72–73, 77; pro-British sympathies of, 68; resentment of revisionists, 83–86; on slavery and race, 69–71, 110, 112; traditionist philosophy of, 109–15, 208; visits England, 68, 77
Bruce, William Cabell, 105, 224n85
Buddhism, 160
Burke, Edmund: and American conservatism, 167; and C. H. Cooley, 207–9; on civility, 18; "little platoons" of, 23, 62; and nature of tradition, 19, 64, 168; and partnership of generations, 1, 34, 43, 124–25; and South, 109–10, 244n96; and T. M. Cooley, 207, 259n107; and "Whig" history, 51
Burrow, J. W., 51, 56

Calhoun, John C., 92
Caruthers, William A., 96, 243n79
Cash, Wilbur J., 72
cavaliers: and liberty, 82, 97–98, 101–3, 115; as Virginia immigrants, 19, 66, 84, 96, 99–100, 106, 244n87; in Virginia tradition, 83, 86–87, 93, 95–106, 243n70

Charles I, King, 98, 101–2, 116–17
Charles II, King, 101–2, 104
Civil War, 22, 38, 58, 73, 76, 96
Clark, George Rogers, 81, 100
Coleridge, Samuel Taylor, 248n38
Commons, John R., 170
Comte, Auguste, 15, 21, 49, 62, 200
Congar, Yves, 122, 129, 216
Constitutional Convention (1787), 57, 101
Conway, Moncure, 75, 90
Cooke, John Esten, 86, 90–91, 96–98,
    101–2, 104
Cooley, Charles Horton: introduced, 23;
    on American culture, 193–94, 210,
    256n73; antitraditionalist views of,
    186; and architecture, 187–89, 191,
    200, 209, 213; and behaviorism, 199,
    258n86; on communications, 185,
    196–97, 212–13, 260n118; criticisms
    of, 211–13, 260n117; death of, 189,
    214–15; democratic ideal of, 193–94,
    202; and E. A. Ross, 23, 184, 187, 197;
    early life of, 188, 190–91, 193; and H.
    Spencer, 188, 195–96, 257n76; health
    of, 188, 190; on "I" and "We," 23,
    183, 189–90, 197, 202–3, 206–8, 215;
    and immigrants, 182–85, 192–93,
    221; as interactionist, 196; "looking-
    glass self," 189, 197, 205; and
    Modernism, 222; "primary group,"
    23, 155, 184–86, 189, 193, 197,
    210–12, 258n82, 259n111, 260n117; as
    Progressive, 86, 191, 201–3, 208, 210,
    222; religious views of, 23, 191–93,
    200–203, 205–6; and social process,
    198–99, 203–4, 210, 257n79
Cooley, Thomas M., 188, 207, 259n107
Cram, Ralph Adams: introduced,
    22–23; as Anglo-Catholic, 22, 121–23,
    128–29, 160, 221, 246n9; as antimod-
    ernist, 126, 247n21; as architect, 22,
    118–21, 123–24, 147, 156, 247n23;

considers expatriation, 118; cyclical
    theory of, 22–23, 145–48, 155, 157,
    160–61, 223; on democracy, 136,
    140–46, 152–54, 157, 223–24; early
    life of, 119–21, 143, 246n9; and
    European traditionalists, 148–52; and
    Gothic, 123–24, 139–40, 146–47, 154,
    158; and H. Adams, 138–39; on "im-
    perial modernism," 22, 119, 126, 142,
    152–53, 161, 217, 221; as Jacobite,
    116–17; and Japan, 159–61; and
    Modernism, 119, 222; and monasti-
    cism, 23, 154–56, 158, 183; neo-me-
    dievalism of, 118, 123, 138–41,
    147–48, 151–54, 157–58, 223; in
    1930s, 148; and "progressive evolu-
    tion," 119, 127, 131, 145–46, 151, 158;
    on right to beauty, 141; and sacramen-
    talism, 22, 129–30, 147; "walled
    towns," 64, 134, 156–57, 224
Craven, Wesley Frank, 83

Darwin, Charles, 6, 31, 40–41, 178, 191
Daughters of the American Revolution, 16
Davidson, Donald, 31–32
Dawson, Christopher, 250n70
Declaration of Independence, 80–81,
    100, 144
Dewey, John, 142, 188, 196, 201,
    260n118
Diggins, John P., 197, 201, 213, 220
Disraeli, Benjamin, 248n38
Distributists, 148
Dodd, William E., 78
Dudley, Thomas, 26–29, 39

Eckenrode, Hamilton James, 84
Edwards, Jonathan, 44, 158
Eggleston, Edward, 35, 37, 39
Eliot, T. S., 24, 63, 127–28, 218–19, 222,
    232n18
Elizabeth I, Queen, 82, 101

Ely, Richard T., 170

Emerson, Ralph Waldo: and C. H. Cooley, 184, 186, 191–92, 204, 208, 256n68; as heir of Puritanism, 44; hostility of, to tradition, 2, 158; and Middle Ages, 135; and R. A. Cram, 120; on self-reliance and slavery, 92; and study of the past, 13

Fascism, 148, 150–51

Fenollosa, Ernest, 159

Fischer, David Hackett, 90, 231n13, 244n87

Fiske, John: introduced, 21; as advocate of federalism, 129; on American Indians, 48, 60–62; anthropological views of, 60, 62–63; career of, 39, 41–42, 63; death of, 42; early life of, 40, 53, 233n31; as evolutionist, 47–48, 50, 63–65, 133, 196, 223, 234n52; as expansionist, 39–42, 49–51, 55–67, 73, 154–55, 236n81; and faith in progress, 46–49; and the home, 50, 54, 65, 107, 235n56; on immigration, 60; as mythologist, 41; on nature of tradition, 6, 62–64, 166, 169, 173, 196, 216; on New England towns, 21, 52–54, 56–58, 71, 76, 164, 183; personality of, 40–41; as positivist, 40–41, 43, 45; racial views of, 41, 59, 60–62, 69; reception of, in South, 66; religious views of, 40–45, 50, 65, 234n44; on Spanish conquests, 61–62; and "Teutonic Idea," 40, 55–56, 58, 60–63, 67, 76, 215

Ford, Worthington Chauncey, 78

Foucault, Michel, 229n28

Franklin, Benjamin, 1, 55, 79, 105

Freeman, Edward A., 51–53, 56, 67, 238n8

Frothingham, A. L., 137

Gaines, Francis Pendleton, 90

Gaines, Joseph Edmunds, 108

George III, King, 69, 104

Giddings, Franklin H., 164, 188, 210

Gildersleeve, Basil L., 239n20

Gilman, Daniel Coit, 30

Glasgow, Ellen, 84

Goethe, Johann Wolfgang von, 191

Goldman, Emma, 170, 253n20

Goodhue, Bertram Grosvenor, 120

Goodwin, Maud Wilder, 100

Grady, Henry, 81, 97

Guiney, Louise I., 117, 122, 146, 156

Hamilton, Alexander, 117

Harold, King, 28, 100

Hart, Albert Bushnell, 78

Hawthorne, Nathaniel, 8

Hearn, Lafcadio, 159

Henderson, Archibald, 77

Henry VIII, King, 131

Henry, Patrick, 83, 93, 101–2, 243n79

Herder, Johann, 20, 115

heritage, 4–5, 12, 23, 216

Hobsbawm, Eric, 3

Holmes, Oliver Wendell, Jr., 205

honor, southern culture of, 241n52

Hooker, Thomas, 27

Howells, William Dean, 40, 42

Ingle, Edward, 67

Jackson, Andrew, 13, 94, 141

Jackson, Thomas "Stonewall," 98–99

Jacksonian Democracy, 30, 149

Jacobitism, 17, 116–17, 131

James, Henry, 2, 8, 118

James, William, 129, 198, 204–7, 259n101

James I, King, 69, 82

Jamestown tercentenary, 88–89, 94

Jarves, James Jackson, 136

Jefferson, Thomas: and Anglo-Saxon precedents, 13, 28; antitraditionalism of, 1; and democracy, 80–81, 117; as descendant of cavaliers, 100, 101; for "natural aristocracy," 152; and town meeting, 54; universalism of, 76; as Virginia hero, 110; and yeoman farm, 71–72

John, King, 69

Jones, Augustine, 26–30, 39, 137, 216

Kelley, Florence, 184

Kempis, Thomas à, 23, 192–93, 208, 213–15

Lamennais, Robert de, 15

Latané, John T., 77

Lears, T. J. Jackson, 5, 126

Lee, "Lighthouse Harry," 104

Lee, Robert E.: as cavalier, 22, 98–99, 101, 103–4, 223; genealogy of, 103–4; identified with Washington, 104; as social ideal, 79, 114, 239n26

Leo XIII, Pope, 120, 152

Lethaby, William R., 124, 246n18

Lewis, R. W. B., 2

Lewis, Wyndham, 14

Lincoln, Abraham, 17, 78–81, 83, 88, 239n26, 240n31

Littré, Émile, 47

Locke, John, 8

Lowell, James Russell, 2

MacIntyre, Alasdair, 7, 64, 220

Madison, James, 87

Madariaga, Salvador de, 149–50, 250n70

Mahone, Gen. William, 72–73

Maine, Sir Henry, 15, 51–52, 163

Marcuse, Herbert, 144

Marsh, George Perkins, 34

Mathews, Lois Kimball, 38–39

Mead, George Herbert, 189, 196

Menand, Louis, 218

Mencken, H. L., 167, 211–12

Mills, C. Wright, 213, 260n117

Modernism: C. H. Cooley and, 205, 212, 222; and cosmic homelessness, 224; dated Fiske's history, 42; R. A. Cram and, 118–19, 125–28, 142; and tradition, 23–24, 63–64, 217–19, 223

Moore, Charles Herbert, 136–37

Morgan, Louis Henry, 60, 62

Morris, William, 120

Mount Vernon Ladies' Association, 16

Mumford, Lewis, 250n70

Muzzey, David S., 79

New England: and Anglo-American tradition, 21; expansion of, 38–39, 44; and federalism, 52, 56; rivalry with South, 66, 68, 74–75, 95–96, 99; towns, 21, 23, 30, 35–37, 52–54, 56–58, 71, 183

Newman, John Henry, Cardinal, 120

Nisbet, Robert A., 15, 163

North, Arthur Tappan, 127

Norton, Charles E., 120, 135–36, 248n45

Oakeshott, Michael, 7

Order of the White Rose, 116–19, 131. *See also* Jacobitism

Ortega y Gasset, José, 149–51

Orton, William Aylott, 149, 151

Oxford Movement, 122

Page, Rosewell, 92

Page, Thomas Nelson: on aristocracy and democracy, 88, 91, 96, 103, 241n54; and cavaliers, 86, 97, 99, 101, 114; and English tradition, 67, 69; fiction of, 73, 92, 97; love of home, 75, 87, 107; opposes Readjuster move-

ment, 72–73; and P. A. Bruce, 105; on slavery and race, 69, 72, 92; tercentenary address of, 88–89
Paine, Thomas, 110
Park, Robert, 189
Parkman, Francis, 48
Parrington, Vernon Louis, 43
Parsons, Talcott, 205
Pater, Walter, 120
Peabody, Robert S., 137–38
Pelikan, Jaroslav, 4, 19, 49, 220, 230n30
Picasso, Pablo, 127
Pitt, William, the Elder, 59
Plumb, J. H., 6
Postmodernism, 24, 218
Pound, Ezra, 24, 218
Progressive movement: C. H. Cooley and, 191, 203, 208, 260n118; E. A. Ross and, 170, 178, 182; and social science, 162, 164, 167; in Virginia, 72–73, 77
Pugin, Augustus Charles, 133, 248n38
Puritans: as Anglo-Saxons, 28–29, 38–39, 55; Cooley's affinity with, 189; Cram's rebellion against, 121, 126; and democracy, 44, 56; double view of, 26–29; rejected tradition, 1; in sectional controversy, 75, 80–81, 95, 99–101; and typology, 29, 63

Raleigh, Sir Walter, 100
Randall, T. Henry, 121–22
Randolph, John, of Roanoke, 90, 105, 244n85, 245n100
Richardson, Henry Hobson, 124
Riesman, David, 181
Roman Catholic Church: Cram and, 121; Protestant rejection of, 43–44, 132, 135; teaching methods of, 79; tradition in, 4, 122, 129, 216; upward mobility in, 143
Roosevelt, Franklin D., 148

Roosevelt, Theodore, 188, 208
Rorty, Richard, 7, 220
Ross, Edward Alsworth: and anomie, 224–25; as antitraditionalist, 167, 208, 217; on bondage of custom, 172–74, 181; and C. H. Cooley, 170, 184–87, 197; career of, 171; defines custom and tradition, 4; on European pessimism, 171–72; and feminism, 174; on immigrants, 174–77, 254n33; and L. F. Ward, 170, 172–73; as Progressive, 23, 170, 174, 176–80, 182, 253n20; and social control, 171, 178–79, 213; on tradition and heredity, 173; on tradition and individuality, 178–82; travels abroad, 174
Royce, Josiah, 64, 203
Rupert, Prince, 98–99, 243n70
Ruskin, John, 133

Said, Edward, 61
Santayana, George, 120
Schaffle, A. E. F., 196
Schorske, Carl, 126, 132, 217
Scott, Sir Walter, 34, 92
Seddon, James A., 105
Shand-Tucci, Douglas, 120–21, 126
Shils, Edward, 3–4, 7, 19, 50, 189
Sloane, William M., 10–12
Smith, Adam, 214
Smith, John, 66, 82, 94
Southern Agrarians, 31, 64, 148
Spencer, Herbert: and C. H. Cooley, 188, 194–96, 203–4; and Fiske, 40–43, 46–48, 56; and social continuity, 15
Spender, Stephen, 10, 18, 33, 218
Spengler, Oswald, 145, 250n70
Spotswood, Alexander, 67
Stanard, Mary Newton, 82
Stanford, Jane Lathrop, 170
Stith, William, 82
Stuart, J. E. B., 243n70

Stubbs, William, 39, 42, 51
Sumner, William Graham: and continuity of tradition, 15; on folkways and tradition, 165–67; "Forgotten Man" of, 153, 166; and social change, 162

Tarde, Gabriel de, 180–81, 195, 200
Tennyson, Alfred, Lord, 13, 58, 216
Thomas, George H., 101
Thomas, W. I., 189
Thoreau, Henry David, 1, 25, 191, 193, 204, 216, 245n100
Tönnies, Ferdinand, 15, 163, 181, 185–86
Transcendentalism, 1–2, 44, 119, 130, 186, 191
Trent, William Peterfield, 101
Turner, Frederick Jackson, 30–32, 34, 38, 111, 132, 170
Twain, Mark, 167
Tyler, John, President, 92–94
Tyler, Lyon Gardiner: introduced, 21–22; on aristocracy and democracy, 66, 89–92, 94, 96, 103; and cavaliers, 100–101; as college president, 66, 76, 78, 93; and defense of South, 77–81, 87, 94; as historian, 93, 106; and Jeffersonian democracy, 93–94; and Modernism, 222; praise of Fiske, 66; pro-British, 68; resentment of revisionists, 83–86, 244n85; on slavery and race, 70; on Virginia and the Union, 87; and women's rights, 76–77
Tyler, Wat, 93
Typology: applied to Puritans, 29, 39; in E. A. Freeman, 238n8; in Fiske, 56, 63; as linkage, 20, 24; and R. A. Cram, 22, 140, 146, 148, 223; in Virginia history, 69, 81, 102, 223

Unitarianism, 30, 119, 122, 135

Van Rensselaer, Mariana, 136
Viollet-le-Duc, Eugène Emmanuel, 133
Virginia: African Americans in, 60–71; aristocracy and democracy in, 81–87, 89–92, 103; English tradition in, 67–69, 74–75, 101, 111, 113–14; Fiske on, 52, 54, 66; Jamestown settlement, 80, 82–83, 88–89, 94–95; plantations and farms in, 72, 74, 112–13, 155, 183, 242n57; priority of, in America, 79–80, 82, 86–87, 89, 115, 241n46; Progressive movement in, 72–73, 77; quest for vindication, 71–72, 115; and Readjuster movement, 73; role in national expansion, 67, 73; slavery in, 70–72, 105, 112; as source of tradition, 72, 79
Virginia Company of London, 69, 82

Wagner, Richard, 120, 126–27
Ward, Lester Frank, 167–70, 197, 208
Washington, George, 22, 80–81, 87, 101–4, 141
Watterson, Henry, 75, 81, 240n31
Weaver, Richard, 110, 245n100
Weber, Max, 7, 163
Weeden, William B., 36–39, 54, 152
Wendell, Barrett, 258n82
Wentworth, Charles, 120
Wertenbaker, Thomas Jefferson, 83–86, 97, 103, 106
Whitman, Walt, 120
Williams, Roger, 26
Wilson, Woodrow, 68–69, 81, 92, 101, 208, 223
Winthrop, John, 26
World War I: American sentiments in, 68, 84, 118; disruption of, 108, 145–47, 151, 156; horror of, 130, 157, 206
World War II, 24, 161, 221
Wright, Frank Lloyd, 124